Taste of Home

WHAT CAN I BRING?

360+ DISHES FOR PARTIES, PICNICS & POTLUCKS

TASTE OF HOME BOOKS • RDA ENTHUSIAST BRANDS, LLC • MILWAUKEE, WI

© 2023 RDA Enthusiast Brands, LLC.
1610 N. 2nd St., Suite 102, Milwaukee WI 53212-3906

Visit us at **tasteofhome.com** for other *Taste of Home* books and products.

International Standard Book Number:
978-1-62145-891-3

Chief Content Officer, Home & Garden: Jeanne Sidner
Content Director: Mark Hagen
Associate Creative Director: Raeann Thompson
Senior Editor: Christine Rukavena
Senior Art Director: Courtney Lovetere
Editor: Amy Glander
Senior Designer: Jazmin Delgado

Deputy Editor, Copy Desk : Dulcie Shoener
Copy Editor: Cathy Jakicic
Contributing Designer: Jennifer Ruetz

Cover Photography:
Photographer: Dan Roberts
Set Stylist: Stacey Genaw
Food Stylists: Shannon Norris, Ellen Crowley

Pictured on front cover:
Easy Deviled Eggs, p. 27; Hot Italian Party Sandwiches, p. 48; Old-Fashioned Macaroni & Cheese, p. 105

Pictured on back cover:
Chocolate Peanut Treats, p. 288; Strawberry Spinach Salad with Candied Walnuts, p. 164

Printed in China
3 5 7 9 10 8 6 4 2

P. 117

FIND THE BEST BRING-A-DISH RECIPE

The secret to any fantastic get-together is amazing food. Whether you've been invited to a church supper, family reunion, pancake breakfast, charity bake sale or casual backyard barbecue, the first question that pops into your mind is, "What can I bring?"

Finding the perfect contribution is now easier than ever thanks to the collection of easy-to-make, easy-to-take dishes inside *Taste of Home What Can I Bring?* This brand-new cookbook is your biggest and best source for 361 impressive feed-a-crowd dishes—all guaranteed to have guests piling their plates high and begging for the recipe!

Find party-pleasing favorites—hot and savory appetizers, comforting casseroles, sunny breakfast specialties, colorful salads and sides, marvelous sandwiches, even dreamy desserts—to put the finishing touch on a fabulous spread.

In addition to a bevy of big-batch and make-ahead recipes, you'll find those that are suitable for specific holidays and gatherings as well as a chapter devoted to slow-cooker classics that will save you time in the kitchen. Each of these versatile home-cooked dishes has been tested and approved by our staff of Test Kitchen experts, so you can cook with confidence and trust that every dish will be a winner.

You'll also find practical pointers for transporting food and keeping dishes hot and cold on the buffet, easy ways to impress the host, plus other handy how-to tricks for making the most of your culinary creations.

Brimming with gorgeous full-color photos, dozens of clever cooking and entertaining tips, and hundreds of must-try recipes, *What Can I Bring?* makes it a snap to wow your hungry crowd!

P. 253

P. 210

CONTENTS

GUIDE TO BRING-A-DISH SUCCESS

BRING YOUR A-GAME TO GATHERINGS WITH THESE EASY IDEAS

You know who they are: the mom who makes the perfect casserole for the church supper, the neighbor who contributes the best dessert to the block party, the guy whose appetizer receives cheers at the barbecue. Well, at *Taste of Home* we think it's about time you start counting yourself among these cooks!

With the 361 crowd-pleasing recipes in *What Can I Bring?*, bring-a-dish success is as easy as apple pie. Simply follow these practical pointers, prepare a recipe from this book and become the life of the party!

PLAN AHEAD

Who has time to set a dinner on the table, let alone whip up dozens of cupcakes for a bake sale? You do...with a little planning, that is. Be realistic about the time you have available, and choose a recipe that best fits your schedule. Look for **MA** throughout this book, and consider those recipes first if time is tight.

USE YOUR SLOW COOKER

When it comes to making and taking a dish to a get-together, slow cookers are ideal travel vessels. Not only do they simmer large-yield recipes on their own, but they also keep food warm on buffets. See page 232 for an entire chapter of slow-cooker greats.

TRAVEL SAFELY

All the recipes inside *What Can I Bring?* travel well, but we recommend planning accordingly. A four-layer cake may not be the best option for a long drive. Sturdy cardboard boxes prevent slow cookers and casserole dishes from sliding around in car trunks, so ask your grocer for any clean boxes you could have. Secure lids with rubber bands.

THINK OUTSIDE THE BOX

Salads, dips and brownies are welcome at shared-dish events, but why not wow the crowd with a change-of-pace item? Consider something like Strawberry & Cream Bruschetta (p. 38), Mini Rosemary-Roast Beef Sandwiches (p. 45), or Jalapeno Mac & Cheese (p. 270).

BUILD A DIY MULTILEVEL TOTE

If you have more dishes than hands to hold them, use a cooling rack with folding legs. Fold out the legs and use the rack to create sturdy, stable levels inside a carrying tote without crushing what's below. You can also build layers by propping a sheet pan with ring molds or cans.

ENSURE A NO-SLIP TRIP

Place grippy drawer liners or silicone baking mats in the car before loading your food. The liners will keep dishes from sliding and contain any errant spills. An old yoga mat works well for this too.

KEEP A LID ON IT

Use a bungee cord, painter's tape or a thick ribbon to keep the lid of your slow cooker or Dutch oven in place. Secure the cord around the handles and over the top. Now you're ready to transport without risk of a mess.

BRING A SALAD

It's easy to serve a crisp salad even when you're far from home. Bring the fixings in a serving bowl along with the utensils. Toss it all together at your destination. Hold off on adding salad dressing or croutons until it's time to serve. Adding these too early can result in soggy salad greens or the croutons absorbing moisture and losing their crunch.

FROSTING IS GOOD GLUE

If you're transporting a cake to a special event, make it easier to tote with this little tip: Secure the cake (or cardboard cake circle, if you're using one) onto the presentation plate with a dab of frosting. This makes the cake less likely to slide around, even if you have to brake suddenly.

PACK A TOUCH-UP KIT

Make a little touch-up kit of decorations and frosting (just in case) to take with your decorated cake. Pack the items with a clean dish towel and offset spatula. Take the frosting in its pastry bag.

POTLUCK POINTERS

- Before selecting your recipe, ask the host if any guests have food allergies.

- Tell the host what you're bringing and stick to it.

- Bring a dish that's ready to serve or requires minimal setup or kitchen space at the party.

- Bring your contribution intact. Don't arrive with a slice of cake missing because your spouse wanted to sample it first.

- Bring food on/in a decorative serving piece. Leave that piece as a hostess gift.

- Share extra copies of your recipe.

- No time to cook? Offer to bring beverages, plates, napkins, plastic utensils, condiments or even a centerpiece.

- After the party, offer to clean up or do dishes.

- Leave leftovers at the party. Don't pack a to-go plate for home; take food home only if the host asks you to do so.

FOOD SAFETY TIPS

- If the party is outdoors, set up the buffet in a cool area—like in a garage, in the shade of a building or under a big tree. Stash coolers also in the shade to keep drinks colder.

- Have plenty of ice to pack around dishes to keep them cold. The food will taste better when it's properly chilled and you won't have to worry about the risk of any foodborne illnesses.

- Likewise, keep hot foods hot. Hot foods should not be out at room temperature for more than 2 hours (less if it's hotter). Set chafing dishes, slow cookers, and grills or ovens to the low setting to keep food warm. Remember to pack an extra extension cord for buffets.

MORE WAYS TO CONNECT WITH US:

APPETIZERS, DIPS & SPREADS

These easy hot bites, dips and sippers ensure there's plenty of yummy goodness to pass around at your next potluck.

P. 35

P. 37

P. 25

AVOCADO SALSA

MINI GRILLED CHEESE

Folks will love this easy adaptation of the classic grilled cheese sandwich. Take them to your next party, or store some in the freezer to pull out when you're having soup or salad for lunch. My family loves to nibble on them anytime.
—*Anita Curtis, Camarillo, CA*

TAKES: 30 min. • **MAKES:** 8 dozen

- 1 cup butter, softened
- 2 jars (5 oz. each) sharp American cheese spread, softened
- 1 large egg
- 1 can (4 oz.) chopped green chiles, drained
- ¼ cup salsa
- 2 cups shredded cheddar cheese
- 2 loaves (1½ lbs. each) thinly sliced sandwich bread, crusts removed

1. Preheat oven to 350°. Cream butter, cheese spread and egg until smooth. Stir in the chiles, salsa and cheddar cheese. Spread about 1 Tbsp. cheese mixture on each slice of 1 loaf of bread.
2. Top with remaining bread; spread with more cheese mixture. Cut each sandwich into 4 squares or triangles; place on a baking sheet lined with parchment. Bake until cheese is melted, 10-15 minutes.
Freeze option: Place cooled appetizers on a baking sheet. Freeze for 1 hour. Remove from the baking sheet and store in freezer in an airtight container until needed. To bake frozen, place on a greased baking sheet. Bake at 350° for 15-20 minutes or until bubbly and browned.
1 piece: 77 cal., 4g fat (2g sat. fat), 10mg chol., 168mg sod., 7g carb. (1g sugars, 0 fiber), 2g pro.

AVOCADO SALSA

I first made this recipe for a party, and it was an absolute success. People love the garlic, corn and avocado combination.
—*Susan Vandermeer, Ogden, UT*

PREP: 20 min. + chilling
MAKES: about 7 cups

- 1⅔ cups (about 8¼ oz.) frozen corn, thawed
- 2 cans (2¼ oz. each) sliced ripe olives, drained
- 1 medium sweet red pepper, chopped
- 1 small onion, chopped
- 5 garlic cloves, minced
- ⅓ cup olive oil
- ¼ cup lemon juice
- 3 Tbsp. cider vinegar
- 1 tsp. dried oregano
- ½ tsp. salt
- ½ tsp. pepper
- 4 medium ripe avocados, peeled
  Tortilla chips

1. Combine the corn, olives, red pepper and onion. In another bowl, mix the next 7 ingredients. Pour over corn mixture; toss to coat. Refrigerate, covered, overnight.
2. Just before serving, chop avocados; stir into salsa. Serve with tortilla chips.
¼ cup: 82 cal., 7g fat (1g sat. fat), 0 chol., 85mg sod., 5g carb. (1g sugars, 2g fiber), 1g pro. **Diabetic exchanges:** 1½ fat.

BUFFALO CHICKEN
WINGS

BUFFALO CHICKEN WINGS

Hot wings got their start in Buffalo, New York, in the kitchen of a bar. Cayenne, red hot sauce and spices keep these tangy Buffalo chicken wings good and hot, just like the originals.
—Nancy Chapman, Center Harbor, NH

PREP: 10 min. • COOK: 10 min./batch
MAKES: about 4 dozen

- 5 lbs. chicken wings
  Oil for frying
- 1 cup butter, cubed
- ¼ cup Louisiana-style hot sauce
- ¾ tsp. cayenne pepper
- ¾ tsp. celery salt
- ½ tsp. onion powder
- ½ tsp. garlic powder
  Optional: Celery ribs and ranch or blue cheese salad dressing

1. Cut chicken wings into 3 sections; discard wing tip sections. In an electric skillet, heat 1 in. oil to 375°. Fry wings in oil, a few at a time, for 3-4 minutes on each side or until chicken juices run clear. Drain on paper towels.
2. Meanwhile, in a small saucepan, melt butter. Stir in the hot sauce and spices. Place chicken in a large bowl; add sauce and toss to coat. Remove to a serving plate with a slotted spoon. Serve the wings with celery and ranch or blue cheese salad dressing if desired.
Note: Uncooked chicken wing sections (wingettes) may be substituted for whole chicken wings.
1 piece: 126 cal., 12g fat (4g sat. fat), 25mg chol., 105mg sod., 0 carb. (0 sugars, 0 fiber), 5g pro.

APRICOT TURKEY PINWHEELS

APRICOT TURKEY PINWHEELS

I created these unique pinwheels for a football game using ingredients I had on hand. They were a huge hit! I appreciate how quick and easy they are to prepare.
—Melanie Foster, Blaine, MN

TAKES: 30 min. • MAKES: 16 pinwheels

- 1 sheet frozen puff pastry, thawed
- ¼ cup apricot preserves
- ½ tsp. ground mustard
- ½ cup shredded Monterey Jack cheese
- ¼ lb. sliced deli turkey

1. Unfold puff pastry; layer with apricot preserves, mustard, cheese and turkey. Roll up jelly-roll style. Cut into 16 slices. Place cut side down on a parchment-lined baking sheet.
2. Bake at 400° for 15-20 minutes or until golden brown.
Freeze option: Freeze cooled appetizers in a resealable freezer container. To use, reheat appetizers on a parchment-lined baking sheet in a preheated 400° oven until crisp and heated through.
1 appetizer: 108 cal., 5g fat (2g sat. fat), 6mg chol., 135mg sod., 12g carb. (2g sugars, 1g fiber), 3g pro.
Ham & Brie Pinwheels: Omit mustard. Substitute 4 oz. diced Brie cheese for Monterey Jack and deli ham for the turkey.

HAM & SWISS BRAIDS

Satisfy hearty appetites with these golden loaves. Each slice is a hot sandwich packed with ham, broccoli and Swiss cheese. Hot pepper sauce adds a nice kick, while refrigerated crescent rolls makes them extra easy to put together.
—*Donna McCord, Fishers, IN*

PREP: 30 min. • **BAKE:** 20 min.
MAKES: 2 loaves (6 servings each)

- ¾ cup mayonnaise
- 2 Tbsp. Dijon mustard
- 2 Tbsp. honey
- ⅛ tsp. hot pepper sauce
- 2 cups chopped fully cooked ham (about 10 oz.)
- 1 cup shredded Swiss cheese or crumbled goat cheese
- 1 cup chopped fresh broccoli florets
- 1 cup chopped fresh spinach
- 2 tubes (8 oz. each) refrigerated crescent rolls
- 1 large egg white, lightly beaten

1. Preheat oven to 375°. For the filling, mix first 4 ingredients; stir in the ham, cheese and vegetables.

2. Unroll 1 tube of crescent dough onto an ungreased baking sheet; seal perforations to form 1 long rectangle. Spoon half of the filling lengthwise down the center of the rectangle, covering a third of the width. On each long side, cut 1-in. wide strips at an angle to within ½ in. of filling. Starting at 1 end, fold alternating strips at an angle across filling; seal ends. Brush with egg white. Repeat with the remaining dough and filling.

3. Bake 20-25 minutes or until dark golden brown, rotating the pans halfway through baking. Cool 5 minutes before slicing.

1 piece: 306 cal., 21g fat (6g sat. fat), 27mg chol., 721mg sod., 20g carb. (7g sugars, 0 fiber), 11g pro.

HAM & SWISS BRAIDS

CHEESY MEATBALL SLIDERS

1. Preheat oven to 350°. Combine the ground beef, bread crumbs, pesto and egg; mix lightly but thoroughly. Shape into 12 meatballs; place on a greased rack in a 15x10x1-in. baking pan. Bake until browned and a thermometer reads 160°, about 35 minutes. Toss with sauce; set aside.
2. Meanwhile, without separating rolls, cut horizontally in half; arrange bottom halves in a greased 13x9-in. baking dish. Place half the cheese slices over roll bottoms; sprinkle with oregano. Add meatballs and sauce. Top with remaining cheese slices and bun tops.
3. Combine butter, olive oil, garlic, Italian seasoning and red pepper flakes; brush over buns. Bake, covered, for 20 minutes. Uncover; sprinkle with Parmesan and shredded mozzarella.
4. Bake, uncovered, until cheese is melted, 10-15 minutes longer. Sprinkle with basil before serving.

1 slider: 514 cal., 25g fat (12g sat. fat), 120mg chol., 856mg sod., 39g carb. (15g sugars, 3g fiber), 33g pro.

BRING IT

If you're taking these sliders to a potluck, keep things easy by making some of the recipe components ahead of time. For example, bake the meatballs in advance and combine them with the sauce in a covered container. You can also prepare the flavored butter that will be brushed on the rolls ahead of time. Just be sure to assemble the sliders close to serving time so the rolls don't get soggy.

CHEESY MEATBALL SLIDERS

These sliders are a fun way to serve meatballs at your party without using a slow cooker. Made on mini Hawaiian rolls, they have a hint of sweetness to balance out the wonderful Italian seasonings.
—Taste of Home *Test Kitchen*

PREP: 1 hour • **BAKE:** 30 min.
MAKES: 12 servings

- 2 lbs. lean ground beef (90% lean)
- 1 cup Italian-style bread crumbs
- 3 Tbsp. prepared pesto
- 1 large egg, lightly beaten
- 1 jar (24 oz.) pasta sauce
- 1 pkg. (18 oz.) Hawaiian sweet rolls
- 12 slices part-skim mozzarella cheese
- ½ tsp. dried oregano
- ¼ cup melted butter
- 1 Tbsp. olive oil
- 3 garlic cloves, minced
- 1 tsp. Italian seasoning
- ½ tsp. crushed red pepper flakes
- 2 Tbsp. grated Parmesan cheese
- 1 cup shredded part-skim mozzarella cheese or shredded Italian cheese blend
  Minced fresh basil

ITALIAN CHEESE LOAF

Here's a deliciously different sandwich. It's yummy warm from the oven or off the grill at a cookout. The cheese in the filling with garden-fresh ingredients goes great inside crusty bread. I usually serve it with a salad and onion rings.

—Mary Ann Marino, West Pittsburgh, PA

PREP: 15 min. • **BAKE:** 25 min.
MAKES: 12 servings

- 1 loaf (1 lb.) French bread
- 2 cups diced fresh tomatoes
- 1 cup shredded part-skim mozzarella cheese
- 1 cup shredded cheddar cheese
- 1 medium onion, finely chopped
- ¼ cup grated Romano cheese
- ¼ cup chopped ripe olives
- ¼ cup Italian salad dressing
- 1 tsp. minced fresh basil or ¼ tsp. dried basil
- 1 tsp. minced fresh oregano or ¼ tsp. dried oregano

1. Preheat oven to 350°. Cut top half off loaf of bread. Carefully hollow out both halves of loaf, leaving a ½-in. shell (discard removed bread or save for another use).
2. Combine remaining ingredients. Spoon into bottom half of bread, mounding as necessary; replace top. Wrap in foil. Bake until cheese is melted, about 25 minutes. Slice and serve warm.
1 piece: 204 cal., 8g fat (4g sat. fat), 18mg chol., 478mg sod., 23g carb. (3g sugars, 2g fiber), 9g pro.

ITALIAN CHEESE LOAF

SAVORY CUCUMBER SANDWICHES

Italian salad dressing adds flavor to this simple spread. Serve it as a dip with crackers and veggies, or use it as a sandwich filling.

—Carol Henderson, Chagrin Falls, OH

PREP: 15 min. + chilling • **MAKES:** 3 dozen

- 1 pkg. (8 oz.) cream cheese, softened
- ½ cup mayonnaise
- 1 envelope Italian salad dressing mix
- 36 slices snack rye bread
- 1 medium cucumber, sliced
  Snipped fresh dill, optional

1. In a small bowl, combine the cream cheese, mayonnaise and salad dressing mix. Refrigerate for 1 hour.
2. Just before serving, spread mixture over each slice of rye bread; top each with a cucumber slice. If desired, sprinkle with fresh dill.
1 sandwich: 62 cal., 5g fat (2g sat. fat), 7mg chol., 149mg sod., 4g carb. (1g sugars, 0 fiber), 1g pro.

ANTIPASTO KABOBS

ANTIPASTO KABOBS

My husband and I met at a cooking class. It must have been fate because we have loved creating menus and entertaining ever since. These make-ahead kabobs are one of our favorite appetizers to serve at parties.

—*Denise Hazen, Cincinnati, OH*

PREP: 35 min. + marinating
MAKES: 40 appetizers

- 1 pkg. (9 oz.) refrigerated cheese tortellini
- 40 pimiento-stuffed olives
- 40 large pitted ripe olives
- ¾ cup Italian salad dressing
- 40 thin slices pepperoni
- 20 thin slices hard salami, halved

1. Cook tortellini according to package directions; drain and rinse in cold water. In a large bowl, combine the tortellini, olives and salad dressing. Toss to coat; cover mixture and refrigerate for 4 hours or overnight.

2. Drain mixture, discarding marinade. For each appetizer, thread a stuffed olive, a folded pepperoni slice, a tortellini, a folded salami piece and a ripe olive on a toothpick or short skewer.

1 kabob: 66 cal., 5g fat (1g sat. fat), 9mg chol., 315mg sod., 4g carb. (0 sugars, 0 fiber), 2g pro.

FESTIVE HOLIDAY SLIDERS

FESTIVE HOLIDAY SLIDERS

These flavorful mini turkey sandwiches keep well in the refrigerator. I like to have a batch on hand for holiday get-togethers.
—*Pamela Miller, Big Rapids, MI*

TAKES: 30 min. • **MAKES:** 2 dozen

- 1 pkg. (8 oz.) cream cheese, softened
- ½ cup mayonnaise
- ¼ cup Creole mustard
- 2 Tbsp. minced fresh gingerroot
- 1 Tbsp. grated orange zest
- 1½ tsp. prepared horseradish
- 1 cup whole-berry cranberry sauce
- 4 green onions, sliced
- 2 pkg. (12 oz. each) Hawaiian sweet rolls or 24 dinner rolls, split
- 1½ lbs. thinly sliced cooked turkey

1. Beat cream cheese and mayonnaise until smooth. Beat in the mustard, minced ginger, orange zest and horseradish. In another bowl, mix the cranberry sauce and green onions.
2. Spread cream cheese mixture onto roll bottoms. Top with the turkey, cranberry mixture and roll tops.
1 slider: 231 cal., 10g fat (4g sat. fat), 54mg chol., 221mg sod., 22g carb. (10g sugars, 1g fiber), 13g pro.

AUNT KAREN'S SHRIMP SALAD

When unexpected company calls or you need a dish to pass, this salad is the perfect choice. It's quick to put together, too, leaving you more time to spend with your guests.
—*Karen Moore, Jacksonville, FL*

PREP: 10 min. • **COOK:** 10 min. + chilling
MAKES: 24 servings

- 2 lbs. uncooked shrimp (26-30 per lb.), peeled and deveined and halved
- 1 Tbsp. white vinegar
- 1 Tbsp. lemon juice
- ⅓ cup plus 1 Tbsp. mayonnaise, divided
- ½ tsp. garlic salt
- 2 celery ribs, chopped
- 5 hard-boiled large eggs, chopped
- ¼ cup chopped sweet red pepper
- 24 Bibb lettuce leaves or Boston lettuce leaves
     Sliced green onions, optional

1. In a Dutch oven or large saucepan, bring 6 cups water to a boil. Add shrimp; cook, uncovered, until the shrimp turn pink, 3-5 minutes. Drain. Transfer to a large bowl. Add the vinegar, lemon juice, 1 Tbsp. mayonnaise and garlic salt; toss to coat. Refrigerate salad, covered, for at least 4 hours or overnight.
2. To serve, stir in the remaining ⅓ cup mayonnaise, celery, eggs and red pepper. Serve in lettuce leaves. If desired, top with green onions.
¼ cup: 74 cal., 4g fat (1g sat. fat), 85mg chol., 120mg sod., 1g carb. (0 sugars, 0 fiber), 8g pro. **Diabetic exchanges:** 1 lean meat, 1 fat.

TEST KITCHEN TIP

To know when shrimp are cooked (and safe to eat), watch the color. A perfectly cooked shrimp has an opaque pinky color with a sheen.

AUNT KAREN'S
SHRIMP SALAD

FRUIT KABOBS WITH MARGARITA DIP

FRUIT KABOBS WITH MARGARITA DIP

Your adult guests will love the margarita flavor of this cool and creamy dip. Serve the kabobs as either a snack or a dessert.
—Michelle Zapf, Kingsland, GA

TAKES: 25 min.
MAKES: 6 kabobs (1½ cups dip)

3 oz. cream cheese, softened
½ cup sour cream
¼ cup confectioners' sugar
1 Tbsp. lime juice
1 Tbsp. thawed orange juice concentrate
1 Tbsp. tequila
½ cup heavy whipping cream
12 fresh strawberries
6 pineapple chunks
1 medium mango, peeled and cubed
6 seedless red grapes
2 slices pound cake, cubed

In a large bowl, combine the first 6 ingredients. Beat in whipping cream until fluffy. Meanwhile, thread fruits and cake on metal or wooden skewers. Serve skewers with dip.

1 kabob with ¼ cup dip: 273 cal., 18g fat (11g sat. fat), 78mg chol., 97mg sod., 25g carb. (16g sugars, 2g fiber), 3g pro.

TEST KITCHEN TIP

To make this fruit dip a little healthier, use plain Greek yogurt instead of sour cream and replace the heavy whipping cream with low-fat or fat-free whipped topping. You can also substitute the dairy products for dairy-free versions.

STROMBOLI SANDWICH

STROMBOLI SANDWICH

I've made this hot stromboli sandwich many times for parties, and it gets terrific reviews. Feel free to add ingredients and spices to suit your taste.
—Leigh Lauer, Hummelstown, PA

PREP: 20 min. + rising • **BAKE:** 30 min.
MAKES: 10 servings

2 loaves (1 lb. each) frozen bread dough, thawed
¼ lb. sliced ham
¼ lb. sliced pepperoni
¼ cup chopped onion
¼ cup chopped green pepper
1 jar (14 oz.) pizza sauce, divided
¼ lb. sliced mozzarella cheese
¼ lb. sliced bologna
¼ lb. sliced hard salami
¼ lb. slice Swiss cheese
1 tsp. dried basil
1 tsp. dried oregano
¼ tsp. garlic powder
¼ tsp. pepper
2 Tbsp. butter, melted

Let the dough rise in a warm place until doubled. Punch down. Combine loaves and roll into one 15x12-in. rectangle. Layer ham and pepperoni on half of the dough (lengthwise). Sprinkle with onion and green pepper. Top with ¼ cup of pizza sauce. Layer mozzarella, bologna, salami and Swiss cheese over sauce. Sprinkle with basil, oregano, garlic powder and pepper. Spread another ¼ cup of pizza sauce on top. Fold plain half of dough over filling and seal edges well. Place on a greased 15x10x1-in. baking pan. Bake at 375° until golden brown, 30-35 minutes. Brush with the melted butter. Heat the remaining pizza sauce and serve with sliced stromboli.

1 piece: 388 cal., 23g fat (10g sat. fat), 60mg chol., 1175mg sod., 28g carb. (5g sugars, 2g fiber), 19g pro.

CHEESE & PIMIENTO SPREAD

This pimiento and cheese spread is a spicy, modern version of my mother's delicious recipe. Serve it stuffed in celery or spread on crackers or a sandwich.

—*Elizabeth Hester, Elizabethtown, NC*

TAKES: 15 min. • **MAKES:** 2¾ cups

- 12 oz. sharp white cheddar cheese
- 8 oz. reduced-fat cream cheese, softened
- 2 tsp. Worcestershire sauce
- 2 tsp. white vinegar
- ¼ tsp. white pepper
- ¼ tsp. garlic powder
- ¼ tsp. cayenne pepper
- 1 jar (4 oz.) diced pimientos, undrained
  Assorted crackers and vegetables

Shred the cheddar cheese; transfer to a large bowl. Add the cream cheese, Worcestershire sauce, vinegar, pepper, garlic powder and cayenne; beat on low speed until blended. Drain pimientos, reserving 2 Tbsp. juice. Stir in pimientos and reserved juice. Serve with crackers and vegetables.

2 Tbsp.: 90 cal., 7g fat (4g sat. fat), 23mg chol., 150mg sod., 1g carb. (1g sugars, 0 fiber), 5g pro.

READER RAVES

"This is a staple at my house on poker night. It goes great with beer!"

—RAY218, TASTEOFHOME.COM

CHEESE & PIMIENTO SPREAD

GROUND BEEF TACO DIP

What's a football party without taco dip? This version, made with spicy ground beef and fresh toppings, does not disappoint the die-hards. It is full of classic flavors and is a little extra filling for hearty game-day appetites.
—*Errika Perry, Green Bay, WI*

TAKES: 25 min. • MAKES: 24 servings

- 1 lb. lean ground beef (90% lean)
- ¾ cup water
- 2 envelopes taco seasoning, divided
- 2 cups fat-free sour cream
- 1 pkg. (8 oz.) cream cheese, softened
- 2 cups shredded iceberg lettuce
- 1 cup shredded cheddar cheese
- 3 medium tomatoes, finely chopped
- 1 medium green pepper, finely chopped
- 1 can (2¼ oz.) sliced ripe olives, drained

1. In a large skillet, cook and crumble the beef over medium heat until no longer pink, 4-6 minutes; drain. Add water and 1 envelope taco seasoning; cook until thickened. Cool slightly.
2. Beat sour cream, cream cheese and remaining taco seasoning until blended. Spread in a 3-qt. dish; add ground beef. Top with lettuce, cheddar, tomatoes, pepper and olives.
½ cup: 116 cal., 7g fat (3g sat. fat), 30mg chol., 378mg sod., 7g carb. (2g sugars, 0 fiber), 7g pro.

TEST KITCHEN TIP

If you want to amp up the flavor in your taco dip, select an aged sharp cheddar cheese instead of mild. As cheese ages, its flavor becomes more pronounced, adding more spark to your dish.

CHAMPAGNE SIPPER

Here's a terrific cocktail for any special celebration. And because you make it by the pitcher, you can mingle with your guests instead of tending bar.
—*Moffat Frazier, New York, NY*

TAKES: 10 min. • MAKES: 12 servings

- 1½ cups sugar
- 1 cup lemon juice
- 3 cups cold water
- 1½ cups sweet white wine, chilled
- 1 bottle (750 ml) champagne, chilled
  Sliced fresh strawberries, optional

In a 3-qt. pitcher, dissolve sugar in lemon juice. Add cold water and wine. Stir in the champagne. If desired, serve with sliced fresh strawberries.
¾ cup: 168 cal., 0 fat (0 sat. fat), 0 chol., 2mg sod., 28g carb. (26g sugars, 0 fiber), 0 pro.

DILL DIP

Be prepared—you'll likely need to make a double batch of this delightful dip. One is never enough when we have a gathering. It tastes fantastic with just about any vegetable, so you can use whatever you have on hand as a dipper.
—*Kathy Beldorth, Three Oaks, MI*

PREP: 10 min. + chilling • **MAKES:** 2 cups

- 1 **cup mayonnaise**
- 1 **cup sour cream**
- 2 **Tbsp. dried parsley flakes**
- 1 **Tbsp. dried minced onion**
- 2 **tsp. dill weed**
- 1½ **tsp. seasoned salt**
- 1 **tsp. sugar**
  Fresh vegetables or potato chips

In a small bowl, combine the first 7 ingredients. Chill for at least 1 hour. Serve with vegetables or potato chips.
2 Tbsp.: 123 cal., 13g fat (3g sat. fat), 5mg chol., 219mg sod., 1g carb. (1g sugars, 0 fiber), 1g pro.

DID YOU KNOW?

Dill weed is a tangy herb that imparts a slight licorice flavor and grows in a bouquet of wispy, fragrant fronds. Most commonly associated with Scandinavian and German cooking, dill adds a clean, fresh earthiness to foods.

DILL DIP

MINIATURE CORN DOGS

FRIED CINNAMON STRIPS

These sweet chips are a must for your next party. Use holiday cookie cutters to shape the tortillas into fun shapes.
—*Nancy Johnson, Laverne, OK*

TAKES: 25 min. • MAKES: 5 dozen

- 1 cup sugar
- 1 tsp. ground cinnamon
- ¼ tsp. ground nutmeg
- 10 flour tortillas (8 in.)
  Canola oil

1. In a large bowl, combine the sugar, cinnamon and nutmeg; set aside.
2. Cut the tortillas into 3x2-in. strips. Heat 1 in. oil in a cast-iron or other heavy skillet to 375°, fry 4-5 strips at a time until golden brown, 30 seconds on each side. Drain on paper towels.
3. While still warm, place strips in bowl with sugar mixture; shake gently to coat. Serve strips immediately or store in an airtight container.
1 piece: 44 cal., 1g fat (0 sat. fat), 0 chol., 39mg sod., 8g carb. (3g sugars, 0 fiber), 1g pro.

MINIATURE CORN DOGS

Fun-size corn dogs add a little wow to any gathering. Kids and adults love them, so expect them to disappear fast.
—*Deb Perry, Bluffton, IN*

PREP: 25 min. • COOK: 5 min./batch
MAKES: about 3½ dozen

- 1 cup all-purpose flour
- 2 Tbsp. cornmeal
- 1½ tsp. baking powder
- ¼ tsp. salt
  Dash onion powder
- 3 Tbsp. shortening
- ¾ cup 2% milk
- 1 large egg, room temperature
- 1 pkg. (16 oz.) miniature smoked sausages

Oil for deep-fat frying
Spicy ketchup
Mustard

1. In a small bowl, combine the flour, cornmeal, baking powder, salt and onion powder; cut in shortening until crumbly. Whisk milk and egg; stir into flour mixture just until moistened. Dip sausages into the batter.
2. In a cast-iron or other heavy skillet, heat oil to 375°. Fry sausages, a few at a time, until golden brown, 2-3 minutes. Drain on paper towels. Serve corn dogs with the ketchup and mustard.
1 mini corn dog: 68 cal., 6g fat (1g sat. fat), 11mg chol., 136mg sod., 2g carb. (0 sugars, 0 fiber), 2g pro.

THE BEST HUMMUS

Homemade hummus is my go-to appetizer when I need something quick, easy and impressive. Over the years I've picked up a number of tricks that make this the best hummus you'll ever have.
—*James Schend, Pleasant Prairie, WI*

PREP: 25 min. + chilling • **COOK:** 20 min.
MAKES: 1½ cups

- 1 **can (15 oz.) garbanzo beans or chickpeas, rinsed and drained**
- ½ **tsp. baking soda**
- ¼ **cup fresh lemon juice**
- 1 **Tbsp. minced garlic**
- ½ **tsp. kosher salt**
- ½ **tsp. ground cumin**
- ½ **cup tahini**
- 2 **Tbsp. extra virgin olive oil**
- ¼ **cup cold water**
  Optional: Olive oil, roasted garbanzo beans, toasted sesame seeds, ground sumac

1. Place garbanzo beans in a large saucepan; add water to cover by 1 in. Gently rub beans together to loosen outer skin. Pour off water and any skins that are floating. Repeat 2-3 times until no skins float to the surface; drain. Return to the saucepan; add baking soda and enough water to cover by 1 in. Bring to a boil; reduce heat. Simmer, uncovered, until beans are very tender and just starting to fall apart, 20-25 minutes.
2. Meanwhile, in a blender, process lemon juice, garlic and salt until almost a paste. Let stand 10 minutes; strain, discarding solids. Stir in cumin. In a small bowl, stir together tahini and olive oil.
3. Drain beans and add to blender; add cold water. Loosely cover and process until completely smooth. Add lemon mixture and process. With blender running, slowly add tahini mixture, scraping side as needed. Adjust the seasoning with additional salt and cumin if desired.
4. Transfer mixture to a serving bowl; cover and refrigerate at least 30 minutes. If desired, top with additional olive oil and optional toppings.

¼ cup: 250 cal., 19g fat (3g sat. fat), 0 chol., 361mg sod., 15g carb. (2g sugars, 5g fiber), 7g pro.

TEST KITCHEN TIP

Hummus is the perfect make-ahead appetizer to have on hand and it's a great spread to add to charcuterie boards or platters. This recipe creates a nice, thick hummus, but if you still find it's too thin, pop it into the fridge to set. If the hummus is still not as thick as you'd like, simply blend in more chickpeas or tahini.

THE BEST
HUMMUS

HOVER YOUR CAMERA HERE
How to Make a Charcuterie Board Perfect for Any Party

BARBECUE & BEER MEATBALLS

This simple meatball recipe relies on timesaving ingredients like frozen meatballs and barbecue sauce. It's the perfect last-minute appetizer!
—Taste of Home *Test Kitchen*

TAKES: 30 min. • **MAKES:** 20 servings

- 1 pkg. (22 oz.) frozen fully cooked Angus beef meatballs
- 1 cup barbecue sauce
- ⅓ cup beer
  Thinly sliced jalapeno pepper, optional

1. Prepare the meatballs according to package directions.
2. Meanwhile, in a small saucepan, combine barbecue sauce and beer; heat through. Add meatballs; stir to coat. If desired, top with sliced jalapeno.
1 meatball: 106 cal., 6g fat (3g sat. fat), 17mg chol., 338mg sod., 7g carb. (5g sugars, 0 fiber), 4g pro.

READER RAVES

"Wow, super easy and delicious! I made these for New Year's Eve and everyone loved them. Such a simple and yummy appetizer."

—DEBGLASS11, TASTEOFHOME.COM

BARBECUE & BEER
MEATBALLS

CURRIED BEEF BITES

CURRIED BEEF BITES

These appetizers are so fast and easy to prepare. They are always the first to disappear at any party!
—*Karen Kuebler, Dallas, TX*

PREP: 15 min. • **BAKE:** 15 min.
MAKES: 3 dozen

- 12 slices white bread, crusts removed
- 3 Tbsp. butter, melted
- ½ lb. ground beef
- 5 celery ribs, chopped
- ½ cup seasoned bread crumbs
- 2 tsp. curry powder
- ½ tsp. garlic salt
  Optional: Cucumber raita and chopped fresh cilantro

1. Preheat oven to 400°. Flatten bread slices with a rolling pin; brush tops with butter. Set aside.
2. In a large skillet, cook beef and celery over medium heat until beef is no longer pink and celery is tender, 8-10 minutes, breaking beef into crumbles; drain. Stir in the bread crumbs, curry powder and garlic salt.
3. Spoon beef mixture onto bread slices. Roll up and secure with toothpicks. Place on a greased baking sheet. Bake until the roll-ups are golden brown, 12-15 minutes. When the appetizers are cool enough to handle, discard toothpicks and cut each roll-up crosswise into 3 pieces. If desired, serve warm with cucumber raita and chopped fresh cilantro.
1 roll-up: 52 cal., 2g fat (1g sat. fat), 6mg chol., 114mg sod., 6g carb. (1g sugars, 0 fiber), 2g pro.

CHEESY BBQ BEEF DIP

CHEESY BBQ BEEF DIP

Barbecued beef dip is a holiday staple in our house. My husband can't get enough!
—*Selena Swafford, Dalton, GA*

TAKES: 30 min. • **MAKES:** 8 servings

- 1 pkg. (8 oz.) cream cheese, softened
- 1 pkg. (15 oz.) refrigerated fully cooked barbecued shredded beef
- 1 cup shredded cheddar cheese
- ½ cup chopped red onion
- ¾ cup french-fried onions
  Optional toppings: Chopped tomatoes, chopped red onion and minced fresh cilantro
  Tortilla chips

Preheat oven to 350°. Spread the cream cheese onto bottom of a greased 9-in. pie plate. Spread beef evenly on top. Sprinkle with cheddar cheese and red onion. Bake until heated through, 15-20 minutes. Sprinkle with french-fried onions; bake for 5 minutes longer. If desired, top dip with tomatoes, onion and cilantro. Serve with tortilla chips.
¼ cup: 279 cal., 19g fat (10g sat. fat), 57mg chol., 578mg sod., 16g carb. (10g sugars, 0 fiber), 12g pro.

CRANBERRY-LIME SANGRIA

Tart, light and fruity, this party-worthy sangria is a hit any time of the year.
—Katy Joosten, Little Chute, WI

TAKES: 20 min.
MAKES: 13 servings (about 2½ qt.)

- 2 cups water
- 1 cup fresh or frozen cranberries, thawed
- 1 bottle (750 ml) white wine, chilled
- ¾ cup frozen limeade concentrate, thawed
- 1 each medium orange, lime and apple, peeled and diced
- 1 bottle (1 liter) citrus soda, chilled

1. In a small saucepan, combine water and cranberries. Cook over medium heat until berries pop, about 5 minutes. Drain and discard liquid; set the cranberries aside.
2. In a pitcher, combine the wine and limeade concentrate. Stir in the diced fruit and reserved cranberries; add the soda. Serve over ice.

¾ cup: 134 cal., 0 fat (0 sat. fat), 0 chol., 12mg sod., 24g carb. (21g sugars, 1g fiber), 0 pro.

READER RAVES

"This was a hit for the holidays and my friends enjoyed every sip of it. This recipe is going into my favorites!"

—BCANALES21, TASTEOFHOME.COM

HOVER YOUR CAMERA HERE
Everything You Need For a Perfect Home Bar Setup

CRANBERRY-LIME SANGRIA

**EASY
DEVILED EGGS**

EASY DEVILED EGGS
(PICTURED ON COVER)

I drew inspiration for these deviled eggs from the ones served at the Durbin Inn, a well-known restaurant in Rushville, Indiana, that operated from the 1920s until it closed in the late '70s. The eggs are delicious and easy to make.
—*Margaret Sanders, Indianapolis, IN*

TAKES: 15 min. • **MAKES:** 1 dozen

- 6 hard-boiled large eggs
- 2 Tbsp. mayonnaise
- 1 tsp. sugar
- 1 tsp. white vinegar
- 1 tsp. prepared mustard
- ½ tsp. salt
  Paprika

Slice eggs in half lengthwise; remove the yolks and set whites aside. In a small bowl, mash yolks with a fork. Add the mayonnaise, sugar, vinegar, mustard and salt; mix well. Stuff or pipe into egg whites. Sprinkle eggs with paprika. Refrigerate until serving.

1 egg half: 55 cal., 4g fat (1g sat. fat), 94mg chol., 146mg sod., 1g carb. (1g sugars, 0 fiber), 3g pro.

Bacon-Cheddar Deviled Eggs: To the mashed yolks, add ¼ cup mayonnaise, 2 cooked and crumbled bacon strips, 1 Tbsp. finely shredded cheddar cheese, 1½ tsp. honey mustard and ⅛ tsp. pepper. Stuff eggs as directed.

Picnic Stuffed Deviled Eggs: To the mashed yolks, add ¼ cup mayonnaise, 2 Tbsp. drained sweet pickle relish, 1½ tsp. honey mustard, ½ tsp. garlic salt, ¼ tsp. Worcestershire sauce and ⅛ tsp. pepper. Stuff as directed.

Santa Fe Deviled Eggs: To mashed yolks, add 3 Tbsp. each mayonnaise and canned chopped green chiles, 1½ tsp. chipotle pepper in adobo sauce and ¼ tsp. garlic salt. Stuff as directed. Garnish each with 1 tsp. salsa and a sliver of ripe olive.

Crab-Stuffed Deviled Eggs: Prepare 12 hard-cooked eggs. To mashed yolks, add 1 can (6 oz.) crabmeat (drained, flaked and cartilage removed), ⅔ cup mayonnaise, ½ cup finely chopped celery, ½ cup slivered almonds, 2 Tbsp. finely chopped green pepper and ½ tsp. salt. Stuff as directed.

BRIE PHYLLO CUPS

Mini phyllo shells from the freezer section make these elegant bites quick and easy. They look fancy and taste delicious, but they're a snap to put together for a special occasion.
—*Brenda Little, Boise, ID*

TAKES: 20 min. • **MAKES:** 15 appetizers

- 1 pkg. (1.9 oz.) frozen miniature phyllo tart shells
- 3 Tbsp. crushed gingersnaps
- 6 oz. Brie cheese, rind removed, cubed
- ¼ cup spreadable fruit of your choice

Preheat oven to 325°. Place the tart shells on an ungreased baking sheet. Sprinkle about ½ tsp. gingersnap crumbs into each shell; top with Brie and spreadable fruit. Bake tarts for 5 minutes or until the cheese is melted.

1 serving: 83 cal., 4g fat (2g sat. fat), 11mg chol., 100mg sod., 7g carb. (3g sugars, 0 fiber), 3g pro.

CHICKARITOS

SAUSAGE CHEESE PUFFS

People are always surprised when I tell them there are only four ingredients in these tasty bite-sized puffs. Cheesy and spicy, the golden morsels are a fun novelty at a breakfast or brunch, and they also make yummy party appetizers.
—*Della Moore, Troy, NY*

TAKES: 25 min. • **MAKES:** about 4 dozen

- 1 lb. bulk Italian sausage
- 3 cups biscuit/baking mix
- 4 cups shredded cheddar cheese
- ¾ cup water

1. Preheat oven to 400°. In a large skillet, cook sausage over medium heat until meat is no longer pink, 5-7 minutes, breaking sausage into crumbles; drain.
2. In a large bowl, combine the biscuit mix and cheese; stir in sausage. Add water and toss with a fork until moistened. Shape into 1½-in. balls. Place 2 in. apart on ungreased baking sheets.
3. Bake until puffed and golden brown, 12-15 minutes. Cool on wire racks.
Freeze option: Baked puffs may be frozen. Reheat at 400° for 7-9 minutes or until puffs are heated through (they do not need to thaw first).
1 appetizer: 89 cal., 6g fat (3g sat. fat), 14mg chol., 197mg sod., 6g carb. (0 sugars, 0 fiber), 4g pro.

CHICKARITOS

After our son grew fond of a fast-food restaurant's fried burritos, I created this recipe by substituting beef with chicken and skipping the frying. It's been a hit with our family ever since!
—*Nancy Coates, Oro Valley, AZ*

PREP: 30 min. • **BAKE:** 20 min.
MAKES: 3 dozen

- 3 cups finely chopped cooked chicken
- 1½ cups shredded sharp cheddar cheese
- 1 can (4 oz.) chopped green chiles
- 4 green onions, finely chopped
- 1 tsp. hot pepper sauce
- 1 tsp. garlic salt
- ¼ tsp. paprika
- ¼ tsp. ground cumin
- ¼ tsp. pepper
- 2 pkg. (17.3 oz. each) frozen puff pastry, thawed
- 1 large egg, beaten
  Salsa and guacamole

1. Preheat oven to 425°. In a large bowl, combine chicken, cheese, chiles, onions, pepper sauce and seasonings.
2. Unfold 1 sheet of puff pastry onto a lightly floured surface. Roll into a 12x9-in. rectangle. Cut into nine 4x3-in. rectangles.
3. Place 2 Tbsp. filling across the center of each rectangle. Brush edges of pastry with water and roll up pastry around filling. Press edges with a fork to seal. Repeat with remaining pastry and filling. Refrigerate, covered, until ready to bake.
4. Place pastries on a lightly greased baking sheet, seam side down. Brush tops with egg. Bake 20-25 minutes or until golden brown. Serve warm with salsa and guacamole.
1 appetizer: 213 cal., 12g fat (4g sat. fat), 31mg chol., 294mg sod., 16g carb. (0 sugars, 2g fiber), 11g pro.

SAUSAGE CHEESE PUFFS

CARAMEL CHEX MIX

This crunchy snack is loaded with cereal, pretzels and nuts—and coated with a not-too-sweet brown sugar mixture. Set out a bowl at your party and watch it disappear by the handful.
—Samantha Moyer, Oskaloosa, IA

PREP: 10 min. • BAKE: 15 min. + cooling
MAKES: 3 qt.

- 2 cups each Rice Chex, Corn Chex and Wheat Chex
- 2 cups miniature pretzels
- 2 cups pecan halves
- 2 cups salted cashews
- ¾ cup butter, cubed
- ¾ cup packed brown sugar

1. In a large bowl, combine the cereal, pretzels and nuts. In a small saucepan, combine butter and brown sugar. Bring to a boil; cook and stir until thickened, about 2 minutes. Pour over cereal mixture; toss to coat.

2. Spread into 2 greased 15x10x1-in. baking pans. Bake mix at 350° for 8 minutes. Stir; bake 6 minutes longer. Transfer mix to waxed paper-lined baking sheets. Cool completely. Store in airtight containers.

¾ cup: 383 cal., 27g fat (8g sat. fat), 23mg chol., 333mg sod., 34g carb. (14g sugars, 3g fiber), 6g pro.

HOVER YOUR CAMERA HERE
20 Host and Hostess Gifts (That Aren't a Bottle of Wine)

CARAMEL CHEX MIX

**MINI
CHEESE BALLS**

SPINACH & CRAB DIP

We love this recipe! I've lightened it up considerably without losing any of the original's richness, and no one can tell the difference. I also serve it as a topping on baked potatoes.
—*Sandie Heindel, Liberty, MO*

TAKES: 25 min. • **MAKES:** 4 cups

- 1 pkg. (10 oz.) frozen chopped spinach, thawed and squeezed dry
- 1 pkg. (8 oz.) reduced-fat cream cheese, cubed
- 1 cup plain yogurt
- ½ cup grated Parmesan cheese
- ½ cup Miracle Whip Light
- 2 garlic cloves, minced
- 1 tsp. crushed red pepper flakes
- ¼ tsp. salt
- ¼ tsp. pepper
- 1 can (6 oz.) lump crabmeat, drained
  Assorted crackers or baked tortilla chip scoops

1. In a large saucepan over low heat, combine the first 9 ingredients. Cook and stir until cream cheese is melted. Stir in crab; heat through.
2. Transfer to a serving bowl; serve with crackers. Refrigerate leftovers.
¼ cup: 89 cal., 6g fat (3g sat. fat), 26mg chol., 256mg sod., 3g carb. (2g sugars, 1g fiber), 6g pro.

BRING IT
Transfer this dip to a small 1- or 2-qt. slow cooker to transport it easily in a car. This will also keep it hot at a party.

MINI CHEESE BALLS

These mini cheese balls are the perfect quick appetizer for any party. Roll them in toasted sesame seeds, fresh rosemary and/or paprika to add even more flavor.
—*Judy Spivey, Ennice, NC*

PREP: 30 min. + chilling
MAKES: 36 cheese balls

- 1 pkg. (8 oz.) cream cheese, softened
- 2 cups shredded sharp cheddar cheese
  Optional toppings: Toasted sesame seeds, minced fresh rosemary and paprika
  Optional garnishes: Halved rye crisps and rolled tortilla chips

In a large bowl, combine cheeses. Shape into 36 balls; roll the balls in toppings as desired. Cover and refrigerate for 8 hours or overnight. Before serving, press a rye crisp or rolled tortilla chip into the top of each cheese ball if desired,
1 cheese ball: 47 cal., 4g fat (2g sat. fat), 13mg chol., 61mg sod., 1g carb. (0 sugars, 0 fiber), 2g pro.

PINEAPPLE CHEESE BALL

Pineapple lends a fruity tang to this fun and tasty appetizer. Instead of forming one large cheese ball, you could make two smaller balls—one to serve before a meal and one to take to a party.
—*Anne Halfhill, Sunbury, OH*

PREP: 20 min. + chilling
MAKES: 1 cheese ball (3 cups)

- 2 pkg. (8 oz. each) cream cheese, softened
- 1 can (8 oz.) unsweetened crushed pineapple, drained
- ¼ cup finely chopped green pepper
- 2 Tbsp. finely chopped onion
- 2 tsp. seasoned salt
- 1½ cups chopped walnuts
  Optional: Assorted crackers and fresh vegetables

In a small bowl, beat cream cheese, pineapple, green pepper, onion and seasoned salt until blended. Cover and refrigerate for 30 minutes. Shape into a ball (mixture will be soft); coat in walnuts. Cover and refrigerate overnight. Serve with crackers and vegetables if desired.

2 Tbsp.: 87 cal., 8g fat (2g sat. fat), 10mg chol., 155mg sod., 3g carb. (1g sugars, 1g fiber), 3g pro.

PINEAPPLE CHEESE BALL

BUTTERSCOTCH MULLED CIDER

Only five minutes of preparation is needed for this dynamite slow-cooked drink. You will love the sweet taste of butterscotch and cinnamon in this hot apple cider.
—*Karen Mack, Webster, NY*

PREP: 5 min. • **COOK:** 3 hours
MAKES: 18 servings

- 1 gallon apple cider or juice
- 2 cups butterscotch schnapps liqueur
- 8 cinnamon sticks (3 in.)
  Optional: Apple pieces and additional cinnamon sticks

In a 6-qt. slow cooker, combine the first 3 ingredients. Cover and cook on low for 3-4 hours or until heated through. If desired, garnish with apple pieces and additional cinnamon sticks.
1 cup: 128 cal., 0 fat (0 sat. fat), 0 chol., 22mg sod., 27g carb. (23g sugars, 0 fiber), 0 pro.

READER RAVES

"This is so good and easy to throw together. It's an instant signature drink with no effort—warm, sweet, boozy and cinnamony. I have made it part of my Christmas Eve tradition."

—**KREDHEAD, TASTEOFHOME.COM**

SPINACH & TURKEY PINWHEELS

Need an awesome snack for game day? My kids love these easy four-ingredient turkey pinwheels. Go ahead and make these treats the day before—they won't get soggy!
—*Amy Van Hemert, Ottumwa, IA*

TAKES: 15 min. • **MAKES:** 4 dozen

- 1 carton (8 oz.) spreadable garden vegetable cream cheese
- 8 flour tortillas (8 in.)
- 4 cups fresh baby spinach
- 1 lb. sliced deli turkey

Spread cream cheese over tortillas. Layer with spinach and turkey. Roll up tightly. If not serving immediately, cover pinwheels and refrigerate. To serve, cut each roll crosswise into 6 pieces.
1 pinwheel: 51 cal., 2g fat (1g sat. fat), 9mg chol., 144mg sod., 5g carb. (0 sugars, 0 fiber), 3g pro.

PROSCIUTTO-WRAPPED ASPARAGUS WITH RASPBERRY SAUCE

Grilling prosciutto with the asparagus gives this dish a salty crunch that's perfect for dipping into a sweet glaze. When a delicious appetizer is this easy to prepare, you owe it to yourself to try it!
—Noelle Myers, Grand Forks, ND

TAKES: 30 min. • **MAKES:** 16 appetizers

- ⅓ lb. thinly sliced prosciutto or deli ham
- 16 fresh asparagus spears, trimmed
- ½ cup seedless raspberry jam
- 2 Tbsp. balsamic vinegar

1. Cut the prosciutto slices in half. Wrap a piece of prosciutto around each asparagus spear; secure ends with toothpicks.

2. Grill asparagus, covered, on a greased rack over medium heat for 6-8 minutes or until prosciutto is crisp, turning once. Discard toothpicks.

3. In a small microwave-safe bowl, microwave jam and vinegar on high for 15-20 seconds or until the jam is melted. Serve with asparagus.

1 asparagus spear with 1½ tsp. sauce: 50 cal., 1g fat (0 sat. fat), 8mg chol., 184mg sod., 7g carb. (7g sugars, 0 fiber), 3g pro. **Diabetic exchanges:** ½ starch.

TEST KITCHEN TIP

Fine grit can lurk in asparagus tips. To get rid of it, fill a bowl with cold water and soak the asparagus for a few minutes, then thoroughly rinse off. That should rid the stems of any unpleasant sandiness.

PROSCIUTTO-WRAPPED ASPARAGUS WITH RASPBERRY SAUCE

CITRUS & WHITE GRAPE PARTY PUNCH

JALAPENO POPPER POCKET

For a fresh take on classic fried poppers, we stuff chicken, cheeses and jalapenos inside puff pastry and bake.
—*Sally Sibthorpe, Shelby Township, MI*

PREP: 15 min. • BAKE: 20 min. + standing
MAKES: 12 servings

- 2 **cups chopped rotisserie chicken (about 10 oz.)**
- 1 **carton (8 oz.) spreadable chive and onion cream cheese**
- 1 **cup shredded pepper jack or Monterey Jack cheese**
- 1 **can (4 oz.) diced jalapeno peppers**
- 1 **sheet frozen puff pastry, thawed**
- 1 **large egg, lightly beaten**

1. Preheat oven to 425°. In a bowl, mix the chicken, cream cheese, pepper jack cheese and peppers.
2. On a lightly floured surface, unfold puff pastry; roll into a 13-in. square. Place on a parchment-lined baking sheet. Spread half with chicken mixture to within ½ in. of edges. Fold remaining half over filling; press edges with a fork to seal.
3. Brush lightly with the beaten egg. Cut slits in pastry. Bake 20-25 minutes or until golden brown. Let the poppers stand for 10 minutes before cutting.
1 piece: 237 cal., 15g fat (6g sat. fat), 58mg chol., 252mg sod., 13g carb. (1g sugars, 2g fiber), 12g pro.

CITRUS & WHITE GRAPE PARTY PUNCH

I was looking for a party punch that wouldn't stain expensive prom dresses and tuxedos. All the teens loved this one! You can mix the first four ingredients ahead of time, refrigerate and add the soda right before serving.
—*Karen Ballance, Wolf Lake, IL*

TAKES: 5 min. • MAKES: 32 servings (4 qt.)

- 4 **cups white grape juice, chilled**
- 1 **can (12 oz.) frozen lemonade concentrate, thawed**
- 1 **can (12 oz.) frozen orange juice concentrate, thawed**
- 2 **bottles (2 liters each) lemon-lime soda, chilled**
  Optional: Lemon slices, orange slices and green grapes

In a punch bowl, combine grape juice, lemonade concentrate and orange juice concentrate. Add soda; serve immediately. If desired, garnish with fruit.
½ cup: 119 cal., 0 fat (0 sat. fat), 0 chol., 17mg sod., 30g carb. (26g sugars, 0 fiber), 0 pro.

GRILLED GLAZED DRUMMIES

GRILLED GLAZED DRUMMIES

My family prefers these mild, slightly sweet chicken wings to traditional hot ones. They are a favorite at so many gatherings, especially game-day parties.
—*Laura Mahaffey, Annapolis, MD*

PREP: 10 min. + marinating • **GRILL:** 15 min.
MAKES: about 2 dozen

- 1 cup ketchup
- ⅓ cup reduced-sodium soy sauce
- 4 tsp. honey
- ¾ tsp. ground ginger
- ½ tsp. garlic powder
- 3 lbs. fresh or frozen chicken drumettes, thawed
  Optional: Sliced green onions and ranch dressing

1. In a small bowl, combine the first 5 ingredients. Pour 1 cup marinade into a large shallow dish. Add the chicken; turn to coat. Cover and refrigerate for at least 4 hours or overnight to marinate. Cover and refrigerate remaining marinade for basting.
2. Drain chicken, discarding marinade. Grill, covered, over medium heat until juices run clear, 15-20 minutes, turning and basting occasionally with reserved marinade. If desired, top with sliced green onions and serve with ranch dressing.
1 drummy: 141 cal., 9g fat (2g sat. fat), 43mg chol., 311mg sod., 3g carb. (3g sugars, 0 fiber), 11g pro.

KALAMATA CHEESECAKE APPETIZER

The rich, savory cheesecake filling tames the bold taste of kalamata olives, so even those who shy away from kalamatas will be glad they sampled this creamy appetizer. For a milder flavor, use the more common black or green olives.
—*Theresa Kreyche, Tustin, CA*

PREP: 30 min. • **BAKE:** 25 min. + chilling
MAKES: 24 servings

KALAMATA CHEESECAKE APPETIZER

- 1¼ cups seasoned bread crumbs
- ½ cup finely chopped pecans
- ⅓ cup butter, melted

FILLING

- 11 oz. cream cheese, softened
- 1 cup sour cream
- 1 Tbsp. all-purpose flour
- ¼ tsp. salt
- ¼ tsp. pepper
- 1 large egg, room temperature
- 1 large egg yolk, room temperature
- ½ cup pitted kalamata olives, chopped
- 2 tsp. minced fresh rosemary
  Optional: Halved pitted kalamata olives and fresh rosemary sprigs

1. In a small bowl, combine bread crumbs and pecans; stir in butter. Press onto the bottom of a greased 9-in. springform pan.

Place the pan on a baking sheet. Bake at 350° for 12 minutes. Cool on a wire rack.
2. In a large bowl, beat cream cheese, sour cream, flour, salt and pepper until smooth. Add egg and egg yolk; beat on low speed just until combined. Fold in chopped olives and minced rosemary. Pour over crust. Return pan to baking sheet.
3. Bake for 25-30 minutes or until the center is almost set. Cool on a wire rack for 10 minutes. Loosen the edge of the cheesecake from pan with a knife. Cool 1 hour longer. Refrigerate overnight.
4. Remove rim from pan. If desired, top the cheesecake with halved olives and rosemary sprigs.
1 piece: 142 cal., 12g fat (6g sat. fat), 45mg chol., 223mg sod., 6g carb. (1g sugars, 0 fiber), 3g pro.

STRAWBERRY & CREAM BRUSCHETTA

QUICK
TURKEY NACHOS SNACK

My husband is one of the biggest snackers around. I keep the ingredients on hand so I can whip up a batch of these nachos any time a craving calls.
—*Kathy Faulk, East Hartford, CT*

TAKES: 30 min. • **MAKES:** 8 servings

- 1 lb. ground turkey
- 1 pkg. (1¼ oz.) taco seasoning
- ¾ cup water
- 1 pkg. (12 oz.) tortilla chips
- ½ cup shredded Monterey Jack cheese
- ½ cup shredded cheddar cheese
- 2 cups shredded lettuce
- ½ cup sour cream
- ½ cup salsa
- 4 green onions, chopped

1. In a large nonstick skillet over medium heat, cook turkey until no longer pink, breaking into crumbles; drain. Add taco seasoning and water. Bring to a boil. Reduce heat; simmer, uncovered, until thickened, 8-10 minutes.
2. Arrange tortilla chips on an ungreased baking sheet. Top with turkey and cheese. Broil 4 in. from the heat until cheese is melted, 2-3 minutes. Top with lettuce, sour cream, salsa and onions.
1 serving: 400 cal., 21g fat (7g sat. fat), 54mg chol., 760mg sod., 35g carb. (1g sugars, 2g fiber), 18g pro.

STRAWBERRY & CREAM BRUSCHETTA

Here's a dessert take on bruschetta. Sweet, cinnamony toasts are topped with a cream cheese mixture, strawberries and almonds. They are like miniature cheesecakes and so yummy!
—*Christi Meixner, Aurora, IL*

TAKES: 25 min. • **MAKES:** 2 dozen

- 1 French bread baguette (8 oz.), cut into 24 slices
- ¼ cup butter, melted
- 3 Tbsp. sugar
- ½ tsp. ground cinnamon
- 1 pkg. (8 oz.) cream cheese, softened
- ¼ cup confectioners' sugar
- 2 tsp. lemon juice
- 1 tsp. grated lemon zest
- 2½ cups fresh strawberries, chopped
- ⅓ cup slivered almonds, toasted

1. Preheat oven to 375°. Place bread on an ungreased baking sheet; brush with butter. Combine sugar and cinnamon; sprinkle over bread. Bake 4-5 minutes on each side or until lightly crisp.
2. In a small bowl, beat cream cheese, confectioners' sugar, and lemon juice and zest until blended; spread over toast. Top with strawberries; sprinkle with almonds.
1 appetizer: 94 cal., 6g fat (3g sat. fat), 15mg chol., 70mg sod., 8g carb. (4g sugars, 1g fiber), 2g pro.

QUICK
TURKEY NACHOS
SNACK

CHICKEN CRESCENT WREATH

Here's an impressive-looking dish that's a snap to prepare. Even when my time is limited, I can still serve this delicious crescent wreath. The red pepper and green broccoli add a festive touch.
—*Marlene Denissen, St. Croix Falls, WI*

PREP: 15 min. • **BAKE:** 20 min.
MAKES: 16 servings

- 2 tubes (8 oz. each) refrigerated crescent rolls
- 1 cup shredded Colby-Monterey Jack cheese
- ⅔ cup condensed cream of chicken soup, undiluted
- ½ cup chopped fresh broccoli
- ½ cup chopped sweet red pepper
- ¼ cup chopped water chestnuts
- 1 can (5 oz.) white chicken, drained, or ¾ cup cubed cooked chicken
- 2 Tbsp. chopped onion

1. Arrange crescent rolls on a 12-in. pizza pan, forming a ring with pointed ends facing the outer edge of pan and wide ends overlapping.
2. Combine the remaining ingredients; spoon over wide ends of rolls. Fold points over filling and tuck under wide ends (filling will be visible).
3. Bake at 375° for 20-25 minutes or until golden brown.
Freeze option: Securely wrap the cooled wreath in foil; freeze. To use, remove from freezer 30 minutes before reheating. Remove the wreath from foil; reheat on a greased baking sheet in a preheated 325° oven until heated through.
1 piece: 151 cal., 8g fat (2g sat. fat), 11mg chol., 357mg sod., 14g carb. (3g sugars, 0 fiber), 6g pro.

SIMPLE GUACAMOLE

Because avocados can brown quickly, it's best to make this guacamole right before the party. If you do have to make it a little in advance, place the avocado pit in the guacamole until serving.
—*Heidi Main, Anchorage, AK*

TAKES: 10 min. • **MAKES:** 1½ cups

- 2 medium ripe avocados
- 1 Tbsp. lemon juice
- ¼ cup chunky salsa
- ⅛ to ¼ tsp. salt

Peel and chop avocados; place in a small bowl. Sprinkle with lemon juice. Add salsa and salt; mash with a fork to a coarse consistency. Refrigerate until serving.
2 Tbsp.: 53 cal., 5g fat (1g sat. fat), 0 chol., 51mg sod., 3g carb. (0 sugars, 2g fiber), 1g pro.

CHICKEN
CRESCENT
WREATH

FETA CHEESE-STUFFED TOMATOES

FETA CHEESE-STUFFED TOMATOES

These tempting cheese-stuffed tomatoes are bursting with fresh flavor. Use the small end of a melon scoop to easily remove the pulp.
—*Laura LeRoy, Waxhaw, NC*

TAKES: 25 min. • **MAKES:** 2 dozen

- 24 firm cherry tomatoes
- 3   oz. cream cheese, softened
- ⅓ cup crumbled feta cheese
- ¼ cup sour cream
- 1   green onion, finely chopped
- ¾ tsp. lemon juice
- ⅛ to ¼ tsp. dried oregano
     Coarsely ground pepper, optional

1. Cut a thin slice off the top of each tomato. Scoop out and discard pulp. Invert tomatoes onto paper towels to drain.
2. In a small mixing bowl, beat the cream cheese, feta cheese, sour cream, onion, lemon juice and oregano until blended. Pipe or spoon mixture into tomatoes. If desired, sprinkle with black pepper. Chill until serving.
1 stuffed tomato: 25 cal., 2g fat (1g sat. fat), 6mg chol., 28mg sod., 1g carb. (1g sugars, 0 fiber), 1g pro.

TEST KITCHEN TIP

To save time, you can prep the tomatoes and filling the night before your party, then fill the tomatoes before guests arrive. If you don't have oregano on hand, substitute dried basil.

GARDEN-FRESH SEAFOOD COCKTAIL

For something cool on a hot day, we mix shrimp and crabmeat with crunchy veggies straight from the garden. Look for adobo seasoning in your grocery store's ethnic food section.
—*Teri Rasey, Cadillac, MI*

PREP: 15 min. + chilling • **MAKES:** 6 cups

- ¾ lb. peeled and deveined cooked shrimp (31-40 per lb.)
- 1 container (8 oz.) refrigerated jumbo lump crabmeat, drained
- 3 celery ribs, chopped
- 1 medium cucumber, peeled, seeded and chopped
- 1 medium sweet orange pepper, chopped
- 2 plum tomatoes, seeded and chopped
- ½ cup red onion, finely chopped
- 1 to 2 jalapeno peppers, seeded and finely chopped
- ¼ cup minced fresh cilantro
- 3 Tbsp. lime juice
- 1 Tbsp. olive oil
- 2¼ tsp. adobo seasoning

Combine the first 9 ingredients. Whisk together the lime juice, oil and adobo seasoning; drizzle over shrimp mixture and toss gently to coat. Refrigerate at least 1 hour, tossing gently every 20 minutes. Serve shrimp mixture in cocktail glasses.
¾ cup: 103 cal., 3g fat (0 sat. fat), 92mg chol., 619mg sod., 5g carb. (2g sugars, 1g fiber), 15g pro.

STRAWBERRY WATERMELON LEMONADE

STRAWBERRY WATERMELON LEMONADE

The nutrition department at my local hospital inspired me to create this refreshing summer sipper. I tweaked their recipe slightly to create this drink full of sweet-tart flavor.
—*Dawn Lowenstein, Huntingdon Valley, PA*

TAKES: 20 min.
MAKES: 12 servings (3 qt.)

- ¼ cup sugar
- 2 cups boiling water
- ½ lb. fresh strawberries, hulled and quartered (about 2 cups)
- 12 cups cubed watermelon (about 1 medium)
- 1 can (12 oz.) frozen lemonade concentrate, thawed
- 3 Tbsp. lemon juice
  Ice cubes

Dissolve sugar in boiling water. Place strawberries and watermelon in a blender in batches; cover and process until blended. Pour blended fruit though a fine mesh strainer; transfer to a large pitcher. Stir in lemonade concentrate, lemon juice and sugar water. Serve over ice.
1 cup: 119 cal., 0 fat (0 sat. fat), 0 chol., 7mg sod., 34g carb. (30g sugars, 1g fiber), 1g pro.

PIZZA PUFFS

PIZZA PUFFS

What's more fun than a pizza puff? Skip store-bought brands and sample this homemade version. You can substitute any meat or vegetable for the pepperoni and any cheese for the mozzarella.
—*Vivi Taylor, Middleburg, FL*

TAKES: 30 min. • **MAKES:** 20 servings

- 1 loaf (1 lb.) frozen pizza dough, thawed
- 20 slices pepperoni
- 8 oz. part-skim mozzarella cheese, cut into 20 cubes
- ¼ cup butter
- 2 small garlic cloves, minced
  Dash salt
  Marinara sauce, warmed
  Optional: Crushed red pepper flakes and grated Parmesan cheese

1. Preheat oven to 400°. Shape dough into 1½-in. balls; flatten into ⅛-in. thick circles. Place 1 pepperoni slice and 1 cheese cube in center of each circle; wrap the dough around pepperoni and cheese. Pinch edges to seal; shape into a ball. Repeat with the remaining dough, cheese and pepperoni. Place seam side down on greased baking sheets; bake until light golden brown, 10-15 minutes. Cool slightly.
2. Meanwhile, in a small saucepan, melt butter over low heat. Add garlic and salt, taking care not to brown butter or garlic; brush over puffs. Serve with marinara sauce; if desired, sprinkle with red pepper flakes and Parmesan.

Freeze option: Cover and freeze unbaked pizza puffs on waxed paper-lined baking sheets until firm. Transfer to a freezer container; seal and return to freezer. To use, preheat oven to 400°; bake pizza puffs on greased baking sheets as directed, increasing baking time as necessary until golden brown.

1 pizza puff: 120 cal., 6g fat (3g sat. fat), 15mg chol., 189mg sod., 11g carb. (1g sugars, 0 fiber), 5g pro.

MINI ROSEMARY-
ROAST BEEF
SANDWICHES

Remove roast from skillet; let stand 1 hour.
Refrigerate roast, covered, for at least
2 hours, until cold.
4. Place giardiniera in a food processor;
pulse until finely chopped. In a bowl, mix
mayonnaise, mustard and horseradish.
5. To serve, thinly slice cold beef. Serve
on rolls with the mayonnaise mixture and
giardiniera relish.

**1 sandwich with about 2 tsp. mayonnaise
mixture and 4 tsp. giardiniera:** 220 cal.,
9g fat (3g sat. fat), 50mg chol., 466mg sod.,
18g carb. (7g sugars, 1g fiber), 17g pro.

PARTY PITAS

Whenever the ladies of our church host a
shower, these pita sandwiches appear on
the menu. Not only are they easy and
delicious, they add color to the table.
—*Janette Root, Ellensburg, WA*

TAKES: 15 min. • **MAKES:** 16 pieces

- 1   pkg. (8 oz.) cream cheese, softened
- ½   cup mayonnaise
- ½   tsp. dill weed
- ¼   tsp. garlic salt
- 4   whole pita breads
- 1½ cups fresh baby spinach
- 1   lb. shaved fully cooked ham
- ½   lb. thinly sliced Monterey Jack
      cheese

1. Mix the first 4 ingredients. Carefully
cut each pita horizontally in half; spread
2 Tbsp. mixture onto each cut surface.
2. On 4 pita halves, layer spinach, ham and
cheese. Top with remaining pita halves.
Cut each sandwich into 4 wedges; secure
with toothpicks.

1 piece: 225 cal., 15g fat (6g sat. fat), 45mg
chol., 557mg sod., 10g carb. (1g sugars,
0 fiber), 12g pro.

MINI ROSEMARY-
ROAST BEEF SANDWICHES

Roast beef sandwiches never last long at
a party, especially if you dollop them with
mayo, mustard, horseradish and pickled
giardiniera relish.
—*Susan Hein, Burlington, WI*

PREP: 25 min. + chilling
BAKE: 50 min. + chilling
MAKES: 2 dozen

- 1   beef top round roast (3 lbs.)
- 3   tsp. kosher salt
- 2   tsp. crushed dried rosemary
- 2   Tbsp. olive oil, divided
- 2   tsp. pepper
- 2   cups mild giardiniera, drained
- 1   cup reduced-fat mayonnaise
- 2   Tbsp. stone-ground mustard
- 1   to 2 Tbsp. prepared horseradish
- 24 Hawaiian sweet rolls, split

1. Sprinkle roast with salt and rosemary.
Cover and refrigerate at least 8 hours or
up to 24 hours.
2. Preheat oven to 325°. Uncover roast and
pat dry. Rub roast with 1 Tbsp. oil; sprinkle
with pepper. In a large cast-iron or other
ovenproof skillet, heat remaining 1 Tbsp.
oil over medium-high heat. Brown roast
on both sides.
3. Transfer roast to oven; roast until a
thermometer reads 135° for medium-rare,
50-60 minutes. (Temperature of roast will
continue to rise about 10° upon standing.)

EASY
STRAWBERRY SALSA

EASY STRAWBERRY SALSA

My salsa is sweet and colorful, with just a little bit of a bite from jalapeno peppers. I use fresh strawberries and my own home-grown vegetables, but you can also use produce available year-round. It's delicious with tortilla chips or even as a garnish to grill chicken or pork.
—*Dianna Wara, Washington, IL*

PREP: 20 min. + chilling
MAKES: 16 servings

- 3 cups chopped seeded tomatoes (about 4 large)
- 1⅓ cups chopped fresh strawberries
- ½ cup finely chopped onion (about 1 small)
- ½ cup minced fresh cilantro
- 1 to 2 jalapeno peppers, seeded and finely chopped
- ⅓ cup chopped sweet yellow or orange pepper
- ¼ cup lime juice
- ¼ cup honey
- 4 garlic cloves, minced
- 1 tsp. chili powder
  Baked tortilla chip scoops

In a large bowl, combine the first 10 ingredients. Refrigerate, covered, at least 2 hours. Serve with chips.
Note: Wear disposable gloves when cutting hot peppers; the oils can burn skin. Avoid touching your face.
¼ cup: 33 cal., 0 fat (0 sat. fat), 0 chol., 4mg sod., 8g carb. (6g sugars, 1g fiber), 1g pro.
Diabetic exchanges: ½ starch.

TEST KITCHEN TIP

As the salsa chills in the fridge, the tomatoes will start to break down. To keep your salsa from getting too watery, always scoop out the inner pulp and seeds from tomatoes before chopping and adding them to the salsa.

PANCETTA, PEAR & PECAN PUFFS

PANCETTA, PEAR & PECAN PUFFS

I was recently at a wedding reception where the menu was all small bites. Here's my rendition of the pear pastries they served. They're the perfect combo of savory and sweet.
—*Arlene Erlbach, Morton Grove, IL*

PREP: 25 min. • BAKE: 10 min. + cooling
MAKES: 2 dozen

- 1 sheet frozen puff pastry, thawed
- 6 oz. cream cheese, softened
- 2 Tbsp. honey
- ⅛ tsp. salt
- ⅛ tsp. pepper
- ¼ cup crumbled fresh goat cheese
- 3 Tbsp. crumbled crisp pancetta or crumbled cooked bacon
- 3 Tbsp. finely chopped peeled ripe pear
- 2 Tbsp. finely chopped pecans, toasted

1. Preheat the oven to 400°. On a lightly floured surface, unfold puff pastry. Using a 1¾-in. round cookie cutter, cut sheet into 24 circles. Transfer circles to parchment-lined baking sheets. Bake until golden brown, 10-12 minutes. Cool completely on a wire rack.
2. Meanwhile, beat cream cheese, honey, salt and pepper until well blended. Fold in goat cheese, pancetta, pear and pecans.
3. Halve each cooled pastry circle. Spoon the cream cheese mixture over bottom pastry halves; cover with top halves. Serve at room temperature.
1 puff: 105 cal., 7g fat (3g sat. fat), 13mg chol., 178mg sod., 8g carb. (2g sugars, 1g fiber), 2g pro.

DILLY CHEESE BALL

HOT ITALIAN PARTY SANDWICHES
(PICTURED ON COVER)

It doesn't get easier or more delicious than these warm Italian sandwiches. They're wonderful as a party app or to feed your hungry crew when you want something quick and easy.
—*Joan Hallford, North Richland Hills, TX*

PREP: 20 min. • **BAKE:** 15 min.
MAKES: 12 sandwiches

- 1 pkg. (12 oz.) Hawaiian sweet rolls
- ½ cup mayonnaise
- 2 Tbsp. prepared pesto
- 6 slices part-skim mozzarella or provolone cheese
- 6 thin slices deli ham
- 9 thin slices hard salami
- 6 thin slices deli pastrami
- 1¼ cups giardiniera
- ½ cup shredded Parmesan cheese
- 1 cup fresh basil leaves
- ½ cup sliced red onion
- ¼ cup prepared zesty Italian salad dressing
  Pepperoncini

1. Preheat oven to 350°. Cut the rolls horizontally in half; place roll bottoms in a greased 11x7-in. baking dish. Mix mayonnaise and pesto until combined. Spread over cut sides of rolls. Layer bottoms with mozzarella cheese, ham, salami, pastrami, giardiniera, shredded Parmesan cheese, basil leaves and red onion. Place bun tops over filling and gently press to flatten.
2. Bake for 10 minutes. Remove from oven; brush with the salad dressing. Bake until golden brown and cheese is melted, about 5 minutes longer. Cool slightly before cutting. Serve with pepperoncini, and additional giardiniera if desired.
1 sandwich: 290 cal., 17g fat (6g sat. fat), 44mg chol., 1026mg sod., 20g carb. (7g sugars, 1g fiber), 15g pro.

DILLY CHEESE BALL

My whole family devours this herby cheese spread—even my son, the chef. Serve it with your favorite crackers.
—*Jane Vince, London, ON*

PREP: 10 min. + chilling • **MAKES:** 2½ cups

- 1 pkg. (8 oz.) cream cheese, softened
- 1 cup dill pickle relish, drained
- ¼ cup finely chopped onion
- 1½ cups shredded cheddar cheese
- 1 Tbsp. Worcestershire sauce
- 2 Tbsp. mayonnaise
- 2 Tbsp. minced fresh parsley
  Assorted crackers

Beat the first 6 ingredients until smooth. Shape into a ball; wrap and refrigerate several hours. Sprinkle with parsley; serve with crackers.
2 Tbsp.: 100 cal., 8g fat (4g sat. fat), 22mg chol., 244mg sod., 5g carb. (1g sugars, 0 fiber), 3g pro.

READER RAVES
"My family and I love this! We make it for every holiday now."
—SARAH20S, TASTEOFHOME.COM

BREAKFAST FOR A BUNCH

Get ready to load your plate with all your a.m. faves. These mouthwatering sunny specialties will make brunch the highlight of your weekend!

P. 72

P. 54

P. 80

HAM & CHEDDAR BRUNCH RING

HOVER YOUR CAMERA HERE
The Ultimate
Easter Brunch
Checklist

1. Preheat oven to 375°. Unroll crescent dough and separate into triangles. On an ungreased 12-in. pizza pan, arrange triangles in a ring with points toward the outside and wide ends overlapping to create a 3-in.-diameter hole in the center. Press overlapping dough to seal. Fold ham slices lengthwise and place on top of the wide end of each triangle. Sprinkle with half the cheese.

2. In a large bowl, beat 10 eggs; add the chopped peppers. In a large skillet, cook green onions in oil over medium heat until tender, 2-3 minutes. Add the garlic; cook 30 seconds. Pour in egg mixture; cook and stir until eggs are thickened and no liquid egg remains. Spoon egg mixture over cheese on the wide end of the triangles; sprinkle with remaining cheese. Fold pointed ends of triangles over filling, tucking points under to form a ring with a small hole in the center (filling will be visible). Beat the remaining egg; brush over pastry. If desired, sprinkle pastry with sesame seeds.

3. Bake until golden brown and heated through, 20-25 minutes. If desired, top with parsley to serve.

1 serving: 313 cal., 19g fat (5g sat. fat), 282mg chol., 735mg sod., 15g carb. (5g sugars, 0 fiber), 19g pro.

TEST KITCHEN TIP

You can substitute bacon for the ham or use your favorite shredded cheese in place of the cheddar. For extra flair, garnish each serving of this egg ring with chopped tomato, cilantro, salsa or sour cream.

HAM & CHEDDAR BRUNCH RING

It's surprisingly easy to transform ordinary breakfast standbys into next-level brunch centerpieces. This looks and smells so good, you might have to fend off guests en route from oven to table. Dig in!
—*James Schend, Pleasant Prairie, WI*

PREP: 25 min. • **BAKE:** 20 min.
MAKES: 8 servings

- 1 tube (8 oz.) refrigerated crescent rolls
- 10 pieces thinly sliced deli ham
- 1 cup shredded cheddar cheese, divided
- 11 large eggs, divided use
- ¾ cup roasted sweet red peppers, drained and chopped
- 4 green onions, thinly sliced
- 1 Tbsp. olive oil
- 1 tsp. minced garlic
- 2 tsp. sesame seeds, optional
  Chopped fresh parsley, optional

SHIITAKE & MANCHEGO SCRAMBLE

SHIITAKE & MANCHEGO SCRAMBLE

This savory breakfast dish takes everyday scrambled eggs up a few notches. The rich flavor is so satisfying in the morning, and it's even better served with buttery toasted Italian bread.
—*Thomas Faglon, Somerset, NJ*

TAKES: 25 min. • **MAKES:** 8 servings

- 2 Tbsp. extra virgin olive oil, divided
- ½ cup diced onion
- ½ cup diced sweet red pepper
- 2 cups thinly sliced fresh shiitake mushrooms (about 4 oz.)
- 1 tsp. prepared horseradish
- 8 large eggs, beaten
- 1 cup heavy whipping cream
- 1 cup shredded Manchego cheese
- 1 tsp. kosher salt
- 1 tsp. coarsely ground pepper

1. In a large nonstick skillet, heat 1 Tbsp. olive oil over medium heat. Add onion and red pepper; cook and stir until crisp-tender, 2-3 minutes. Add mushrooms; cook and stir until tender, 3-4 minutes. Stir in horseradish; cook 2 minutes more.
2. In a small bowl, whisk together the remaining ingredients and remaining 1 Tbsp. olive oil. Pour into skillet; cook and stir until eggs are thickened and no liquid egg remains.

1 serving: 274 cal., 24g fat (12g sat. fat), 234mg chol., 405mg sod., 4g carb. (2g sugars, 1g fiber), 11g pro.

GRITS & BACON CASSEROLE

 GRITS & BACON CASSEROLE

A Mississippi home cook gave me her recipe for grits casserole. It baked like traditional custard. I garnish it with parsley, crumbled bacon and cheese.
—*Theresa Liguori, Elkridge, MD*

PREP: 20 min. + cooling • **COOK:** 1¼ hours
MAKES: 8 servings

- 4½ cups water
- ½ tsp. salt
- ¼ tsp. pepper
- 1 cup quick-cooking grits
- 8 large eggs
- 8 bacon strips, cooked and crumbled
- 1 cup shredded Gouda cheese

1. Preheat oven to 350°. In a large saucepan, bring water, salt and pepper to a boil. Slowly stir in grits. Reduce heat to medium-low; cook, covered, until thickened, about 5 minutes, stirring occasionally. Remove from heat. Pour grits into a greased 2½-qt. souffle dish; cool completely.
2. In a large bowl, whisk eggs; pour over grits. Sprinkle with bacon and cheese.
3. Place casserole in a larger baking pan; add 1 in. of hot water to larger pan. Bake, covered, 45 minutes. Uncover; bake until knife inserted in the center comes out clean, 30-40 minutes. Let casserole stand 5-10 minutes before serving.

To make ahead: Refrigerate unbaked casserole, covered, several hours or overnight. To use, preheat oven to 350°. Remove casserole from refrigerator while oven heats. Place casserole in a larger baking pan; add 1 in. of hot water to larger pan. Bake, as directed, increasing time as necessary for a knife inserted in the center to come out clean. Let stand 5-10 minutes before serving.

1 piece: 227 cal., 12g fat (5g sat. fat), 210mg chol., 480mg sod., 16g carb. (1g sugars, 1g fiber), 14g pro.

GLAZED FRUIT MEDLEY

APPLE BUTTER BREAD PUDDING

This is one of my mother's best recipes! I'm sure your family will be delighted with it, too. Serve it as a special breakfast treat or even as a dessert.
—*Jerri Gradert, Lincoln, NE*

PREP: 20 min. + standing • **BAKE:** 50 min.
MAKES: 12 servings

- ⅓ cup raisins
- 1 cup apple butter
- 6 croissants, split

CUSTARD

- 8 large eggs
- 3 cups 2% milk
- 1½ cups sugar
- 2 tsp. vanilla extract
- ¼ tsp. salt

STREUSEL

- ½ cup all-purpose flour
- ½ cup packed brown sugar
- ¼ tsp. salt
- ¼ cup cold butter

1. Place raisins in a small bowl. Cover with boiling water; let stand for 5 minutes. Drain and set aside.
2. Combine apple butter and raisins. Spread over croissant bottoms; replace tops. Cut each croissant into 3 pieces; place in a greased 13x9-in. baking dish.
3. In a large bowl, combine the eggs, milk, sugar, vanilla and salt. Pour mixture over croissants; let stand for 30 minutes or until bread is softened.
4. In a small bowl, combine the flour, brown sugar and salt. Cut in butter until mixture resembles coarse crumbs. Sprinkle over top.
5. Bake, uncovered, at 350° until a knife inserted in the center comes out clean, 50-60 minutes. Serve warm. Refrigerate any leftovers.
1 serving: 433 cal., 14g fat (7g sat. fat), 175mg chol., 422mg sod., 68g carb. (51g sugars, 1g fiber), 9g pro.

GLAZED FRUIT MEDLEY

The orange dressing on this salad complements the fresh fruit flavors beautifully. It's perfect for a spring or summer brunch.
—*Karen Bourne, Magrath, AB*

PREP: 20 min. + chilling
MAKES: 10 servings

- 2 cups orange juice
- 1 cup sugar
- 2 Tbsp. cornstarch
- 3 cups cubed honeydew melon
- 3 medium firm bananas, sliced
- 2 cups green grapes
- 2 cups halved fresh strawberries

1. In a small saucepan, mix the orange juice, sugar and cornstarch until smooth. Bring to a boil, stirring constantly; cook and stir for 2 minutes or until thickened. Transfer to a small bowl; cool slightly. Refrigerate, covered, for at least 2 hours.
2. Just before serving, combine the fruit in a large serving bowl. Drizzle with orange juice mixture; toss gently to coat.
¾ cup: 188 cal., 1g fat (0 sat. fat), 0 chol., 7mg sod., 47g carb. (41g sugars, 2g fiber), 1g pro.
Apple-Ginger Glazed Fruit: Omit first 3 ingredients. In a small saucepan, mix 2 cups unsweetened apple juice, ¼ cup honey, 2 Tbsp. finely chopped crystallized ginger and 2 Tbsp. lemon juice. Bring to a boil over medium-high heat. Cook and stir 2 minutes or until mixture is reduced to 1½ cups. Remove from heat. Cool. Mix 4 tsp. chopped fresh mint into fruit and drizzle with cooled glaze.

APPLE BUTTER
BREAD PUDDING

GET-UP-AND-GO GRANOLA

My family loves to have this soul-warming granola before hiking, biking or even when camping. It smells delicious while baking and you can easily make it in large batches for special occasions or to send in gift packages to loved ones.
—*Sabrina Olson, Otsego, MN*

PREP: 15 min. • **BAKE:** 30 min. + cooling
MAKES: 7½ cups

   6   cups old-fashioned oats
   ½   cup unblanched almonds, coarsely chopped
   ¼   cup packed brown sugar
   ¼   cup flaxseed
   ¼   cup canola oil
   ¼   cup honey
   1   Tbsp. maple syrup
   1   tsp. apple pie spice
   ½   tsp. salt
   ½   tsp. vanilla extract
   ½   cup dried cranberries
   ½   cup raisins

1. Preheat oven to 300°. In a large bowl, combine oats, almonds, brown sugar and flax. In a microwave-safe dish, whisk oil, honey, maple syrup, pie spice and salt. Microwave on high for 30-45 seconds or until heated through, stirring once. Stir in vanilla. Pour over oat mixture; toss to coat.
2. Spread evenly in a 15x10x1-in. baking pan coated with cooking spray. Bake until golden brown, 30-40 minutes, stirring every 10 minutes. Cool completely on a wire rack. Stir in cranberries and raisins. Store in an airtight container.
½ cup: 255 cal., 10g fat (1g sat. fat), 0 chol., 84mg sod., 40g carb. (15g sugars, 5g fiber), 7g pro.

GET-UP-AND-GO GRANOLA

MAPLE-WALNUT STICKY BUNS

2. Turn dough onto a floured surface; knead 6-8 minutes or until smooth and elastic. Place in a greased bowl, turning once to grease the top. Cover dough and refrigerate overnight.

3. Pour syrup into a greased 13x9-in. baking dish; sprinkle with walnuts. In a small bowl, mix sugar and cinnamon. Punch down dough; turn onto a lightly floured surface. Roll the dough into a 24x8-in. rectangle. Spread with butter to within ½ in. of edges; sprinkle with cinnamon sugar. Roll up jelly-roll style, starting with a long side; pinch seam to seal. Cut into 24 slices.

4. Place in prepared baking dish, cut side down. Cover with a kitchen towel; let rise in a warm place until doubled, about 30 minutes. Preheat the oven to 350°.

5. Bake 30-35 minutes or until golden brown. Cool 5 minutes before inverting buns onto a platter.

1 bun: 159 cal., 5g fat (1g sat. fat), 13mg chol., 114mg sod., 26g carb. (12g sugars, 1g fiber), 3g pro.

TEST KITCHEN TIP

To make sure your active dry yeast (not quick-rise yeast) is alive and active, you should proof it first. To do this, dissolve 1 tsp. sugar and 1 package of yeast in ¼ cup warm water (110° to 115°). Let stand for 5-10 minutes. If the mixture foams up, the yeast mixture can be used because the yeast is active. If it does not foam, the yeast should be discarded.

MA

MAPLE-WALNUT STICKY BUNS

Mmm! These ooey-gooey goodies will have everyone licking maple syrup from their fingers—and reaching for seconds.
—*Nancy Foust, Stoneboro, PA*

PREP: 45 min. + chilling • **BAKE:** 30 min.
MAKES: 2 dozen

- 1 pkg. (¼ oz.) active dry yeast
- 1 cup warm water (110° to 115°)
- ½ cup mashed potatoes (without added milk and butter)
- 1 large egg, room temperature
- 2 Tbsp. shortening
- 2 Tbsp. sugar
- 1 tsp. salt
- 3 to 3½ cups all-purpose flour

TOPPING
- 1 cup maple syrup
- ¾ cup coarsely chopped walnuts

FILLING
- ⅓ cup sugar
- 1½ tsp. ground cinnamon
- 3 Tbsp. butter, softened

1. In a small bowl, dissolve yeast in warm water. In a large bowl, combine potatoes, egg, shortening, sugar, salt, yeast mixture and 1 cup flour; beat on medium speed until smooth. Stir in enough remaining flour to form a soft dough.

STUFFED HAM & EGG BREAD

My son, Gus, loves anything with ham and eggs, so I created this comforting stuffed bread with him in mind. I later added the tomatoes to the recipe, and he still gives it a big thumbs-up.
—*Karen Kuebler, Dallas, TX*

PREP: 25 min. • **BAKE:** 20 min.
MAKES: 8 servings

- 2 tsp. canola oil
- 1 can (14½ oz.) diced tomatoes, drained
- 6 large eggs, lightly beaten
- 2 cups chopped fully cooked ham
- 1 tube (11 oz.) refrigerated crusty French loaf
- 2 cups shredded sharp cheddar cheese

1. Preheat oven to 400°. In a large nonstick skillet, heat oil over medium heat. Add tomatoes; cook and stir until juices are evaporated, 12-15 minutes. Add eggs; cook and stir until they are thickened and and no liquid egg remains, 3-4 minutes. Remove from heat; stir in ham.

2. Unroll dough onto a greased baking sheet. Sprinkle cheese lengthwise down one half of the dough to within 1 in. of the edges. Top with egg mixture. Fold dough over the filling, pinching to seal; tuck the ends under.

3. Bake 17-20 minutes or until deep golden brown. Cut into slices.

1 piece: 321 cal., 17g fat (7g sat. fat), 188mg chol., 967mg sod., 22g carb. (3g sugars, 1g fiber), 22g pro.

QUICK & EASY SAUSAGE GRAVY

Breakfast doesn't get any heartier or more satisfying than this home-style classic. No one will leave the table hungry!
—*John Wilhelm, Richmond, VA*

TAKES: 25 min. • **MAKES:** 8 servings

- 2 lbs. bulk pork sausage
- ⅓ cup all-purpose flour
- 3 tsp. pepper
- 2 tsp. sugar
- ½ tsp. salt
- 2 cups 2% milk
- 2 cans (5 oz. each) evaporated milk
  Cooked biscuits

1. In a Dutch oven, cook the sausage over medium heat until no longer pink, breaking into crumbles (do not drain), 8-10 minutes. Add the flour, pepper, sugar and salt; cook and stir until blended, about 2 minutes.

2. Stir in milks; bring to a boil. Reduce heat; simmer, uncovered, until thickened, 3-5 minutes, stirring occasionally. Serve with biscuits.

¾ cup: 446 cal., 34g fat (12g sat. fat), 93mg chol., 1075mg sod., 14g carb. (7g sugars, 0 fiber), 20g pro.

STUFFED HAM & EGG BREAD

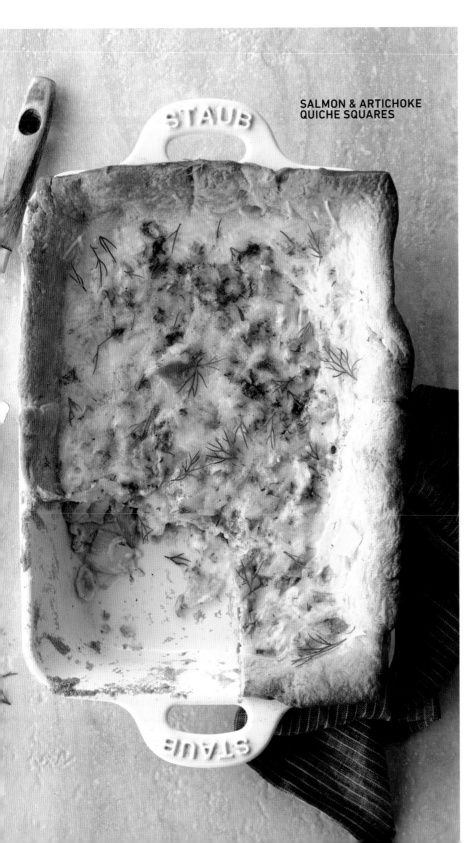

SALMON & ARTICHOKE
QUICHE SQUARES

SALMON & ARTICHOKE QUICHE SQUARES

Salmon, goat cheese and artichoke hearts elevate this special quiche and make it taste extra delicious. Baked in an 11x7-in. dish, it comes together easily and makes enough to serve a hungry brunch crowd.
—*Jeanne Holt, St. Paul, MN*

PREP: 15 min. • **BAKE:** 40 min. + cooling
MAKES: 15 servings

- 1   tube (8 oz.) refrigerated crescent rolls
- ⅔ cup shredded Parmesan cheese, divided
- ½ cup crumbled goat cheese
- 1   cup thinly sliced smoked salmon fillets
- 1   cup water-packed artichoke hearts, drained
- ¼ cup chopped green onions (green portion only)
- 2   Tbsp. finely chopped fresh dill
- ¼ tsp. pepper
- 5   large eggs
- 1   cup heavy whipping cream

1. Preheat oven to 350°. Unroll crescent roll dough into a long rectangle; place in an ungreased 11x7-in. baking dish. Press dough over bottom and up sides of dish, pressing perforations to seal.
2. Sprinkle with ⅓ cup Parmesan cheese. Top with the goat cheese, salmon and artichoke hearts. Sprinkle with onions, chopped dill and pepper. Whisk the eggs and cream; pour over salmon mixture. Sprinkle with the remaining ⅓ cup Parmesan cheese.
3. Bake until a knife inserted in center comes out clean, 40-45 minutes (loosely cover with foil if edges are getting too dark). Cool 20 minutes. Cut into squares.
1 square: 179 cal., 13g fat (7g sat. fat), 89mg chol., 330mg sod., 8g carb. (2g sugars, 0 fiber), 8g pro.

ORANGE-GLAZED BACON

Just when you thought bacon couldn't get any better, our Test Kitchen staff whipped up this tasty recipe starring the favorite breakfast meat drizzled with a sweet orange glaze.

—Taste of Home *Test Kitchen*

PREP: 20 min. • **BAKE:** 25 min.
MAKES: 8 servings

- ¾ cup orange juice
- ¼ cup honey
- 1 Tbsp. Dijon mustard
- ¼ tsp. ground ginger
- ⅛ tsp. pepper
- 24 bacon strips (1 lb.)

1. Preheat the oven to 350°. In a small saucepan, combine the first 5 ingredients. Bring to a boil; cook until liquid is reduced to ⅓ cup.

2. Place bacon on a rack in an ungreased 15x10x1-in. baking pan. Bake the bacon for 10 minutes; drain.

3. Drizzle half of glaze over bacon. Bake for 10 minutes. Turn bacon and drizzle with remaining glaze. Bake until golden brown, 5-10 minutes longer. Place bacon on waxed paper until set. Serve warm.

3 glazed bacon strips: 146 cal., 8g fat (3g sat. fat), 21mg chol., 407mg sod., 12g carb. (11g sugars, 0 fiber), 7g pro.

ORANGE-GLAZED BACON

 MA

BEAR'S BREAKFAST BURRITOS

Everyone loves these hearty burritos. It's so convenient to freeze some and then bake them for a lazy Saturday breakfast.
—*Larry & Sandy Kelley, Grangeville, ID*

PREP: 30 min. • **COOK:** 15 min.
MAKES: 12 servings

- 2 pkg. (22½ oz. each) frozen hash brown patties
- 15 large eggs, lightly beaten
- 2 Tbsp. chili powder
- 2 Tbsp. garlic salt
- 1 Tbsp. ground cumin
- ½ lb. uncooked chorizo or bulk spicy pork sausage
- 6 jalapeno peppers, seeded and minced
- 1 large green pepper, chopped
- 1 large sweet red pepper, chopped
- 1 large onion, chopped
- 1 bunch green onions, chopped
- 3 cups salsa
- 12 flour tortillas (12 in.), warmed
- 4 cups shredded Monterey Jack cheese
  Sour cream, optional

1. Cook the hash browns according to package directions; crumble and keep warm. Meanwhile, in a large bowl, whisk the eggs, chili powder, garlic salt and cumin. Set aside.

2. Crumble chorizo into a large cast-iron or other heavy skillet; add the jalapenos, peppers and onions. Cook and stir over medium heat until chorizo is fully cooked; drain. Add egg mixture; cook and stir until eggs are set. Stir in salsa.

3. Spoon ½ cup hash browns and ½ cup egg mixture off center on each tortilla; sprinkle with ⅓ cup cheese. Fold sides and ends over filling and roll up. If desired, serve with sour cream.

Note: Wear disposable gloves when cutting hot peppers; the oils can burn skin. Avoid touching your face.

Freeze option: Cool the remaining burritos to room temperature. Wrap each burrito in waxed paper and foil. Freeze for up to 1 month. To use frozen burritos, remove foil and waxed paper. Place burritos 2 in. apart on an ungreased baking sheet. Preheat oven to 350°. Bake, uncovered, until heated through, 50-55 minutes.

1 burrito: 584 cal., 27g fat (12g sat. fat), 290mg chol., 2151mg sod., 58g carb. (5g sugars, 9g fiber), 27g pro.

READER RAVES

"One of my family's all-time favorites! I try to keep these in the freezer. We even take them camping with us—just take the waxed paper off, wrap them back up with the foil and set over an open fire."

—FIRE291, TASTEOFHOME.COM

HOVER YOUR CAMERA HERE
Essential Etiquette Tips for Hosting Overnight Guests

CHUNKY BREAKFAST COOKIES

GROUND BEEF SNACK QUICHES

CHUNKY BREAKFAST COOKIES

Who says cookies aren't for breakfast? We devour these hearty bites in the a.m., especially when we're on the run. Add any dried fruits and nuts you have on hand.
—*Lea Langhoff, Round Lake, IL*

PREP: 20 min. • **BAKE:** 15 min./batch
MAKES: 16 cookies

⅔ cup butter, softened
⅔ cup packed brown sugar
1 large egg, room temperature
1 large egg yolk, room temperature
1½ cups old-fashioned oats
¾ cup all-purpose flour
¾ cup whole wheat flour
1 tsp. baking soda
½ tsp. salt
1 cup semisweet chocolate chunks
1 cup chopped dates
½ cup sweetened shredded coconut

1. Preheat oven to 350°. In a large bowl, cream butter and brown sugar until light and fluffy, 5-7 minutes. Beat in egg and egg yolk. In another bowl, mix oats, flours, baking soda and salt; gradually beat into creamed mixture. Stir in remaining ingredients.
2. Shape dough by ¼ cupfuls into balls; flatten to ¾-in. thickness. Place 2 in. apart on ungreased baking sheets.
3. Bake for 13-15 minutes or until golden brown. Cool on pans 2 minutes. Remove to wire racks to cool. Serve warm or at room temperature. To reheat, microwave each cookie on high for 15-20 seconds or just until warmed.
Freeze option: Freeze unbaked cookies in a freezer container, separating layers with waxed paper. To use, place dough portions 2 in. apart on ungreased baking sheets; let stand at room temperature 30 minutes before baking. Bake as directed, increasing time by 1-2 minutes.
1 cookie: 291 cal., 15g fat (9g sat. fat), 44mg chol., 239mg sod., 40g carb. (24g sugars, 3g fiber), 4g pro.

GROUND BEEF SNACK QUICHES

My husband, Cory, is a farmer and he works up a hearty appetite. We often enjoy these meaty mini quiches for supper but they're great for breakfast, too. They taste delicious made with ground beef, but you can also use bacon, ham or sausage.
—*Stacy Atkinson, Rugby, ND*

PREP: 15 min. • **BAKE:** 20 min.
MAKES: 1½ dozen

¼ lb. ground beef
⅛ to ¼ tsp. garlic powder
⅛ tsp. pepper
1 cup biscuit/baking mix
¼ cup cornmeal
¼ cup cold butter, cubed
2 to 3 Tbsp. boiling water
1 large egg
½ cup half-and-half cream
1 Tbsp. chopped green onion
1 Tbsp. chopped sweet red pepper
⅛ to ¼ tsp. salt
⅛ to ¼ tsp. cayenne pepper
½ cup finely shredded cheddar cheese

1. Preheat the oven to 375°. In a large saucepan over medium heat, cook the beef, garlic powder and pepper until meat is no longer pink; crumble beef; drain and set aside.
2. Meanwhile, in a small bowl, combine biscuit mix and cornmeal; cut in butter until crumbly. Add enough water to form a soft dough.
3. Press onto the bottoms and up the sides of greased miniature muffin cups. Place 1 tsp. of the beef mixture into each shell.
4. In a small bowl, combine the egg, cream, onion, red pepper, salt and cayenne; pour over the beef mixture. Sprinkle with cheese.
5. Bake for 20 minutes or until a knife inserted in the center comes out clean.
1 snack quiche: 93 cal., 6g fat (3g sat. fat), 27mg chol., 137mg sod., 7g carb. (0 sugars, 0 fiber), 3g pro.

FAVORITE BANANA CHIP MUFFINS

CHRISTMAS BREAKFAST CASSEROLE

Spicy sausage, herbs and vegetables pack this egg casserole. I make it for my family's Christmas breakfast, but it's a worthy meal addition any time of year.
—*Debbie Carter, O'Fallon, IL*

PREP: 20 min. • **BAKE:** 25 min.
MAKES: 12 servings

- 1   lb. bulk Italian sausage
- 1   cup chopped onion
- 1   jar (7 oz.) roasted red peppers, drained and chopped, divided
- 1   pkg. (10 oz.) frozen chopped spinach, thawed and well drained
- 1   cup all-purpose flour
- ¼   cup grated Parmesan cheese
- 1   tsp. dried basil
- ½   tsp. salt
- 8   large eggs
- 2   cups 2% milk
- 1   cup shredded provolone cheese
       Fresh rosemary sprigs, optional

1. Preheat oven to 425°. In a skillet, cook the sausage and onion over medium heat until the sausage is no longer pink; drain. Transfer to a greased 3-qt. baking dish. Sprinkle with half of the red peppers and all the spinach.
2. In a bowl, combine flour, Parmesan cheese, basil and salt. Combine eggs and milk; add to dry ingredients and mix well. Pour over spinach.
3. Bake until a knife inserted in the center comes out clean, 20-25 minutes. Sprinkle with the provolone cheese and remaining red peppers. Bake until cheese is melted, about 2 minutes longer. Let casserole stand 5 minutes before cutting. Garnish with rosemary if desired.
1 serving: 232 cal., 13g fat (6g sat. fat), 170mg chol., 531mg sod., 13g carb. (4g sugars, 1g fiber), 14g pro.

FAVORITE BANANA CHIP MUFFINS

These banana-studded muffins are one of the first things my husband, U.S. Army Maj. John Duda Jr., requests when he's home from deployment. I make sure to have overripe bananas ready to bake.
—*Kimberly Duda, Sanford, NC*

PREP: 20 min. • **BAKE:** 20 min.
MAKES: 1 dozen

- 1½   cups all-purpose flour
- ⅔   cup sugar
- 1   tsp. baking soda
- ¼   tsp. ground cinnamon
- ⅛   tsp. salt
- 1   large egg, room temperature
- 1⅓   cups mashed ripe bananas (about 3 medium)
- ⅓   cup butter, melted
- 1   tsp. vanilla extract
- ½   cup semisweet chocolate chips

1. Preheat oven to 375°. In a large bowl, whisk flour, sugar, baking soda, cinnamon and salt. In another bowl, whisk the egg, bananas, melted butter and vanilla until blended. Add to flour mixture; stir just until moistened. Fold in chocolate chips.
2. Fill greased or paper-lined muffin cups three-fourths full. Bake 17-20 minutes or until a toothpick inserted in center comes out clean. Cool 5 minutes before removing from pan to a wire rack. Serve warm.
1 muffin: 207 cal., 8g fat (5g sat. fat), 31mg chol., 172mg sod., 33g carb. (18g sugars, 2g fiber), 3g pro. **Diabetic exchanges:** 2 starch, 1½ fat.

TEST KITCHEN TIP

When baking with bananas, use ones that are ripe (or even overripe) to yield the best flavor. If you have a day or two to spare, place bananas and an apple, avocado, peach or tomato in a brown paper bag and keep on your counter. This will trap the ethylene gas of the fruits and quicken the ripening process.

CHRISTMAS
BREAKFAST
CASSEROLE

COLORFUL FRUIT KABOBS

These luscious fruit kabobs are perfect as a summer appetizer, snack or side dish. The citrus glaze clings well and keeps the fruit looking fresh.
—*Ruth Ann Stelfox, Raymond, AB*

TAKES: 15 min. • **MAKES:** 1 cup glaze

Assorted fruit of your choice: Strawberries, seedless red grapes, sliced kiwifruit, sliced star fruit, kumquats, and cubes of cantaloupe, honeydew or pineapple
⅓ cup sugar
2 Tbsp. cornstarch
1 cup orange juice
2 tsp. lemon juice

Alternately thread fruit onto skewers; set aside. In a saucepan, combine the sugar, cornstarch and juices until smooth. Bring to a boil; cook and stir for 1-2 minutes or until thickened. Brush glaze over fruit. Refrigerate until serving.

2 tsp. glaze: 18 cal., 0 fat (0 sat. fat), 0 chol., 0 sod., 5g carb. (4g sugars, 0 fiber), 0 pro.

READER RAVES

"I've made these a couple of times. I used different fruit each time. Strawberries are a must for me. Very easy, tasty and pretty."

—QUEENLALISA, TASTEOFHOME.COM

COLORFUL FRUIT KABOBS

BEST CINNAMON ROLLS

2. Turn the dough onto a floured surface; knead 6-8 minutes or until smooth and elastic . Place in a greased bowl, turning once to grease the top. Cover the dough and let rise in a warm place until doubled, about 1 hour.

3. Mix brown sugar and cinnamon. Punch down dough; divide in half. On a lightly floured surface, roll 1 portion into an 11x8-in. rectangle. Brush with 2 Tbsp. butter; sprinkle with half the brown sugar mixture to within ½ in. of edges. Roll up jelly-roll style, starting with a long side; pinch seam to seal. Cut into 8 slices; place in a greased 13x9-in. pan, cut side down. Cover with a kitchen towel. Repeat with remaining dough and filling. Let rise in a warm place until doubled, about 1 hour. Preheat oven to 350°.

4. Bake until golden brown, 20-25 minutes. Cool on wire racks.

5. For frosting, beat butter, cream cheese, vanilla and salt until blended; gradually beat in confectioners' sugar. Spread over tops. Refrigerate leftovers.

1 roll: 364 cal., 15g fat (9g sat. fat), 66mg chol., 323mg sod., 53g carb. (28g sugars, 1g fiber), 5g pro.

TEST KITCHEN TIP
Knead the dough just until it is smooth and elastic. To tell if it's ready, press it with your finger. If the indentation stays, the dough still needs more kneading. If it springs back to its original shape, your dough is ready to rest.

BEST CINNAMON ROLLS

Surprise a neighbor with a batch of oven-fresh cinnamon rolls slathered in cream cheese frosting. These breakfast treats make Christmas morning or any special occasion even more memorable.
—*Shenai Fisher, Topeka, KS*

PREP: 40 min. + rising
BAKE: 20 min.
MAKES: 16 rolls

1 pkg. (¼ oz.) active dry yeast
1 cup warm 2% milk (110° to 115°)
½ cup sugar
⅓ cup butter, melted
2 large eggs, room temperature
1 tsp. salt
4 to 4½ cups all-purpose flour
FILLING
¾ cup packed brown sugar
2 Tbsp. ground cinnamon
¼ cup butter, melted, divided
FROSTING
½ cup butter, softened
¼ cup cream cheese, softened
½ tsp. vanilla extract
⅛ tsp. salt
1½ cups confectioners' sugar

1. Dissolve yeast in warm milk. In another bowl, combine sugar, butter, eggs, salt, yeast mixture and 2 cups flour; beat on medium speed until smooth. Stir in enough remaining flour to form a soft dough (dough will be sticky).

MUSTARD HAM STRATA

I had this at a bed-and-breakfast years ago. The innkeepers were kind enough to give me the recipe—now I make it often.
—*Dolores Zornow, Poynette, WI*

PREP: 15 min. + chilling • **BAKE:** 45 min.
MAKES: 12 servings

- 12 slices day-old bread, crusts removed, cubed
- 1½ cups cubed fully cooked ham
- 1 cup chopped green pepper
- ¾ cup shredded cheddar cheese
- ¾ cup shredded Monterey Jack cheese
- ⅓ cup chopped onion
- 7 large eggs
- 3 cups 2% milk
- 3 tsp. ground mustard
- 1 tsp. salt

1. In a 13x9-in. baking dish coated with cooking spray, layer bread cubes, ham, green pepper, cheeses and onion. In a large bowl, combine eggs, milk, mustard and salt. Pour over top. Cover strata and refrigerate overnight.

2. Remove strata from the refrigerator 30 minutes before baking. Preheat oven to 325°. Bake, uncovered, 45-50 minutes or until a knife inserted in center comes out clean. Let stand 5 minutes before cutting.

1 piece: 198 cal., 11g fat (5g sat. fat), 153mg chol., 648mg sod., 11g carb. (4g sugars, 1g fiber), 13g pro. **Diabetic exchanges:** 2 medium-fat meat, 1 starch.

BRUNCH RISOTTO

This light, flavorful and inexpensive risotto makes a surprising addition to a traditional brunch menu. It's gotten lots of rave reviews from my friends.
—*Jennifer Dines, Brighton, MA*

PREP: 10 min. • **COOK:** 30 min.
MAKES: 8 servings

- 5¼ to 5¾ cups reduced-sodium chicken broth
- ¾ lb. Italian turkey sausage links, casings removed
- 2 cups uncooked arborio rice
- 1 garlic clove, minced
- ¼ tsp. pepper
- 1 Tbsp. olive oil
- 1 medium tomato, chopped

1. In a large saucepan, heat broth and keep warm. In a large nonstick skillet, cook the turkey sausage until no longer pink, breaking it into crumbles; drain and set aside.

2. In the same skillet, saute the rice, garlic and pepper in oil for 2-3 minutes. Return sausage to skillet. Carefully stir in 1 cup heated broth. Cook and stir until all of the liquid is absorbed.

3. Add remaining broth, ½ cup at a time, stirring constantly. Allow liquid to absorb between additions. Cook just until risotto is creamy and rice is almost tender, about 20 minutes total. Add tomato and heat through. Serve immediately.

⅔ cup: 279 cal., 6g fat (2g sat. fat), 23mg chol., 653mg sod., 42g carb. (1g sugars, 1g fiber), 12g pro. **Diabetic exchanges:** 2½ starch, 1 lean meat, ½ fat.

MUSTARD HAM STRATA

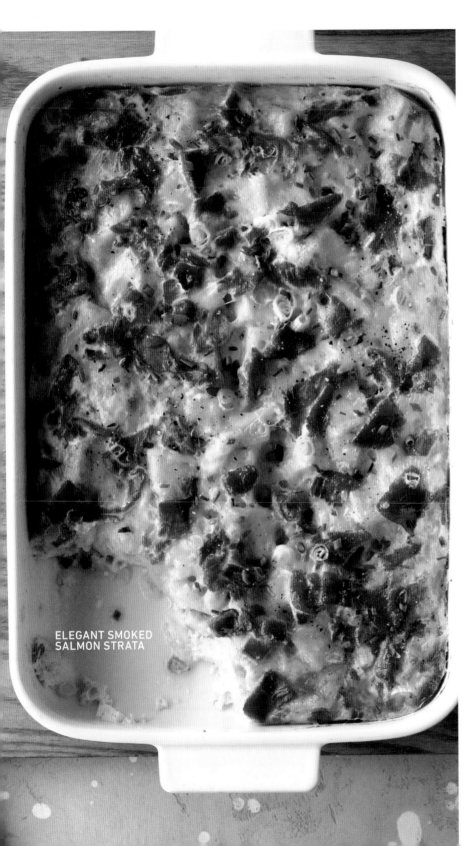

ELEGANT SMOKED SALMON STRATA

ELEGANT SMOKED SALMON STRATA

This fancy overnight egg bake is ideal for guests. In the morning, you can simply let it come to room temperature and whip up side dishes as it bakes. Then get ready for all the compliments!
—*Lisa Speer, Palm Beach, FL*

PREP: 30 min. + chilling
BAKE: 55 min. + standing
MAKES: 12 servings

- 4 cups cubed ciabatta bread
- 2 Tbsp. butter, melted
- 2 Tbsp. olive oil
- 2 cups shredded Gruyere or Swiss cheese
- 2 cups shredded white cheddar cheese
- 10 green onions, sliced
- ½ lb. smoked salmon or lox, coarsely chopped
- 8 large eggs
- 4 cups 2% milk
- 4 tsp. Dijon mustard
- ¼ tsp. salt
- ¼ tsp. pepper
  Creme fraiche or sour cream and minced chives

1. In a large bowl, toss bread cubes with butter and oil; transfer to a greased 13x9-in. baking dish. Sprinkle with cheeses, onions and salmon. In another bowl, whisk the eggs, milk, mustard, salt and pepper; pour over top. Cover and refrigerate overnight.

2. Remove from refrigerator 30 minutes before baking. Preheat oven to 350°. Cover and bake for 30 minutes. Uncover; bake until a knife inserted in the center comes out clean, 25-30 minutes longer. Let stand for 10 minutes before serving. Serve with creme fraiche and chives.

1 piece: 359 cal., 21g fat (11g sat. fat), 194mg chol., 845mg sod., 21g carb. (6g sugars, 1g fiber), 22g pro.

CREAMY STRAWBERRY FRENCH TOAST BAKE

On Sunday mornings, I like to take it easy, but I also want my family to have a nice breakfast. This indulgent make-ahead recipe allows me to sleep in but still feel like a fabulous mom. Win!
—*Alynn Hansen, Mona, UT*

PREP: 30 min. + chilling • **BAKE:** 40 min.
MAKES: 8 servings

- 3 cups sliced fresh strawberries, divided
- 2 Tbsp. sugar
- 1 pkg. (8 oz.) cream cheese, softened
- ½ cup confectioners' sugar
- 1 Tbsp. grated orange zest
- 1 Tbsp. orange juice
- 1 tsp. vanilla extract
- 1 loaf (1 lb.) cinnamon bread, cut into 1-in. pieces
- 5 large eggs
- 1 cup half-and-half cream
    Sweetened whipped cream

1. Toss 2 cups strawberries with sugar. In another bowl, beat the next 5 ingredients until smooth. Place half the bread in a greased 13x9-in. baking dish. Spoon the cream cheese mixture over bread. Layer with strawberry mixture and remaining bread. Whisk the eggs and cream until blended; pour over top. Refrigerate, covered, overnight.
2. Preheat oven to 350°. Remove casserole from refrigerator while oven heats. Bake, uncovered, until a knife inserted in the center comes out clean, 40-45 minutes. Let stand 5 minutes before serving. Top with whipped cream and the remaining 1 cup strawberries.

1 piece: 431 cal., 21g fat (10g sat. fat), 160mg chol., 382mg sod., 47g carb. (24g sugars, 5g fiber), 13g pro.

CREAMY STRAWBERRY FRENCH TOAST BAKE

CARAMEL APPLE STRATA

If you're hosting brunch, try this overnight strata. It tastes like a sticky bun and won't dry out as coffee cakes sometimes do.
—*Kelly Boe, Whiteland, IN*

PREP: 20 min. + chilling
BAKE: 50 min. + standing
MAKES: 12 servings

- 2 cups packed brown sugar
- ½ cup butter, cubed
- ¼ cup corn syrup
- 3 large apples, peeled and chopped
- 2 Tbsp. lemon juice
- 1 Tbsp. sugar
- 1 tsp. apple pie spice
- 1 loaf (1 lb.) day-old cinnamon bread
- ½ cup chopped pecans
- 10 large eggs
- 1 cup 2% milk
- 1 tsp. salt
- 1 tsp. vanilla extract

1. In a small saucepan, combine brown sugar, butter and corn syrup. Bring to a boil over medium heat, stirring constantly. Cook and stir 2 minutes or until thickened. Set aside.
2. In a small bowl, combine apples, lemon juice, sugar and pie spice. Arrange half of the bread slices in a greased 13x9-in. baking dish. Top with apples; drizzle with half the caramel sauce. Sprinkle with pecans; top with remaining bread.
3. In a large bowl, combine eggs, milk, salt and vanilla. Pour over top. Cover and refrigerate strata overnight. Cover and refrigerate remaining caramel sauce.
4. Remove the strata from refrigerator 30 minutes before baking. Bake strata, uncovered, at 350° for 50-55 minutes or until a knife inserted in center comes out clean. Let stand 10 minutes before cutting.
5. In a microwave, heat reserved caramel sauce. Drizzle warm sauce over strata.
1 piece: 462 cal., 19g fat (7g sat. fat), 198mg chol., 472mg sod., 67g carb. (49g sugars, 4g fiber), 10g pro.

COFFEE MILK

It's the official state drink of Rhode Island, and once you taste it, you'll understand why it has so many fans!
—*Karen Barros, Bristol, RI*

TAKES: 5 min.
MAKES: 8 servings (about 1 cup each)

- 2 qt. cold 2% or whole milk
- 1 cup Eclipse coffee syrup

In a large pitcher, mix milk and coffee syrup until blended.
1 cup: 135 cal., 5g fat (3g sat. fat), 18mg chol., 122mg sod., 15g carb. (12g sugars, 0 fiber), 8g pro.
To make your own coffee milk syrup:
Brew ½ cup finely ground coffee with 2 cups cold water in a coffeemaker. Combine brewed coffee and 1 cup sugar in a saucepan; simmer until reduced by half, about 30 minutes. Refrigerate syrup until cold or up to 2 weeks. Use as directed.
Yield: 1 cup syrup.

MOCHA CINNAMON ROLLS

I came up with this recipe because I love cinnamon rolls and coffee-flavored treats. It's a perfect combination that works for breakfast, dessert or a snack.
—*Victoria Mitchel, Gettysburg, PA*

PREP: 45 min. + rising • **BAKE:** 25 min.
MAKES: 1 dozen

- 1 pkg. (¼ oz.) active dry yeast
- 1 cup warm 2% milk (110° to 115°)
- ¼ cup sugar
- ¼ cup butter, melted
- 2 Tbsp. instant coffee granules
- 1 large egg yolk, room temperature
- 1½ tsp. vanilla extract
- ¾ tsp. salt
- ½ tsp. ground nutmeg
- 2½ to 3 cups all-purpose flour

FILLING
- ¾ cup chopped pecans
- ⅔ cup semisweet chocolate chips
- ¼ cup sugar
- 2 Tbsp. instant coffee granules
- ½ tsp. ground cinnamon
- ¼ cup butter, softened
- ¼ cup butter, melted

FROSTING
- 1 oz. cream cheese, softened
- 1 cup confectioners' sugar
- 3 Tbsp. heavy whipping cream
- ¾ tsp. instant coffee granules
- ⅛ tsp. vanilla extract

1. In a large bowl, dissolve yeast in warm milk. Add sugar, butter, coffee granules, egg yolk, vanilla, salt, nutmeg and 2 cups flour. Beat on medium speed until smooth. Stir in enough remaining flour to form a soft dough (dough will be sticky).
2. Turn onto a floured surface; knead until smooth and elastic, 6-8 minutes. Place in a greased bowl, turning once to grease top. Cover and let rise in a warm place until doubled, about 1 hour. Place the pecans, chocolate chips, sugar, instant coffee granules and cinnamon in a food processor; process until finely chopped. Punch dough down; turn onto a floured surface. Roll into an 18x12-in. rectangle; spread with softened butter. Sprinkle the pecan mixture over dough to within ½ in. of edges.
3. Roll up jelly-roll style, starting with a long side; pinch seam to seal. Cut into 12 slices. Place rolls, cut side down, in a greased 13x9-in. baking pan. Cover and let rise until doubled, about 1 hour.
4. Preheat oven to 350°. Drizzle rolls with melted butter. Bake until golden brown, 22-28 minutes. Place pan on a wire rack. In a small bowl, beat frosting ingredients until smooth. Spread over rolls. Serve rolls warm.

1 roll: 406 cal., 23g fat (11g sat. fat), 55mg chol., 259mg sod., 48g carb. (25g sugars, 2g fiber), 5g pro.

THE BEST QUICHE LORRAINE

Nestled in a buttery crust, this quiche is the perfect addition to a special brunch.
—*Shannon Norris, Cudahy, WI*

PREP: 1 hour • **BAKE:** 1¼ hours + cooling
MAKES: 8 servings

Dough for single-crust deep-dish pie
- 1 pkg. (12 oz.) thick-sliced bacon strips, coarsely chopped
- 3 large sweet onions, chopped
- 1 Tbsp. minced fresh thyme
- ½ tsp. coarsely ground pepper
- ⅛ tsp. ground nutmeg
- 1½ cups shredded Gruyere cheese
- ½ cup grated Parmesan cheese
- 8 large eggs
- 2 cups 2% milk
- 1 cup heavy whipping cream

1. On a lightly floured surface, roll the dough to a 14-in. circle. Transfer to a 9-in. springform pan; press firmly against the bottom and side. Refrigerate while preparing filling.
2. In a large skillet, cook the bacon over medium heat until crisp, stirring occasionally. Remove with a slotted spoon; drain on paper towels. Discard drippings, reserving 1 Tbsp. in pan. Add onions to drippings; cook and stir over medium heat until caramelized, 20-25 minutes.
3. Stir in the thyme, pepper and nutmeg; remove from the heat. Cool slightly. Stir in cheeses and reserved bacon; spoon into crust. Preheat oven to 350°. In a large bowl, whisk eggs, milk and cream until blended; pour over top. Place springform pan on a rimmed baking sheet.
4. Bake on a lower oven rack until a knife inserted near the center comes out clean, 75-85 minutes. Cool on a wire rack for 15 minutes. Loosen side from pan with a knife. Remove rim from pan.
Note: To make dough for crust, combine 1½ cups all-purpose flour and ¼ tsp. salt; cut in ⅔ cup cold butter until crumbly. Gradually add 3-6 Tbsp. ice water, tossing with a fork until the dough holds together when pressed. Shape into a disk; wrap and refrigerate 1 hour.

1 piece: 671 cal., 49g fat (27g sat. fat), 308mg chol., 841mg sod., 33g carb. (10g sugars, 2g fiber), 25g pro.

THE BEST
QUICHE LORRAINE

HOME FRIES

HOME FRIES

When I was little, my dad and I would get up early on Sundays and make these for the family. The rest of the gang would be awakened by the tempting aroma.
—*Teresa Koide, Manchester, CT*

PREP: 25 min. • **COOK:** 15 min./batch
MAKES: 8 servings

- 1 lb. bacon, chopped
- 8 medium potatoes (about 3 lbs.), peeled and cut into ½-in. pieces
- 1 large onion, chopped
- 1 tsp. salt
- ½ tsp. pepper

1. In a large skillet, cook chopped bacon over medium-low heat until crisp. Remove bacon from pan with a slotted spoon and drain on paper towels. Remove bacon drippings from pan and reserve.
2. Working in batches, add ¼ cup bacon drippings, potatoes, onion, salt and pepper to pan; toss to coat. Cook and stir over medium-low heat until the potatoes are golden brown and tender, 15-20 minutes, adding more drippings as needed. Stir in cooked bacon; serve immediately.
1 cup: 349 cal., 21g fat (8g sat. fat), 33mg chol., 681mg sod., 31g carb. (3g sugars, 2g fiber), 10g pro.

BREAKFAST BURRITO CASSEROLE

A friend gave me this recipe and I modified it to fit our family. It's perfect for a brunch, because you can prep it the night before and bake it the next morning.
—*Krista Yoder, Abbeville, SC*

PREP: 25 min. • **BAKE:** 30 min.
MAKES: 8 servings

- 8 large eggs
- ⅓ cup 2% milk
- ½ tsp. salt
- ½ tsp. pepper
- 1 lb. bulk pork sausage
- 1 cup sour cream

BREAKFAST BURRITO CASSEROLE

- 1 can (10¾ oz.) condensed cream of chicken soup, undiluted
- 4 flour tortillas (10 in.), cut into 1-in. pieces
- 1⅓ cups salsa, divided
- ⅔ cup shredded cheddar cheese
- ⅔ cup shredded part-skim mozzarella cheese
  Optional: Enchilada sauce and thinly sliced green onions

1. Preheat oven to 350°. Whisk together eggs, milk, salt and pepper. In a large skillet coated with cooking spray, cook and stir egg mixture over medium heat until thickened and no liquid egg remains; remove scrambled eggs from skillet.
2. In the same skillet, cook and crumble sausage over medium heat until no longer pink, 5-7 minutes; drain. Stir together sour cream and soup. Spread half the sour cream mixture in an ungreased 13x9-in. baking dish. Layer with half the tortilla pieces, half the salsa, the scrambled eggs, the sausage, and the remaining tortillas and sour cream mixture. Top with the remaining salsa; sprinkle with cheeses.
3. Bake, uncovered, until heated through, 30-35 minutes. If desired, serve with enchilada sauce and sliced green onions.
To make ahead: Refrigerate unbaked casserole, covered, several hours or overnight. To use, preheat oven to 350°. Remove casserole from refrigerator while oven heats. Bake as directed, increasing time by 5 minutes.
1 cup: 506 cal., 34g fat (14g sat. fat), 243mg chol., 1419mg sod., 27g carb. (5g sugars, 2g fiber), 22g pro.

WILD BLUEBERRY MUFFINS

CARAMELIZED BACON TWISTS

Whenever my grandchildren come over, these sweet chewy bacon strips are a big hit. Lining the pan with foil before baking helps cut down on cleanup.
—*Jane Paschke, University Park, FL*

TAKES: 30 min. • **MAKES:** about 3 dozen

- ½ cup packed brown sugar
- 2 tsp. ground cinnamon
- 1 lb. bacon strips

1. Preheat oven to 350°. Line a 15x10x1-in. pan with foil.
2. In a shallow bowl, mix brown sugar and cinnamon. Cut bacon strips crosswise in half; dip in sugar mixture to coat. Twist 2 or 3 times, then place in prepared pan. Bake until browned and crisp, 15-20 minutes.
Freeze option: Freeze cooled bacon twists in freezer containers, separating layers with waxed paper. If desired, reheat in a microwave oven or on a foil-lined baking sheet in a preheated 350° oven before serving.
1 bacon twist: 35 cal., 2g fat (1g sat. fat), 5mg chol., 81mg sod., 3g carb. (3g sugars, 0 fiber), 2g pro.

TEST KITCHEN TIP
Looking for extra-crisp bacon? Place a metal cooling rack on top of the aluminum-lined pan and lay the raw bacon on top. This will allow the bacon to cook from all sides.

WILD BLUEBERRY MUFFINS

Nothing is better than a warm blueberry muffin in the morning. These muffins are the best I have ever made. The wild blueberries make them extra special.
—*Dewey Grindle, Blue Hill, ME*

PREP: 15 min. • **BAKE:** 20 min.
MAKES: 1 dozen

- ¼ cup butter, softened
- ⅓ cup sugar
- 1 large egg, room temperature
- 2⅓ cups all-purpose flour
- 4 tsp. baking powder
- ½ tsp. salt
- 1 cup 2% milk
- 1 tsp. vanilla extract
- 1½ cups fresh or frozen wild blueberries or 1 can (15 oz.) water-packed wild blueberries, well drained

STREUSEL TOPPING
- ½ cup sugar
- ⅓ cup all-purpose flour
- ½ tsp. ground cinnamon
- ¼ cup cold butter, cubed

1. Preheat oven to 375°. In a bowl, cream the butter and sugar until light and fluffy, 5-7 minutes. Add egg; mix well. Combine flour, baking powder and salt; add to the creamed mixture alternately with milk. Stir in vanilla. Gently fold in blueberries.
2. Fill greased or paper-lined muffin cups two-thirds full. For streusel topping, in a small bowl, combine the sugar, flour and cinnamon; cut in the butter until crumbly. Sprinkle over the muffins. Bake until a toothpick comes out clean, 20-25 minutes.
1 muffin: 252 cal., 9g fat (5g sat. fat), 41mg chol., 325mg sod., 39g carb. (17g sugars, 1g fiber), 4g pro.

CARAMELIZED
BACON TWISTS

MA

MAPLE BACON FRENCH TOAST BAKE

Our family loves Sunday brunch. Each season I try to bring a new flavor to the table. This French toast bake reminds us of fall. Whole or 2% milk works best, but I use regular almond milk because I can't consume dairy and it works, too!
—*Peggie Brott, Milford, KS*

PREP: 35 min. + chilling • **BAKE:** 50 min.
MAKES: 12 servings

8	cups cubed bread
8	large eggs
2	cups 2% milk
½	cup packed brown sugar
⅓	cup maple syrup
½	tsp. ground cinnamon
1	lb. bacon strips, cooked and crumbled

1. Place bread in a greased 13x9-in. baking dish. In a large bowl, whisk eggs, milk, brown sugar, syrup and cinnamon. Pour over bread. Sprinkle with crumbled bacon. Refrigerate, covered, 4 hours or overnight.
2. Remove casserole from the refrigerator 30 minutes before baking. Preheat oven to 350°. Bake, uncovered, until a knife inserted in the center comes out clean, 50-60 minutes. Let stand 5-10 minutes before serving.
1 piece: 256 cal., 10g fat (3g sat. fat), 141mg chol., 426mg sod., 29g carb. (18g sugars, 1g fiber), 12g pro.

MAPLE BACON FRENCH TOAST BAKE

SPICY BREAKFAST LASAGNA

PEACHY DUTCH PANCAKE

After my daughter attended a slumber party, she raved about a Dutch pancake they had for breakfast. She asked her friend's mom for the recipe so we could make it at home. This is my version.
—*Carol Rogers, Tipton, IA*

TAKES: 30 min. • **MAKES:** 8 servings

- ¼ cup butter, cubed
- 2 cups fresh or frozen thinly sliced peaches, thawed and drained
- 4 large eggs
- 1¼ cups fat-free milk
- ½ tsp. almond extract
- 1¼ cups all-purpose flour
- ½ cup sugar
- ¾ tsp. salt
  Warm peach preserves and maple syrup

1. Preheat the oven to 425°. Place butter in a 13x9-in. baking dish. Place in oven for 3-4 minutes or until the butter is melted; carefully swirl to coat bottom and sides of dish. Carefully add peaches; return to oven for 3-4 minutes or until bubbly.

2. Meanwhile, in a large bowl, whisk eggs until frothy. Add milk and extract. Whisk in flour, sugar and salt. Pour into hot baking dish. Bake 10-12 minutes or until puffed and sides are golden brown.

3. Remove from oven; serve immediately with preserves and syrup.

To make ahead: Prepare pancake batter as directed. Refrigerate, covered, several hours or overnight. Remove batter from refrigerator 30 minutes before baking. Preheat oven to 425°. Prepare baking dish as directed. Whisk batter until blended; pour into hot baking dish. Bake, as directed, until puffed and the sides are golden brown.

1 piece: 235 cal., 8g fat (4g sat. fat), 109mg chol., 319mg sod., 33g carb. (18g sugars, 1g fiber), 7g pro.

SPICY BREAKFAST LASAGNA

It's fun to make something new, especially when it gets rave reviews. When I took this dish to our breakfast club at work, people said it woke up their taste buds!
—*Guthrie Torp Jr., Highland Ranch, CO*

PREP: 20 min. + chilling • **BAKE:** 35 min.
MAKES: 16 servings

- 3 cups 4% cottage cheese
- ½ cup minced chives
- ¼ cup sliced green onions
- 18 large eggs
- ⅓ cup 2% milk
- ½ tsp. salt
- ¼ tsp. pepper
- 1 Tbsp. butter
- 8 lasagna noodles, cooked and drained
- 4 cups frozen shredded hash browns, thawed
- 1 lb. bulk pork sausage, cooked and crumbled
- 8 oz. sliced Monterey Jack cheese with jalapeno peppers
- 8 oz. sliced Muenster cheese

1. In a bowl, combine cottage cheese, chives and onions. In another bowl, whisk eggs, milk, salt and pepper until blended. In a large skillet, heat butter over medium heat. Pour in egg mixture; cook and stir until eggs are thickened and no liquid egg remains. Remove from heat.

2. Place 4 lasagna noodles in a greased 13x9-in. baking dish. Layer with 2 cups hash browns, scrambled eggs, sausage and half the cottage cheese mixture. Cover with Monterey Jack cheese. Top with remaining 4 lasagna noodles, hash browns and remaining cottage cheese mixture. Cover with Muenster cheese. Refrigerate, covered, 8 hours or overnight.

3. Remove the dish from the refrigerator 30 minutes before baking. Preheat oven to 350°. Bake, uncovered, until a knife inserted in the center comes out clean, 35-40 minutes. Let casserole stand for 5 minutes before cutting.

1 piece: 366 cal., 23g fat (11g sat. fat), 256mg chol., 640mg sod., 16g carb. (3g sugars, 1g fiber), 23g pro.

SUNRISE SAUSAGE ENCHILADAS

2. In same pan, heat oil over medium-high heat; saute potatoes until lightly browned, 8-10 minutes. Remove from the heat; stir in the seasonings, chiles, sausage and ½ cup cheese.

3. Place ½ cup filling on each tortilla; roll up and place in a greased 13x9-in. baking dish, seam side down. Top with the sauce. Refrigerate enchiladas, covered, several hours or overnight.

4. Preheat oven to 375°. Remove the enchiladas from the refrigerator while oven heats. Bake, covered, 30 minutes. Sprinkle with remaining 1½ cups cheddar cheese. Bake, uncovered, until lightly browned and heated through, an additional 10-15 minutes. Serve with desired toppings.

1 enchilada: 398 cal., 25g fat (9g sat. fat), 48mg chol., 1116mg sod., 30g carb. (2g sugars, 2g fiber), 14g pro.

RUBY BREAKFAST SAUCE

Brighten any breakfast with this delicious cherry sauce spooned over French toast, pancakes or waffles. With a pleasant hint of cranberry flavor, the mixture is also nice served over ham, pork or chicken.
—*Edie DeSpain, Logan, UT*

TAKES: 10 min. • **MAKES:** about 4 cups

- 1 can (21 oz.) cherry pie filling
- 1 can (8 oz.) jellied cranberry sauce
- ¼ cup maple syrup
- ¼ cup orange juice
- 3 Tbsp. butter
  Pancakes or French toast

1. In a microwave-safe bowl, combine pie filling, cranberry sauce, syrup, orange juice and butter.

2. Microwave on high for 2 minutes; stir. Microwave 1-2 minutes longer or until butter is melted and mixture is heated through; stir. Serve over pancakes or French toast.

¼ cup: 97 cal., 2g fat (1g sat. fat), 6mg chol., 32mg sod., 19g carb. (16g sugars, 0 fiber), 0 pro.

(MA)

SUNRISE SAUSAGE ENCHILADAS

These delicious enchiladas are equally good made with cubed ham or sausage. Prepare ahead, refrigerate, and bake when ready for a convenient breakfast.
—*Deb LeBlanc, Phillipsburg, KS*

PREP: 30 min. + chilling • **BAKE:** 40 min.
MAKES: 10 servings

- 1 lb. bulk pork sausage
- 2 Tbsp. canola oil
- 7 cups frozen shredded hash brown potatoes, thawed (20 oz.)
- ½ tsp. salt
- ½ tsp. chili powder
- ¼ tsp. cayenne pepper
- ¼ tsp. pepper
- 1 can (4 oz.) chopped green chiles
- 2 cups shredded cheddar cheese, divided
- 10 flour tortillas (6 in.)
- 2 cans (10 oz. each) green enchilada sauce
  Optional toppings: Chopped red onion, chopped sweet red pepper and chopped fresh cilantro

1. In a large skillet, cook and crumble the sausage over medium heat until no longer pink, 5-7 minutes. Remove from pan with a slotted spoon; discard drippings.

RAISIN BREAD & SAUSAGE MORNING CASSEROLE

RAISIN BREAD & SAUSAGE MORNING CASSEROLE

When we used to have Sunday breakfasts with my grandparents, my mom often made this for Grandpa because he enjoyed it so much. Pork sausage and cinnamon-raisin bread taste surprisingly good together.
—*Carolyn Levan, Dixon, IL*

PREP: 25 min. + chilling • **BAKE:** 35 min.
MAKES: 12 servings

- ½ **lb. bulk pork sausage**
- 1 **loaf (1 lb.) cinnamon-raisin bread, cubed**
- 6 **large eggs**
- 1½ **cups 2% milk**
- 1½ **cups half-and-half cream**
- 1 **tsp. vanilla extract**
- ¼ **tsp. ground cinnamon**
- ¼ **tsp. ground nutmeg**

TOPPING
- 1 **cup chopped pecans**
- 1 **cup packed brown sugar**
- ½ **cup butter, softened**
- 2 **Tbsp. maple syrup**

1. In a large skillet, cook sausage over medium heat 4-6 minutes or until no longer pink, breaking it into crumbles; drain. In a greased 13x9-in. baking dish, combine bread and sausage.
2. In a large bowl, whisk eggs, milk, cream, vanilla, cinnamon and nutmeg until blended; pour over bread. Refrigerate, covered, several hours or overnight.
3. Preheat oven to 350°. Remove casserole from refrigerator while the oven heats. In a small bowl, beat the topping ingredients until blended. Drop by tablespoonfuls over the casserole.
4. Bake, uncovered, 35-45 minutes or until golden brown and a knife inserted in center comes out clean. Let stand for 5-10 minutes before serving.
1 piece: 425 cal., 25g fat (10g sat. fat), 141mg chol., 324mg sod., 41g carb. (26g sugars, 3g fiber), 11g pro.

3. Spoon by ⅓ cupfuls into greased muffin cups. Bake until a knife inserted in the center comes out clean, 20-25 minutes.

Freeze option: Cool baked egg muffins. Place on waxed paper-lined baking sheets, cover and freeze until firm. Transfer to freezer container; return to freezer. To use, place in greased muffin pan, cover loosely with foil and reheat in a preheated 350° oven until heated through. Or microwave each muffin on high 30-60 seconds or until heated through.

1 muffin: 133 cal., 10g fat (4g sat. fat), 224mg chol., 268mg sod., 2g carb. (1g sugars, 0 fiber), 9g pro.

BRING IT

These scrambled egg muffins are ideal for taking to potluck brunches because you can easily transport them in the metal tins you bake them in. Once you get to the party, remove the egg muffins and reheat individual servings on a microwave-safe plate in the microwave for 30-60 seconds. Or place the metal tins in a warm oven for 8-10 minutes or until the egg muffins are thoroughly heated through.

MA

SCRAMBLED EGG MUFFINS

After enjoying scrambled egg muffins at a local restaurant, I came up with this savory version that my husband likes even better. Freeze the extras to reheat on busy mornings.
—*Cathy Larkins, Marshfield, MO*

TAKES: 30 min. • **MAKES:** 1 dozen

- ½ lb. bulk pork sausage
- 12 large eggs
- ½ cup chopped onion
- ¼ cup chopped green pepper
- ½ tsp. salt
- ¼ tsp. garlic powder
- ¼ tsp. pepper
- ½ cup shredded cheddar cheese

1. Preheat the oven to 350°. In a large skillet, cook sausage over medium heat until it is no longer pink, breaking it into crumbles; drain.

2. In a large bowl, beat eggs. Add onion, green pepper, salt, garlic powder and pepper. Stir in the sausage and cheese.

ITALIAN SAUSAGE
EGG BAKE

ITALIAN SAUSAGE EGG BAKE

This hearty entree warms up any breakfast or brunch menu with its herb-seasoned flavor.
—*Darlene Markham, Rochester, NY*

PREP: 20 min. + chilling • **BAKE:** 50 min.
MAKES: 12 servings

- 8 slices white bread, cubed
- 1 lb. Italian sausage links, casings removed, sliced
- 2 cups shredded sharp cheddar cheese
- 2 cups shredded part-skim mozzarella cheese
- 9 large eggs, lightly beaten
- 3 cups 2% milk
- 1 tsp. dried basil
- 1 tsp. dried oregano
- 1 tsp. fennel seed, crushed

1. Place bread cubes in a greased 13x9-in. baking dish; set aside. In a large skillet, cook sausage over medium heat until no longer pink; drain. Spoon sausage over bread; sprinkle with cheeses.
2. In a large bowl, whisk the eggs, milk and seasonings; pour over casserole. Cover and refrigerate overnight.
3. Remove from refrigerator 30 minutes before baking. Bake, uncovered, at 350° for 50-55 minutes or until a knife inserted in the center comes out clean. Let stand for 5 minutes before cutting.
1 piece: 316 cal., 20g fat (10g sat. fat), 214mg chol., 546mg sod., 13g carb. (5g sugars, 1g fiber), 21g pro.

SPIRAL OMELET SUPREME

I love the medley of ingredients in this omelet, but feel free to substitute 2 cups of any combination of your favorite fillings for the vegetables. Use a serrated knife for easy slicing.
—*Debbie Morris, Hamilton, OH*

PREP: 20 min. • **BAKE:** 20 min.
MAKES: 8 servings

- 4 oz. cream cheese, softened
- ¾ cup 2% milk
- ¼ cup plus 2 Tbsp. grated Parmesan cheese, divided
- 2 Tbsp. all-purpose flour
- 12 large eggs
- 2 tsp. canola oil
- 1 large green pepper, chopped
- 1 cup sliced fresh mushrooms
- 1 small onion, chopped
- 1¼ tsp. Italian seasoning, divided
- 1½ cups shredded part-skim mozzarella cheese
- 1 plum tomato, seeded and chopped

1. Preheat oven to 375°. Line bottom and sides of a greased 15x10x1-in. pan with parchment; grease paper.

2. Beat cream cheese until soft; gradually beat in milk. Beat in ¼ cup Parmesan cheese and the flour. In a large bowl, beat eggs until blended. Add cream cheese mixture; mix well. Pour into prepared pan. Bake until set, 20-25 minutes.

3. Meanwhile, in a large skillet, heat oil over medium-high heat; saute pepper, mushrooms and onion until crisp-tender, 3-4 minutes. Stir in 1 tsp. Italian seasoning. Keep warm.

4. Remove the omelet from the oven; top immediately with mozzarella, tomato and pepper mixture. Starting with a short side, roll up omelet jelly-roll style, lifting with the parchment and carefully removing it as you roll. Transfer to a platter. Sprinkle with the remaining 2 Tbsp. Parmesan cheese and ¼ tsp. Italian seasoning.

1 piece: 275 cal., 19g fat (9g sat. fat), 312mg chol., 372mg sod., 8g carb. (4g sugars, 1g fiber), 18g pro.

SPIRAL OMELET SUPREME

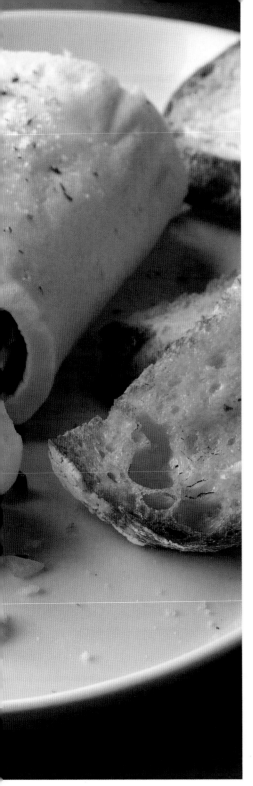

VEGETARIAN EGG STRATA

I used to make this with turkey or chicken sausage, but I adapted it for a vegetarian friend and it was a huge hit. I serve it for brunch with fresh breads or bagels and a big mixed salad featuring arugula, apples and walnuts. It also works well for lunch, served with tomato bisque.
—*Danna Rogers, Westport, CT*

PREP: 25 min. + chilling
BAKE: 45 min. + standing
MAKES: 12 servings

- 1 medium zucchini, finely chopped
- 1 medium sweet red pepper, finely chopped
- 1 cup sliced baby portobello mushrooms
- 1 medium red onion, finely chopped
- 2 tsp. olive oil
- 3 garlic cloves, minced
- 2 tsp. minced fresh thyme or ½ tsp. dried thyme
- ½ tsp. salt
- ¼ tsp. pepper
- 1 loaf (1 lb.) day-old French bread, cubed
- 2 pkg. (5.3 oz. each) fresh goat cheese, crumbled
- 1¾ cups grated Parmesan cheese
- 6 large eggs, lightly beaten
- 2 cups fat-free milk
- ¼ tsp. ground nutmeg

1. In a large skillet, saute zucchini, red pepper, mushrooms and onion in oil until tender. Add garlic, thyme, salt and pepper; saute 1 minute longer.
2. In a 13x9-in. baking dish coated with cooking spray, layer half of the bread cubes, zucchini mixture, goat cheese and Parmesan cheese. Repeat layers.
3. In a small bowl, whisk the eggs, milk and nutmeg. Pour over top. Cover and refrigerate overnight.

4. Remove from refrigerator 30 minutes before baking. Preheat oven to 350°. Bake, uncovered, until a knife inserted in the center comes out clean, 45-50 minutes. Let stand 10 minutes before cutting.
1 piece: 281 cal., 12g fat (6g sat. fat), 140mg chol., 667mg sod., 27g carb. (4g sugars, 2g fiber), 17g pro.

ZUCCHINI QUICHE

I make this unique recipe for so many different occasions. It's popular with company and at potluck dinners, and I've passed it around to many friends. My husband and I are growing lots of zucchini this summer—all for this quiche!
—*Dorothy Collins, Winnsboro, TX*

PREP: 20 min. • **BAKE:** 45 min.
MAKES: 8 servings

- 1 lb. zucchini, thinly sliced
- 2 Tbsp. butter
- 1 pie shell (9 in.), baked
- 1½ cups shredded mozzarella cheese
- 1 cup ricotta cheese
- ½ cup half-and-half cream
- 3 large eggs, lightly beaten
- ¾ tsp. salt
- ½ tsp. dried oregano
- ½ tsp. dried basil
- ¼ tsp. garlic powder
  Dash pepper
  Paprika

1. Preheat oven to 350°. In a small skillet, saute zucchini in butter until tender; drain. Place half the zucchini in the crust. Sprinkle with mozzarella cheese.
2. In a large bowl, combine the ricotta cheese, cream, eggs, salt, oregano, basil, garlic powder and pepper. Pour into crust. Arrange remaining zucchini slices over top. Sprinkle with paprika.
3. Bake for 45 minutes or until a knife inserted in the center comes out clean.
1 piece: 306 cal., 21g fat (11g sat. fat), 129mg chol., 499mg sod., 18g carb. (4g sugars, 1g fiber), 12g pro.

BAKED BLUEBERRY
GINGER PANCAKE

BAKED BLUEBERRY GINGER PANCAKE

We love pancakes, so I came up with this baked version that saves a lot of time in the morning. My kids always gobble these ginger-kissed breakfast squares right up!
—*Erin Wright, Wallace, KS*

TAKES: 30 min. • **MAKES:** 9 servings

- 2 large eggs, room temperature
- 1½ cups 2% milk
- ¼ cup butter, melted
- 2 cups all-purpose flour
- 2 Tbsp. sugar
- 3 tsp. baking powder
- 1½ tsp. ground ginger
- ½ tsp. salt
- 2 cups fresh or frozen unsweetened blueberries
  Maple syrup

1. Preheat the oven to 350°. Combine the eggs, milk and butter. Whisk the next 5 ingredients; add to egg mixture. Spoon the batter into a 9-in. square baking pan coated with cooking spray. Sprinkle the blueberries over top.
2. Bake until a toothpick inserted in center comes out clean, 20-25 minutes. Cut into squares; serve with warm maple syrup.
1 piece: 213 cal., 7g fat (4g sat. fat), 58mg chol., 368mg sod., 31g carb. (8g sugars, 2g fiber), 6g pro. **Diabetic exchanges:** 2 starch, 1½ fat.

TEST KITCHEN TIP
If your little ones aren't fans of ginger, feel free to scale it back or substitute something else, such as ground cinnamon or grated lemon zest. Blueberries make this pancake wonderful, but raspberries, blackberries or chopped strawberries would work well, too.

BACON & EGGS CASSEROLE

BACON & EGGS CASSEROLE
Because it requires so little time to prepare and is such a great hit with family and friends alike, this dish is a favorite of mine to make for brunches. Served with a fruit salad, hot muffins and croissants, it's excellent for an after-church brunch.
—*Deanna Durward-Orr, Windsor, ON*

PREP: 20 min. • **BAKE:** 40 min.
MAKES: 10 servings

- 4 bacon strips
- 18 large eggs
- 1 cup 2% milk
- 1 cup shredded cheddar cheese
- 1 cup sour cream
- ¼ cup sliced green onions
- 1 to 1½ tsp. salt
- ½ tsp. pepper

1. In a large skillet, cook the bacon over medium heat until crisp. Remove to paper towel to drain.
2. In a large bowl, beat eggs. Add the milk, cheese, sour cream, onions, salt and pepper.
3. Pour into a greased 13x9-in. baking dish. Crumble bacon and sprinkle on top. Bake, uncovered, at 325° until knife inserted in center comes out clean, 40-45 minutes. Let stand for 5 minutes.
1 serving: 289 cal., 22g fat (10g sat. fat), 420mg chol., 508mg sod., 4g carb. (3g sugars, 0 fiber), 16g pro.

MAPLE APPLE BAKED OATMEAL

LEEK TART

Satisfying and delicious, this tart has a flaky pastry crust and tasty filling of leeks, bacon and eggs. It makes a nice brunch dish, but you can serve it for any meal.
—*Anneliese Deising, Plymouth, MI*

PREP: 30 min. + chilling • **BAKE:** 30 min.
MAKES: 12 servings

- 2 cups all-purpose flour
- ¼ tsp. salt
- ¼ tsp. sugar
- ½ cup cold butter
- 9 to 11 Tbsp. cold water

FILLING

- 1 lb. thick-sliced bacon, diced
- 3½ lbs. leeks (white portion only), sliced
- 2 Tbsp. all-purpose flour
- 4 large eggs
- 1 cup half-and-half cream
- ½ tsp. salt
- ¼ tsp. pepper
- ⅛ tsp. ground nutmeg

1. In a bowl, combine the flour, salt and sugar; cut in the butter until crumbly. Gradually add water, tossing with a fork until a ball forms. Cover and refrigerate for 30 minutes.
2. In a large skillet, cook bacon over medium heat until crisp. Using a slotted spoon, remove to paper towels. Drain, reserving 2 Tbsp. drippings. Saute leeks in drippings until tender; stir in the bacon. Stir in flour until blended.
3. On a floured surface, roll the dough to ⅛-in. thickness. Transfer to an ungreased 10-in. springform pan. Spoon leek mixture into crust. Trim the crust to ¼ in. above filling; press crust against side of pan. Bake at 400° for 10 minutes.
4. Meanwhile, in a bowl, beat the eggs, cream, salt, pepper and nutmeg. Pour over leek mixture. Bake until a knife inserted in the center comes out clean, 20-25 minutes longer. Serve warm.
1 piece: 352 cal., 18g fat (9g sat. fat), 112mg chol., 482mg sod., 37g carb. (7g sugars, 3g fiber), 11g pro.

MAPLE APPLE BAKED OATMEAL

I've tried many different types of fruit for this recipe, but apple seems to be my family's favorite. I mix the dry and wet ingredients in separate bowls the night before and combine them the next morning when it's ready to be baked.
—*Megan Brooks, Saint Lazare, QC*

PREP: 20 min. • **BAKE:** 25 min.
MAKES: 8 servings

- 3 cups old-fashioned oats
- 2 tsp. baking powder
- 1¼ tsp. ground cinnamon
- ½ tsp. salt
- ¼ tsp. ground nutmeg
- 2 large eggs
- 2 cups fat-free milk
- ½ cup maple syrup
- ¼ cup canola oil
- 1 tsp. vanilla extract
- 1 large apple, chopped
- ¼ cup sunflower kernels or pepitas

1. Preheat oven to 350°. In a large bowl, mix the first 5 ingredients. In a small bowl, whisk eggs, milk, syrup, oil and vanilla until blended; stir into dry ingredients. Let stand 5 minutes. Stir in apple.
2. Transfer mixture to an 11x7-in. baking dish coated with cooking spray. Sprinkle with sunflower kernels. Bake, uncovered, until set and edges are lightly browned, 25-30 minutes.
1 serving: 305 cal., 13g fat (2g sat. fat), 48mg chol., 325mg sod., 41g carb. (20g sugars, 4g fiber), 8g pro. **Diabetic exchanges:** 3 starch, 1½ fat.

LEEK TART

COFFEE CAKE MUFFINS

I combine the dry ingredients for these muffins the night before I plan to bake them. In the morning, I add the remaining items, fill the muffin cups and pop them in the oven. Brown sugar, cinnamon and pecans give them a flavor similar to traditional coffee cake.
—*Margaret McNeil, Germantown, TN*

PREP: 20 min. • **BAKE:** 25 min.
MAKES: 1 dozen

¼ cup packed brown sugar
¼ cup chopped pecans
1 tsp. ground cinnamon
1½ cups all-purpose flour
½ cup sugar
2 tsp. baking powder
¼ tsp. baking soda
¼ tsp. salt
1 large egg, room temperature
¾ cup 2% milk
⅓ cup canola oil
GLAZE
½ cup confectioners' sugar
1 Tbsp. 2% milk
1 tsp. vanilla extract

1. Preheat oven to 400°. In a small bowl, combine the brown sugar, pecans and cinnamon; set aside. In a large bowl, whisk flour, sugar, baking powder, baking soda and salt. In another bowl, whisk egg, milk and oil until blended. Add to flour mixture; stir just until moistened.
2. Spoon 1 Tbsp. muffin batter into each of 12 paper-lined muffin cups. Top each with 1 tsp. nut mixture and about 2 Tbsp. batter. Sprinkle with the remaining nut mixture.
3. Bake until a toothpick inserted in center comes out clean, 22-24 minutes. Cool for 5 minutes before removing from pan to a wire rack. Combine glaze ingredients; spoon over muffins. Serve warm.
1 muffin: 215 cal., 9g fat (1g sat. fat), 17mg chol., 170mg sod., 31g carb. (19g sugars, 1g fiber), 3g pro.

COFFEE CAKE MUFFINS

CHEDDAR-HAM OVEN OMELET

EASY CHEESY LOADED GRITS

A tasty bowl of grits inspired me to develop my own recipe with sausage, green chiles and cheeses. It just might be better than the original.
—*Joan Hallford, North Richland Hills, TX*

PREP: 35 min. • **BAKE:** 50 min. + standing
MAKES: 8 servings

- 1 **lb. mild or spicy bulk pork sausage**
- 1 **small onion, chopped**
- 4 **cups water**
- ½ **tsp. salt**
- 1 **cup quick-cooking grits**
- 3 **cans (4 oz. each) chopped green chiles**
- 1½ **cups shredded sharp cheddar cheese, divided**
- 1½ **cups shredded Monterey Jack cheese, divided**
- 2 **Tbsp. butter**
- ¼ **tsp. hot pepper sauce**
- 2 **large eggs, lightly beaten**
- ¼ **tsp. paprika**
  Chopped fresh cilantro

1. Preheat oven to 325°. In a large skillet, cook sausage and onion over medium heat for 6-8 minutes or until sausage is no longer pink, breaking it into crumbles; drain sausage.
2. In a large saucepan, bring water and salt to a boil. Slowly stir in grits. Reduce heat to medium-low; cook, covered, about 5 minutes or until thickened, stirring occasionally. Remove from heat.
3. Add the green chiles, ¾ cup cheddar cheese, ¾ cup Monterey Jack cheese, butter and pepper sauce; stir until the cheese is melted. Stir in the eggs, then sausage mixture.
4. Transfer to a greased 13x9-in. baking dish. Top with remaining cheeses; sprinkle with paprika. Bake grits, uncovered, until golden brown and set, 50-60 minutes. Let stand 10 minutes before serving. Sprinkle with cilantro.

1 cup: 399 cal., 28g fat (15g sat. fat), 116mg chol., 839mg sod., 19g carb. (2g sugars, 2g fiber), 18g pro.

CHEDDAR-HAM OVEN OMELET

We had a family reunion for 50 relatives from the U.S. and Canada, and it took four pans of this hearty, five-ingredient omelet to feed the crowd. We served fresh fruit and an assortment of muffins to round out our brunch menu.
—*Betty Abrey, Imperial, SK*

PREP: 15 min. • **BAKE:** 40 min. + standing
MAKES: 12 servings

- 16 **large eggs**
- 2 **cups 2% milk**
- 2 **cups shredded cheddar cheese**
- ¾ **cup cubed fully cooked ham**
- 6 **green onions, chopped**

1. Preheat oven to 350°. In a large bowl, whisk eggs and milk. Stir in cheese, ham and onions. Pour mixture into a greased 13x9-in. baking dish.
2. Bake, uncovered, 40-45 minutes or until a knife inserted in the center comes out clean. Let omelet stand for 10 minutes before cutting.

1 piece: 208 cal., 14g fat (7g sat. fat), 314mg chol., 330mg sod., 4g carb. (3g sugars, 0 fiber), 15g pro.

MAIN DISHES

Feed the whole family (and a few more!) with comforting
main dishes that are guaranteed to satisfy even the hungriest of guests.

P. 101

P. 97

P. 117

PEPPERONI PIZZA LOAF

1. Preheat oven to 350°. On a greased baking sheet, roll out dough into a 15x10-in. rectangle. In a small bowl, combine the egg yolks, Parmesan cheese, oil, parsley, oregano, garlic powder and pepper. Brush over the dough.

2. Sprinkle with the pepperoni, mozzarella cheese, mushrooms, pepper rings, green pepper and olives. Roll up, jelly-roll style, starting with a long side; pinch seam to seal and tuck ends under.

3. Position loaf with seam side down; brush with egg whites. Do not let rise. Bake until golden brown and dough is cooked through, 35-40 minutes. Warm the pizza sauce; serve with sliced loaf.

Freeze option: Freeze cooled unsliced pizza loaf in heavy-duty foil. To use, remove from freezer 30 minutes before reheating. Remove from foil and reheat the loaf on a greased baking sheet in a preheated 325° oven until heated through. Serve as directed.

1 piece: 296 cal., 17g fat (6g sat. fat), 66mg chol., 827mg sod., 24g carb. (4g sugars, 2g fiber), 13g pro.

READER RAVES

"So good! I usually hate anything pickled, but the pickled pepper rings make this pizza. Way better than anything you get at restaurants!"

—COOKIEHATCH, TASTEOFHOME.COM

PEPPERONI PIZZA LOAF

Because this savory stromboli relies on frozen bread dough, it comes together in no time. The golden loaf is stuffed with cheese, pepperoni, mushrooms, peppers and olives. I often add a few thin slices of ham too. It's tasty served with warm pizza sauce for dipping.
—*Jenny Brown, West Lafayette, IN*

PREP: 20 min. • **BAKE:** 35 min.
MAKES: 12 pieces

1   loaf (1 lb.) frozen bread dough, thawed
2   large eggs, separated
1   Tbsp. grated Parmesan cheese
1   Tbsp. olive oil
1   tsp. minced fresh parsley
1   tsp. dried oregano
½   tsp. garlic powder
¼   tsp. pepper
8   oz. sliced pepperoni
2   cups shredded part-skim mozzarella cheese
1   can (4 oz.) mushroom stems and pieces, drained
¼ to ½ cup pickled pepper rings
1   medium green pepper, diced
1   can (2¼ oz.) sliced ripe olives
1   can (15 oz.) pizza sauce

SPINACH BEEF MACARONI BAKE

FAVORITE BARBECUED CHICKEN

Is there a better place than Texas to find a fantastic barbecue sauce? That's where this one is from—it's my father-in-law's recipe. We've served it at many family reunions, and we think it's the best!
—*Bobbie Morgan, Woodstock, GA*

PREP: 15 min. • **GRILL:** 35 min.
MAKES: 12 servings

- 2 broiler/fryer chickens (3 to 4 lbs. each), cut into 8 pieces each
  Salt and pepper
BARBECUE SAUCE
- 2 Tbsp. canola oil
- 2 small onions, finely chopped
- 2 cups ketchup
- ¼ cup lemon juice
- 2 Tbsp. brown sugar
- 2 Tbsp. water
- 1 tsp. ground mustard
- ½ tsp. garlic powder
- ¼ tsp. pepper
- ⅛ tsp. salt
- ⅛ tsp. hot pepper sauce

1. Sprinkle chicken pieces with salt and pepper. Grill, skin side down, uncovered, on a greased rack over medium heat for 20 minutes.
2. Meanwhile, in a small saucepan, make the barbecue sauce by heating oil over medium heat. Add the onion; saute until tender. Stir in remaining sauce ingredients and bring to a boil. Reduce heat; simmer, uncovered, for 10 minutes.
3. Turn the chicken; brush with the barbecue sauce. Grill 15-25 minutes longer, brushing frequently with the sauce, until a thermometer reads 165° when inserted in the breast and 170°-175° in the thigh.
1 serving: 370 cal., 19g fat (5g sat. fat), 104mg chol., 622mg sod., 15g carb. (14g sugars, 0 fiber), 33g pro.

SPINACH BEEF MACARONI BAKE

I serve this dish at family gatherings and church suppers and sometimes cut the recipe in half for smaller family dinners. My grandson-in-law and great-grandson often ask me to make it when they stop by to visit.
—*Lois Lauppe, Lahoma, OK*

PREP: 55 min. • **BAKE:** 25 min.
MAKES: 2 casseroles (12 servings each)

- 5¼ cups uncooked elbow macaroni
- 2½ lbs. ground beef
- 2 large onions, chopped
- 3 large carrots, shredded
- 3 celery ribs, chopped
- 2 cans (28 oz. each) Italian diced tomatoes, undrained
- 4 tsp. salt
- 1 tsp. garlic powder
- 1 tsp. pepper
- ½ tsp. dried oregano
- 2 pkg. (10 oz. each) frozen chopped spinach, thawed and squeezed dry
- 1 cup grated Parmesan cheese

1. Cook macaroni according to package directions. Meanwhile, in a large Dutch oven, cook the beef, onions, carrots and celery over medium heat until the meat is no longer pink; drain. Add the tomatoes, salt, garlic powder, pepper and oregano. Bring to a boil. Reduce the heat; cover and simmer for 30 minutes or until the vegetables are tender.
2. Drain macaroni; add the macaroni and spinach to beef mixture. Pour into 2 greased 3-qt. baking dishes. Sprinkle with cheese. Bake, uncovered, at 350° for 25-30 minutes or until heated through.
1 serving: 173 cal., 6g fat (3g sat. fat), 26mg chol., 632mg sod., 18g carb. (4g sugars, 2g fiber), 13g pro.

FAVORITE
BARBECUED CHICKEN

HOVER YOUR
CAMERA HERE
This Is What You
Need to Plan a
Family Reunion
Picnic

ASIAN BARBECUED
SHORT RIBS

ASIAN BARBECUED SHORT RIBS

Here in beef country, we find all sorts of different ways to serve beef. A former boss of mine, who owned a midwestern meat plant, gave me this recipe. It was an immediate hit with my family!
—*Connie McDowell, Lincoln, NE*

PREP: 25 min. • **BAKE:** 1¾ hours
MAKES: 8 servings

- 4 lbs. bone-in beef short ribs
- 1 Tbsp. canola oil
- 1 medium onion, sliced
- ¾ cup ketchup
- ¾ cup water, divided
- ¼ cup reduced-sodium soy sauce
- 2 Tbsp. lemon juice
- 1 Tbsp. brown sugar
- 1 tsp. ground mustard
- ½ tsp. ground ginger
- ¼ tsp. salt
- ⅛ tsp. pepper
- 1 bay leaf
- 2 Tbsp. all-purpose flour
  Optional: Julienned green onions and sesame seeds

1. In a Dutch oven, brown ribs in oil on all sides in batches. Remove ribs; set aside. In the same pan, saute onion until tender, about 2 minutes. Return ribs to the pan.
2. Combine the ketchup, ½ cup water, soy sauce, lemon juice, brown sugar, mustard, ginger, salt, pepper and bay leaf; pour over the ribs.
3. Cover and bake at 325° until ribs are tender, 1¾-2 hours.
4. Remove ribs and keep warm. Discard bay leaf. Skim fat from pan drippings. In a small bowl, combine flour and remaining water until smooth; gradually stir into drippings. Bring to a boil; cook and stir until thickened, about 2 minutes. Serve with ribs. If desired, top with green onions and sesame seeds.
1 serving: 240 cal., 13g fat (5g sat. fat), 55mg chol., 854mg sod., 11g carb. (9g sugars, 1g fiber), 20g pro.

FAVORITE DEEP-DISH PIZZA

FAVORITE DEEP-DISH PIZZA

My kids love to get pizza delivered, but it's expensive and full of calories. I came up with a one-bowl pizza that is healthier than delivery and allows the kids to add the toppings of their choice.
—*Sara LaFountain, Rockville, MD*

PREP: 20 min. • **BAKE:** 20 min.
MAKES: 8 servings

- 1¾ cups whole wheat flour
- 1¾ cups all-purpose flour
- 2 pkg. (¼ oz. each) quick-rise yeast
- 4 tsp. sugar
- 1 tsp. salt
- 1½ cups warm water (120° to 130°)
- ¼ cup olive oil
- 1 can (8 oz.) pizza sauce
- 8 oz. fresh mozzarella cheese, sliced
- 2 cups shredded Italian cheese blend
- ½ tsp. dried oregano
- ½ tsp. Italian seasoning

Optional: Sliced red onion, chopped green pepper, fresh oregano and crushed red pepper flakes

1. In a large bowl, combine wheat flour, 1 cup all-purpose flour, yeast, sugar and salt. Add water and oil; beat until smooth. Stir in enough remaining flour to form a soft dough. Press dough onto the bottom and up the sides of a greased 13x9-in. baking dish.
2. Top with pizza sauce. Place mozzarella slices over sauce. Sprinkle with shredded cheese, oregano and Italian seasoning. If desired, top with red onion and green pepper. Bake, uncovered, at 400° for 20-25 minutes or until golden brown. If desired, top with fresh oregano leaves and crushed red pepper flakes.
1 serving: 449 cal., 20g fat (9g sat. fat), 42mg chol., 646mg sod., 47g carb. (4g sugars, 5g fiber), 19g pro.

PENNSYLVANIA-STYLE PORK ROAST

Our children wouldn't dream of eating sauerkraut until they tasted it with this tender and juicy pork roast at a family celebration. They devoured it and even went back for seconds! Now this dish is a mainstay in my recipe file.
—*Ronda Jay Holcomb, Farmington, NM*

PREP: 10 min. • **COOK:** 2¼ hours + standing
MAKES: 16 servings

- 1 tsp. onion powder
- 1 tsp. garlic powder
- 1 tsp. celery seed, crushed
- 1 tsp. Worcestershire sauce
- ¼ tsp. pepper
- 1 boneless rolled pork loin roast (4 to 5 lbs.)
- 2 cans (14 oz. each) sauerkraut, undrained
- 1 tsp. sugar, optional
- 8 oz. smoked kielbasa or Polish sausage, cut into ½-in. pieces

1. Preheat oven to 350°. In a small bowl, combine the first 5 ingredients; rub over roast. Place roast fat side up in a Dutch oven. Combine sauerkraut and sugar if desired. Spoon sauerkraut and sausage over and around roast.

2. Cover and bake the pork roast until a thermometer inserted in pork reads 145°, 2¼-2¾ hours. Let the roast stand about 15 minutes before slicing.

3 oz. cooked pork: 191 cal., 9g fat (3g sat. fat), 66mg chol., 353mg sod., 2g carb. (1g sugars, 1g fiber), 24g pro.

 CHILI TOTS

Cook once and eat twice with this hearty southwestern casserole. With help from a few convenience products, it quickly goes together before you freeze it or pop it into the oven to bake.
—*Linda Baldwin, Long Beach, CA*

PREP: 15 min. • **BAKE:** 35 min.
MAKES: 2 casseroles (6 servings each)

- 1 lb. ground beef
- 2 cans (15 oz. each) chili without beans
- 1 can (8 oz.) tomato sauce
- 1 can (2¼ oz.) sliced ripe olives, drained
- 1 can (4 oz.) chopped green chiles
- 2 cups shredded cheddar cheese
- 1 pkg. (32 oz.) frozen Tater Tots

1. In a large skillet, cook the beef over medium heat until no longer pink; drain. Stir in the chili, tomato sauce, olives and green chiles. Transfer to 2 greased 8-in. square baking dishes. Sprinkle with the cheese; top with Tater Tots.

2. Cover and bake casseroles at 350° for 35-40 minutes or until heated through.

Freeze option: Before baking, cover the casseroles and freeze for up to 3 months. Remove from freezer 30 minutes before baking (do not thaw). Cover and bake at 350° for 1¼-1½ hours or until casserole is heated through.

1 serving: 297 cal., 18g fat (7g sat. fat), 44mg chol., 761mg sod., 24g carb. (1g sugars, 3g fiber), 15g pro.

PENNSYLVANIA-STYLE PORK ROAST

HEARTY MEATBALL
SUB SANDWICHES

HEARTY MEATBALL SUB SANDWICHES

Making the saucy meatballs in advance and reheating them saves me precious time when expecting company. These satisfying sandwiches are excellent for casual parties.
—*Deena Hubler, Jasper, IN*

TAKES: 30 min. • **MAKES:** 12 servings

- 2 large eggs, lightly beaten
- 1 cup dry bread crumbs
- 2 Tbsp. grated Parmesan cheese
- 2 Tbsp. finely chopped onion
- 1 tsp. salt
- ½ tsp. pepper
- ½ tsp. garlic powder
- ¼ tsp. Italian seasoning
- 2 lbs. ground beef
- 1 jar (28 oz.) spaghetti sauce
- 12 sandwich rolls, split
  Optional: Sliced onion and sliced green pepper

1. In a large bowl, combine the first 8 ingredients. Crumble beef over mixture and mix lightly but throughly. Shape into 1-in. balls. Place the meatballs in a single layer in a 3-qt. microwave-safe dish.
2. Cover and microwave on high for 3-4 minutes. Turn meatballs; cook for 3-4 minutes longer or until no longer pink. Drain. Add spaghetti sauce.
3. Cover and microwave on high for 2-4 minutes or until heated through. Serve meatballs on rolls. If desired, top with additional Parmesan and sliced onion and green peppers.
1 serving: 464 cal., 18g fat (7g sat. fat), 88mg chol., 1013mg sod., 49g carb. (10g sugars, 3g fiber), 26g pro.

HAM SALAD

I first made this ham salad for a shower, and everyone raved about it. Now when I go to a potluck, I take it, along with copies of the recipe.
—*Patricia Reed, Pine Bluff, AR*

TAKES: 15 min. • **MAKES:** 10 servings

- ¾ cup mayonnaise
- ½ cup finely chopped celery
- ¼ cup sliced green onions
- 2 Tbsp. minced fresh chives
- 1 Tbsp. honey
- 2 tsp. spicy brown mustard
- ½ tsp. Worcestershire sauce
- ½ tsp. seasoned salt
- 5 cups diced fully cooked ham or turkey
- ⅓ cup chopped pecans and almonds, toasted
  Slider buns, split, optional

1. Mix the first 8 ingredients. Stir in the ham. Refrigerate, covered, until serving.
2. Stir in pecans before serving. If desired, serve on buns.

½ cup ham salad: 254 cal., 20g fat (3g sat. fat), 43mg chol., 1023mg sod., 4g carb. (2g sugars, 1g fiber), 16g pro.

TEST KITCHEN TIP

This ham salad recipe is perfect for using up the leftovers from a honey-glazed ham—a ham recipe with relatively neutral ingredients that will mix well with spicy brown mustard and Worcestershire sauce. If you want to play it safe, cut away the edges (and with it, most of the glaze) of your leftover ham to avoid any potential less-than-desirable flavor combinations.

HAM SALAD

BIG-BATCH JAMBALAYA

I make this dish for football-watching parties because it feeds so many people. Of course, it's good any time of year!
—Kecia McCaffrey, South Dennis, MA

PREP: 25 min. • **COOK:** 55 min.
MAKES: 13 servings (3¼ qt.)

- 1 boneless skinless chicken breast, cubed
- 3 Tbsp. olive oil, divided
- ½ lb. cubed fully cooked ham
- ½ lb. smoked kielbasa or Polish sausage, cubed
- 2 medium green peppers, coarsely chopped
- 2 medium onions, coarsely chopped
- 6 garlic cloves, minced
- 2 cans (14½ oz. each) beef broth
- 1 can (28 oz.) crushed tomatoes
- 1½ cups water
- ¾ cup Dijon mustard
- ¼ cup minced fresh parsley
- 2 Tbsp. Worcestershire sauce
- 1½ to 2 tsp. cayenne pepper
- ½ tsp. dried thyme
- 1½ cups uncooked long grain rice
- 1 lb. uncooked medium shrimp, peeled and deveined

1. In a Dutch oven, cook chicken in 1 Tbsp. oil until no longer pink; remove and set aside. In the same pan, cook and stir the ham, kielbasa, peppers and onions in remaining oil until onions are tender. Add garlic; cook 1 minute longer.
2. Stir in the broth, tomatoes, water, mustard, parsley, Worcestershire, cayenne and thyme. Bring to a boil. Reduce the heat; cover and simmer for 10 minutes.
3. Add rice and return to a boil. Reduce heat; cover and simmer for 25-30 minutes or until rice is tender. Stir in shrimp and chicken; cook 2-4 minutes longer or until shrimp turn pink.
1 cup: 288 cal., 11g fat (3g sat. fat), 71mg chol., 1185mg sod., 30g carb. (2g sugars, 2g fiber), 18g pro.

MELON ARUGULA SALAD WITH HAM

I love the boost of healthy antioxidants in this fresh melon salad that I serve to my summer dining guests. I save the melon rinds to cut into large wedges and use as serving dishes. It makes a beautiful presentation, and cleanup is a breeze!
—Shawn Jackson, Fishers, IN

TAKES: 20 min. • **MAKES:** 8 servings

- ¼ cup olive oil
- 3 Tbsp. white wine vinegar
- 3 Tbsp. honey
- 3 cups cubed watermelon
- 2 cups cubed honeydew
- 2½ cups cubed fully cooked ham
- 1 small cucumber, coarsely chopped
- 8 cups fresh arugula
- ¾ cup crumbled feta cheese

1. In a large bowl, whisk together the oil, vinegar and honey. Add both melons, ham and cucumber; toss to coat.
2. To serve, arrange arugula on a platter. Top with the melon mixture; sprinkle with feta cheese.
2 cups: 202 cal., 10g fat (3g sat. fat), 32mg chol., 646mg sod., 17g carb. (15g sugars, 2g fiber), 12g pro. **Diabetic exchanges:** 2 lean meat, 1½ fat, 1 vegetable, ½ fruit.

BURGERS WITH SPICY DILL SALSA

When I make burgers or hot dogs for barbecues or boating, I create a topping that tastes like pickle relish meets tomato salsa. You can pile it on anything!
—*Valonda Seward, Coarsegold, CA*

PREP: 20 min. • **GRILL:** 10 min./batch
MAKES: 12 servings (3 cups salsa)

- 1 jar (10 oz.) dill pickle relish
- 3 plum tomatoes, seeded and finely chopped
- 1 small white onion, finely chopped
- ½ cup finely chopped red onion
- ½ cup minced fresh cilantro
- 1 Tbsp. olive oil
- 1 to 2 serrano peppers, seeded and chopped

BURGERS

- 3 lbs. ground beef
- 2 tsp. salt
- 1 tsp. pepper
- 12 hamburger buns, split

1. In a bowl, mix the first 7 ingredients. In another bowl, combine beef, salt and pepper; mix lightly but thoroughly. Shape into twelve ½-in.-thick patties.

2. In 2 batches, grill burgers, covered, over medium heat or broil 4 in. from heat for 4-5 minutes on each side or until a thermometer reads 160°. Serve burgers with salsa.

Note: Wear disposable gloves when cutting hot peppers; the oils can burn skin. Avoid touching your face.

1 burger with ¼ cup salsa: 371 cal., 16g fat (6g sat. fat), 70mg chol., 926mg sod., 31g carb. (4g sugars, 2g fiber), 25g pro.

HOVER YOUR CAMERA HERE
How to Throw an Epic Backyard Party

BURGERS WITH SPICY DILL SALSA

FAVORITE BAKED SPAGHETTI

2. In a large bowl, whisk the eggs, Parmesan cheese and butter. Drain spaghetti; add to egg mixture and toss to coat.

3. Place half of the spaghetti mixture in a greased 13x9-in. or 3-qt. baking dish. Top with half of the cottage cheese, meat sauce and mozzarella cheese. Repeat the layers. Place the baking dish on a rimmed baking sheet.

4. Cover the dish and bake for 40 minutes. Uncover and bake until heated through, 20-25 minutes longer. Let casserole stand for 15 minutes before serving. If desired, sprinkle with basil.

1¼ cups: 526 cal., 24g fat (13g sat. fat), 127mg chol., 881mg sod., 45g carb. (9g sugars, 3g fiber), 31g pro.

Baked Spaghetti Puttanesca: Add 1 Tbsp. minced garlic while cooking the ground beef mixture. After draining, stir in 3 Tbsp. rinsed and drained capers, 1 cup coarsely chopped black olives, 3 finely chopped anchovy fillets and ¾ tsp. red pepper flakes. Proceed as directed, topping the casserole with additional olives and capers before serving.

TEST KITCHEN TIP
Our Test Kitchen recommends using small-curd cottage cheese because it will melt right in. Ricotta is a great substitute if you prefer a milder flavor and finer texture.

FAVORITE BAKED SPAGHETTI
This is my grandchildren's most-loved dish. It feels like such a special dinner and is so cozy for winter.
—*Louise Miller, Westminster, MD*

PREP: 25 min. • **BAKE:** 1 hour + standing
MAKES: 10 servings

- 1   pkg. (16 oz.) spaghetti
- 1   lb. ground beef
- 1   medium onion, chopped
- 1   jar (24 oz.) pasta sauce
- ½   tsp. seasoned salt
- 2   large eggs
- ⅓   cup grated Parmesan cheese
- 5   Tbsp. butter, melted
- 2   cups 4% cottage cheese
- 4   cups shredded part-skim mozzarella cheese
     Chopped fresh basil, optional

1. Preheat oven to 350°. Cook spaghetti according to the package directions for al dente. Meanwhile, in a large skillet, cook beef and onion over medium heat until beef is no longer pink and onion is tender, 6-8 minutes, breaking beef into crumbles; drain. Stir in pasta sauce and seasoned salt; set aside.

OLD-FASHIONED
MACARONI & CHEESE

OLD-FASHIONED MACARONI & CHEESE

(PICTURED ON COVER)

Bring back the taste of days gone by with this ooey-gooey mac-and-cheese classic. A little ground mustard and hot pepper sauce give it just the right spice.
—*James Backman, Centralia, WA*

PREP: 15 min. • **BAKE:** 45 min.
MAKES: 16 servings

- 3½ cups uncooked elbow macaroni
- ¼ cup butter, cubed
- ¼ cup all-purpose flour
- 1 tsp. salt
- ¾ tsp. ground mustard
- ½ tsp. pepper
  Few dashes hot pepper sauce
- 3½ cups whole milk
- 5 cups shredded cheddar cheese, divided

1. Preheat oven to 350°. Cook macaroni in boiling water until almost tender; drain. Meanwhile, in a Dutch oven, melt butter over medium heat. Stir in the flour, salt, mustard, pepper and pepper sauce until smooth. Cook and stir until bubbly, about 1 minute. Stir in cooked macaroni, milk and 4 cups cheese.

2. Transfer the mixture to an ungreased 13x9-in. baking dish. Cover and bake until bubbly, 45-50 minutes. Uncover; sprinkle with the remaining 1 cup cheese. Let stand for 5 minutes before serving.

1 cup: 267 cal., 17g fat (10g sat. fat), 48mg chol., 425mg sod., 17g carb. (3g sugars, 1g fiber), 12g pro.

MEXICAN MANICOTTI

MEXICAN MANICOTTI

I serve this hearty entree with Spanish rice, homemade salsa and tortilla chips. I've also made it without ground beef for our friends who are vegetarians.
—*Lucy Shifton, Wichita, KS*

PREP: 15 min. + chilling • **BAKE:** 65 min.
MAKES: 8 servings

- 1 lb. lean ground beef
- 1 can (16 oz.) refried beans
- 2½ tsp. chili powder
- 1½ tsp. dried oregano
- 1 pkg. (8 oz.) uncooked manicotti shells
- 2½ cups water
- 1 jar (16 oz.) picante sauce
- 2 cups sour cream
- 1 cup shredded Monterey Jack or Mexican cheese blend
- ¼ cup sliced green onions
  Sliced ripe olives, optional

1. In a large bowl, combine the uncooked beef, beans, chili powder and oregano. Spoon into uncooked manicotti shells; arrange in a greased 13x9-in. baking dish. Combine the water and picante sauce; pour over shells. Cover manicotti and refrigerate overnight.

2. Remove from refrigerator 30 minutes before baking. Bake, covered, at 350° for 1 hour. Uncover; spoon sour cream over the top. Sprinkle with cheese, onions and, if desired, olives. Bake 5-10 minutes longer or until the cheese is melted.

1 serving: 431 cal., 20g fat (12g sat. fat), 90mg chol., 554mg sod., 36g carb. (6g sugars, 4g fiber), 23g pro.

WATERMELON
SHRIMP SALAD

OKTOBERFEST CASSEROLE

In northeastern Ohio, we love German flavors. This delicious casserole is a mashup of three of my favorite dishes: classic cheesy hash brown casserole; bratwursts and sauerkraut; and pretzels and beer cheese. This dish takes less than 10 minutes to mix and uses only one baking dish. It's sure to please everyone any time of the year.
—*Sarah Markley, Ashland, OH*

PREP: 15 min. • **BAKE:** 1½ hours + standing
MAKES: 12 servings

- 2 cans (10½ oz. each) condensed cheddar cheese soup, undiluted
- 1 cup beer or chicken broth
- 1 cup sour cream
- 1 pkg. (32 oz.) frozen cubed hash brown potatoes, thawed
- 1 can (14 oz.) sauerkraut, rinsed and well drained
- 2 cups shredded cheddar cheese
- 1 pkg. (14 oz.) fully cooked bratwurst links, chopped
- 2 cups pretzel pieces

1. Preheat oven to 350°. In a large bowl, whisk soup, beer and sour cream until combined. Stir in potatoes, sauerkraut, cheese and chopped bratwurst. Transfer to a greased 13x9-in. baking dish. Cover and bake for 45 minutes.

2. Uncover; bake 30 minutes. Top with pretzel pieces. Bake until bubbly and heated through, 12-15 minutes longer. Let stand 10 minutes before serving.

Freeze option: Freeze cooled potato mixture in freezer containers. To use, partially thaw casserole in refrigerator overnight. Heat through in a saucepan, stirring occasionally; add broth or water if necessary.

1 serving: 356 cal., 21g fat (10g sat. fat), 49mg chol., 884mg sod., 29g carb. (4g sugars, 3g fiber), 13g pro.

HOVER YOUR CAMERA HERE
How to Cut a Watermelon into Slices, Cubes or Sticks

WATERMELON SHRIMP SALAD

Sweet, spicy and easy to make, this salad travels well in a cooler to picnics and summer gatherings. I love the flavors, the colors, and of course, the happy faces of my guests once they've tried it.
—*Judy Batson, Tampa, FL*

PREP: 30 min. + chilling
MAKES: 10 servings

- 1 seedless watermelon, cut into 1-in. cubes (about 10 cups)
- 1 medium honeydew melon, cut into 1-in. cubes (about 4 cups)
- 2 lbs. peeled and deveined cooked shrimp (31-40 per lb.)
- 2 cups green grapes, halved
- 1 large cucumber, seeded and chopped
- 1 small navel orange, peeled and sectioned
- 1 small red onion, chopped
- 1 jalapeno pepper, seeded and finely chopped
- ⅓ cup lemon juice
- 1 Tbsp. brown sugar
- ¼ tsp. crushed red pepper flakes

In a large bowl, combine the first 8 ingredients. Whisk together the remaining ingredients. Drizzle over shrimp mixture and toss to coat. Refrigerate at least 20 minutes before serving. Toss salad before serving.
2 cups: 309 cal., 2g fat (0 sat. fat), 138mg chol., 158mg sod., 56g carb. (50g sugars, 3g fiber), 21g pro.

OKTOBERFEST
CASSEROLE

THREE-CHEESE MEATBALL MOSTACCIOLI

Whenever my husband travels for work, I make a special dinner for my kids to keep their minds off missing Daddy. This tasty mostaccioli is meatball magic.
—*Jennifer Gilbert, Brighton, MI*

PREP: 15 min. • **BAKE:** 35 min.
MAKES: 10 servings

- 1 pkg. (16 oz.) mostaccioli
- 2 large eggs, lightly beaten
- 1 carton (15 oz.) part-skim ricotta cheese
- 1 lb. ground beef
- 1 medium onion, chopped
- 1 Tbsp. brown sugar
- 1 Tbsp. Italian seasoning
- 1 tsp. garlic powder
- ¼ tsp. pepper
- 2 jars (24 oz. each) pasta sauce with meat
- ½ cup grated Romano cheese
- 1 pkg. (12 oz.) frozen fully cooked Italian meatballs, thawed
- ¾ cup shaved Parmesan cheese
  Optional: Torn fresh basil or fresh oregano leaves

1. Preheat oven to 350°. Cook mostaccioli according to the package directions for al dente; drain. Meanwhile, in a small bowl, mix eggs and ricotta cheese.

2. In a 6-qt. stockpot, cook beef and onion until beef is no longer pink, 6-8 minutes, breaking up beef into crumbles; drain. Stir in brown sugar and seasonings. Add pasta sauce and mostaccioli; toss to combine.

3. Transfer half the pasta mixture to a greased 13x9-in. baking dish. Layer with ricotta mixture and remaining pasta mixture; sprinkle with Romano cheese. Top with meatballs and Parmesan cheese.

4. Bake, uncovered, until heated through, 35-40 minutes. If desired, top with basil or oregano.

1⅓ cups: 541 cal., 23g fat (11g sat. fat), 105mg chol., 1335mg sod., 55g carb. (13g sugars, 5g fiber), 34g pro.

THREE-CHEESE
MEATBALL
MOSTACCIOLI

TERIYAKI SHISH KABOBS

MOIST TURKEY BREAST

My family always requests this turkey at family gatherings. The Italian dressing adds a nice zip that you don't find in other recipes. If you'd like, you can make a flavorful gravy from the pan drippings.
—*Cindy Carlson, Ingleside, TX*

PREP: 10 min. • **BAKE:** 2 hours + standing
MAKES: 14 servings

- 1 bone-in turkey breast (about 7 lbs.)
- 1 tsp. garlic powder
- ½ tsp. onion powder
- ½ tsp. salt
- ¼ tsp. pepper
- 1½ cups Italian dressing

1. Place turkey breast in a greased 13x9-in. baking dish. Combine the seasonings; sprinkle over the turkey. Pour dressing over the top.
2. Cover turkey and bake at 325° until a thermometer reads 170°, 2-2½ hours, basting occasionally with pan drippings. Let stand for 10 minutes before slicing.
6 oz. cooked turkey: 406 cal., 22g fat (5g sat. fat), 122mg chol., 621mg sod., 2g carb. (1g sugars, 0 fiber), 47g pro.
Roasted Turkey: Combine 1¾ tsp. garlic powder, ¾ tsp. each onion powder and salt, and ½ tsp. pepper; sprinkle over a 12- to 14-pound turkey. Place in a roasting pan; top with 2½ cups Italian dressing. Cover and bake at 325° for 3-3½ hours or until a thermometer inserted in thigh reads 180°, basting occasionally with the pan drippings. Let turkey stand for 20 minutes before carving.

READER RAVES
"Absolutely delicious, moist and easy to prepare. Everyone commented on the terrific taste."

—MUM0819, TASTEOFHOME.COM

TERIYAKI SHISH KABOBS

When I was a teenager, our family lived on the island Guam in the South Pacific, where my father worked for an airline. One of my mother's friends gave her this tangy-sweet recipe, and we enjoyed it often. Now I make it for my family, and they're big fans as well.
—*Suzanne Pelegrin, Ocala, FL*

PREP: 20 min. + marinating
GRILL: 15 min. • **MAKES:** 8 servings

- 1 cup sugar
- 1 cup reduced-sodium soy sauce
- 1 cup ketchup
- 2 tsp. garlic powder
- 2 tsp. ground ginger
- 2 lbs. beef top sirloin steak, cut into 1½-in. cubes
- 2 to 3 small zucchini, cut into 1-in. slices
- ½ lb. medium fresh mushrooms
- 1 large green or sweet red pepper, cut into 1-in. pieces
- 1 small onion, cut into 1-in. pieces
- 2 cups cubed fresh pineapple

1. For marinade, mix first 5 ingredients. In a large bowl or shallow dish, add half the marinade and the beef; turn to coat. Cover and reserve remaining marinade. Cover and refrigerate mixture of beef and marinade overnight.
2. On metal or soaked wooden skewers, thread the vegetables and, on separate skewers, thread the beef and pineapple. Discard remaining marinade from beef bowl. Grill kabobs, covered, over medium heat until vegetables are tender and beef reaches desired doneness, 12-15 minutes, turning occasionally.
3. In a small saucepan, bring reserved marinade to a boil, stirring occasionally; cook 1 minute. Remove the vegetables, pineapple and beef from skewers before serving. Serve with sauce.
1 serving: 306 cal., 5g fat (2g sat. fat), 46mg chol., 1203mg sod., 38g carb. (32g sugars, 2g fiber), 27g pro.

MAKEOVER MEATLESS LASAGNA

If you have never tried tofu before, go for it with this recipe. The tofu blends in with all the other ingredients, adding protein without the fat and calories of ground beef or sausage.

—Mary Lou Moeller, Wooster, OH

PREP: 30 min. • **BAKE:** 45 min. + standing
MAKES: 12 servings

- 10 uncooked whole wheat lasagna noodles
- 1½ cups sliced fresh mushrooms
- ¼ cup chopped onion
- 2 garlic cloves, minced
- 1 can (14½ oz.) Italian diced tomatoes, undrained
- 1 can (12 oz.) tomato paste
- 1 pkg. (14 oz.) firm tofu, drained and cubed
- 2 large eggs, lightly beaten
- 3 cups 2% cottage cheese
- ½ cup grated Parmesan cheese
- ½ cup packed fresh parsley leaves
- ½ tsp. pepper
- 2 cups shredded part-skim mozzarella cheese, divided

1. Preheat oven to 375°. Cook noodles according to the package directions for al dente. Meanwhile, in a large saucepan, cook mushrooms and onion over medium heat until tender. Add garlic; cook 1 minute. Add tomatoes and tomato paste; cook and stir until heated through.

2. Pulse the tofu in a food processor until smooth. Add next 5 ingredients; pulse until combined. Drain noodles.

3. Place 5 lasagna noodles into a 13x9-in. baking dish coated with cooking spray, overlapping as needed. Layer with half the tofu mixture, half the sauce and half the mozzarella. Top with remaining noodles, tofu mixture and sauce.

4. Bake, covered, 35 minutes. Sprinkle with the remaining mozzarella. Bake, uncovered, until the cheese is melted, 10-15 minutes. Let stand for 10 minutes before serving.

1 piece: 258 cal., 9g fat (4g sat. fat), 48mg chol., 498mg sod., 26g carb. (9g sugars, 3g fiber), 19g pro. **Diabetic exchanges:** 2 medium-fat meat, 1½ starch.

TEST KITCHEN TIP
There are many types of tofu on the market so you'll want to make sure to pick up one marked firm and not soft.

MAKEOVER
MEATLESS
LASAGNA

POTLUCK FRIED CHICKEN

POTLUCK FRIED CHICKEN

This Sunday dinner staple is first fried and then baked to a crispy golden brown. Well-seasoned with oregano and sage, this classic is sure to satisfy diners at church potlucks or late-summer picnics, too. I love fixing it for family and friends.
—*Donna Kuhaupt, Slinger, WI*

PREP: 40 min. • **BAKE:** 25 min.
MAKES: 12 servings

1½ **cups all-purpose flour**
½ **cup cornmeal**
¼ **cup cornstarch**
3 **tsp. salt**
2 **tsp. paprika**
1 **tsp. dried oregano**
1 **tsp. rubbed sage**
1 **tsp. pepper**
2 **large eggs**
¼ **cup water**
2 **broiler/fryer chickens**
   (3 to 4 lbs. each), cut up
   Oil for frying

1. In a large shallow dish, combine the flour, cornmeal, cornstarch, salt, paprika, oregano, sage and pepper. In a shallow bowl, beat eggs and water. Dip chicken in egg mixture; place in flour mixture, a few pieces at a time, and turn to coat.
2. In an electric skillet, heat 1 in. oil to 375°. Fry the chicken, a few pieces at a time, until golden and crispy, 3-5 minutes on each side.
3. Place in 2 ungreased 15x10x1-in. baking pans. Bake, uncovered, at 350° until juices run clear, 25-30 minutes.
5 oz. cooked chicken: 497 cal., 29g fat (6g sat. fat), 135mg chol., 693mg sod., 20g carb. (0 sugars, 1g fiber), 36g pro.

HOMEMADE SLOPPY JOES

I simmer a big batch of this hot, tangy sandwich filling and freeze the extras. Then on a busy day, I thaw and reheat it for a quick dinner.
—*Sandra Castillo, Janesville, WI*

PREP: 10 min. • **COOK:** 30 min.
MAKES: 12 servings

- 2 lbs. ground beef
- 2 medium onions, chopped
- 2 to 3 garlic cloves, minced
- 2 cups ketchup
- 1 cup barbecue sauce
- ¼ cup packed brown sugar
- ¼ cup cider vinegar
- 2 Tbsp. prepared mustard
- 1 tsp. Italian seasoning
- 1 tsp. onion powder
- ½ tsp. pepper
- 12 hamburger buns, split

In a large skillet, cook beef, onions and garlic over medium heat until the meat is no longer pink, 6-8 minutes, breaking meat into crumbles; drain. Stir in ketchup, barbecue sauce, brown sugar, vinegar, mustard, Italian seasoning, onion powder and pepper. Bring to a boil. Reduce heat; simmer, uncovered, for 20 minutes. Serve on buns.

Freeze option: Freeze cooled meat mixture in freezer containers. To use, partially thaw in refrigerator overnight. Heat through in a saucepan, stirring occasionally; add water if necessary.

1 sandwich: 368 cal., 11g fat (4g sat. fat), 47mg chol., 1029mg sod., 49g carb. (27g sugars, 1g fiber), 18g pro.

HOMEMADE
SLOPPY JOES

BARBECUE SLIDERS

When unexpected guests dropped in, all I had was defrosted sausage and ground beef. We combined the two for juicy burgers on the grill.
—*B.J. Larsen, Erie, CO*

TAKES: 25 min. • **MAKES:** 8 servings

- 1 lb. ground beef
- 1 lb. bulk pork sausage
- 1 cup barbecue sauce, divided
- 16 Hawaiian sweet rolls, split
     Optional: Lettuce leaves, sliced plum tomatoes and red onion

1. In a large bowl, mix beef and sausage lightly but thoroughly. Shape into sixteen ½-in.-thick patties.
2. Grill the patties, covered, over medium heat or broil 4-5 in. from the heat until a thermometer reads 160°, 3-4 minutes on each side. Brush with ¼ cup sauce during the last 2 minutes of cooking. Serve on rolls with remaining barbecue sauce; top as desired.
Freeze option: Place patties on a waxed paper-lined baking sheet; cover and freeze until firm. Remove from pan and transfer to an airtight container; return to freezer. To use, grill frozen patties as directed, increasing time as necessary.
2 sliders: 499 cal., 24g fat (9g sat. fat), 96mg chol., 885mg sod., 47g carb. (23g sugars, 2g fiber), 24g pro.

TEST KITCHEN TIP

Make these sliders with 90% lean ground beef and turkey breakfast sausage and you'll save nearly 100 calories and more than half of the fat per serving.

APPLE-GLAZED HOLIDAY HAM

Each Christmas I'm asked to prepare this entree. I'm happy to oblige because it is easy to assemble, bakes for a few hours unattended and is simply delicious.
—*Emory Doty, Jasper, GA*

PREP: 10 min. • **BAKE:** 2½ hours
MAKES: 15 servings

- 1 spiral-sliced fully cooked bone-in ham (7 to 9 lbs.)
- ½ cup packed brown sugar
- ½ cup unsweetened applesauce
- ½ cup unsweetened apple juice
- ¼ cup maple syrup
- ¼ cup molasses
- 1 Tbsp. Dijon mustard
     Dash ground ginger
     Dash ground cinnamon

1. Place the ham on a rack in a shallow roasting pan. Bake, uncovered, at 325° for 2 hours.
2. In a small saucepan, combine the remaining ingredients. Cook and stir over medium heat until heated through. Brush the ham with some glaze; bake for 30-60 minutes longer or until a thermometer reads 140°, brushing occasionally with the remaining glaze.
4 oz. ham: 242 cal., 6g fat (2g sat. fat), 93mg chol., 1138mg sod., 17g carb. (15g sugars, 0 fiber), 31g pro.

GRILLED RIBEYES WITH BROWNED GARLIC BUTTER

(MA) GREEK CHICKEN BAKE

As soon as the weather turns cool, I know it's time to pull out the recipe for this cozy supper. I assemble it in the morning, then put it in the oven just before dinner.
—Kelly Maxwell, Plainfield, IL

PREP: 30 min. • **BAKE:** 50 min.
MAKES: 8 servings

- 3 Tbsp. olive oil, divided
- 1 medium onion, chopped
- 7 garlic cloves, minced
- 2 tsp. minced fresh thyme or ¾ tsp. dried thyme
- 2 tsp. minced fresh rosemary or ¾ tsp. dried rosemary, crushed
- ¾ tsp. pepper, divided
- 2 lbs. red potatoes, cut into ½-in. cubes
- 2 cans (14½ oz. each) diced tomatoes, undrained
- 2 cups cut fresh green beans (1-in. pieces)
- 2 Tbsp. finely chopped ripe olives
- 8 bone-in chicken thighs (about 3 lbs.), skin removed
- ½ tsp. salt
- ½ cup crumbled feta cheese
  Minced fresh parsley
  Hot cooked orzo pasta, optional

1. Preheat oven to 375°. In a large skillet, heat 1 Tbsp. oil over medium heat. Add the onion; cook and stir until tender, 3-4 minutes. Add garlic, thyme, rosemary and ½ tsp. pepper; cook 1 minute longer. Remove from pan.

2. In same pan, heat the remaining oil over medium heat. Add the potatoes; cook and stir until potatoes are lightly browned. Return the onion mixture to pan; stir in tomatoes, green beans and olives. Cook 1 minute longer.

3. Transfer to a greased 13x9-in. baking dish. Sprinkle the chicken with salt and remaining pepper; place over top of potato mixture. Bake, covered, 40 minutes. Bake, uncovered, 10-15 minutes longer or until a thermometer reads 170°-175°. Sprinkle with feta and parsley. If desired, serve with orzo.

To Make Ahead: Can be made a few hours in advance. Cover and refrigerate. Remove from the refrigerator 30 minutes before baking. Bake as directed.

1 chicken thigh with 1 cup potato mixture: 352 cal., 16g fat (4g sat. fat), 91mg chol., 312mg sod., 23g carb. (3g sugars, 3g fiber), 28g pro. **Diabetic exchanges:** 4 lean meat, 1½ starch, 1½ fat.

TEST KITCHEN TIP

The tastiest part of the chicken, bone-in thighs render tender, juicy meat. The meat is darker and firmer than the white breast meat and needs slightly longer to cook because they have a higher fat content and density.

HOVER YOUR CAMERA HERE
How to Host the Best Summer Grilling Get-Together

GRILLED RIBEYES WITH BROWNED GARLIC BUTTER

Use the grill's smoke to flavor the ribeyes, then slather them with garlicky butter for a standout entree your friends and family will always remember.
—*Arge Salvatori, Waldwick, NJ*

TAKES: 25 min. • **MAKES:** 8 servings

- 6 Tbsp. unsalted butter, cubed
- 2 garlic cloves, minced
- 4 beef ribeye steaks (about 1 in. thick and 12 oz. each)
- 1½ tsp. salt
- 1½ tsp. pepper

1. In a small heavy saucepan, melt the butter with garlic over medium heat. Heat for 4-6 minutes or until butter is golden brown, stirring constantly. Remove butter from heat.
2. Season steaks with salt and pepper. Grill, covered, over medium heat or broil 4 in. from heat 5-7 minutes on each side or until meat reaches desired doneness (for medium-rare, a thermometer should read 135°; medium, 140°; medium-well, 145°).
3. Gently warm garlic butter over low heat. Serve with steaks.
4 oz. cooked beef with 2 tsp. garlic butter: 449 cal., 36g fat (16g sat. fat), 123mg chol., 521mg sod., 1g carb. (0 sugars, 0 fiber), 30g pro.

CARAMELIZED
HAM & SWISS BUNS

CARAMELIZED HAM & SWISS BUNS

My next-door neighbor shared this recipe with me, and I simply cannot improve it! You can make it ahead and cook it quickly when company arrives. The combination of flavors makes it so delicious.
—Iris Weihemuller, Baxter, MN

PREP: 25 min. + chilling • BAKE: 30 min.
MAKES: 1 dozen

1 pkg. (12 oz.) Hawaiian sweet rolls
½ cup horseradish sauce
¾ lb. sliced deli ham
6 slices Swiss cheese, halved
½ cup butter, cubed
2 Tbsp. finely chopped onion
2 Tbsp. brown sugar
1 Tbsp. spicy brown mustard
2 tsp. poppy seeds
1½ tsp. Worcestershire sauce
¼ tsp. garlic powder

1. Without separating rolls, cut rolls in half horizontally; arrange bottom halves of rolls in a greased 9x9-in. baking pan. Spread cut side of roll bottoms with horseradish sauce. Layer with ham and cheese; replace tops.
2. In a small skillet, heat the butter over medium-high heat. Add onion; cook and stir until tender, 1-2 minutes. Stir in the remaining ingredients. Pour over rolls. Refrigerate sandwiches, covered, several hours or overnight.
3. Preheat oven to 350°. Bake, covered, 25 minutes. Bake, uncovered, until golden brown, 5-10 minutes longer.
1 sandwich: 315 cal., 17g fat (9g sat. fat), 61mg chol., 555mg sod., 29g carb. (13g sugars, 2g fiber), 13g pro.

BLT CHICKEN SALAD

BLT CHICKEN SALAD

Featuring all the fun fixings for a BLT chicken sandwich, this salad is so lovable. I can prep the ingredients ahead of time and just throw it all together at the last minute. Barbecue sauce in the dressing gives it unexpected flavor. Even picky eaters love it.
—Cindy Moore, Mooresville, NC

TAKES: 20 min. • MAKES: 8 servings

½ cup mayonnaise
3 to 4 Tbsp. barbecue sauce
2 Tbsp. finely chopped onion
1 Tbsp. lemon juice
¼ tsp. pepper
8 cups torn salad greens
2 large tomatoes, chopped
1½ lbs. boneless skinless chicken breasts, cooked and cubed
10 bacon strips, cooked and crumbled
2 hard-boiled large eggs, sliced

In a small bowl, combine the first 5 ingredients; mix well. Cover and refrigerate until serving. Place salad greens in a large bowl. Sprinkle with tomatoes, chicken and bacon; garnish with eggs. Drizzle with dressing.
1 serving: 281 cal., 19g fat (4g sat. fat), 112mg chol., 324mg sod., 5g carb. (3g sugars, 2g fiber), 23g pro.

**BBQ CHICKEN
SANDWICHES**

CHICKEN & CHILES CASSEROLE

This casserole is easy to prepare and can be made ahead if you have a busy day coming up. It's filling and makes good use of leftover chicken.
—*Lois Keel, Alburquerque, NM*

PREP: 15 min. • BAKE: 1¼ hours
MAKES: 8 servings

  1   cup sour cream
  1   cup half-and-half cream
  1   cup chopped onion
  1   can (4 oz.) chopped green chiles
  1   tsp. salt
  ½   tsp. pepper
  1   pkg. (2 lbs.) frozen shredded
       hash brown potatoes
2½   cups cubed cooked chicken
2½   cups shredded cheddar cheese,
       divided
       Chopped fresh cilantro, optional

1. Preheat oven to 350°. In a large bowl, combine the sour cream, half-and-half cream, onion, chiles, salt and pepper. Stir in the potatoes, cubed chicken and 2 cups shredded cheese.
2. Pour the mixture into a greased 13x9-in. or 3-qt. baking dish. Bake, uncovered, until golden brown, about 1¼ hours. Sprinkle with remaining cheese before serving. If desired, sprinkle with chopped cilantro.
Note: Cooked turkey or ham can be used instead of the chicken.
1½ cups: 410 cal., 21g fat (14g sat. fat), 111mg chol., 647mg sod., 25g carb. (4g sugars, 2g fiber), 26g pro.

MA

BBQ CHICKEN SANDWICHES

These tangy sandwiches are a cinch to make. For a little more spice, eliminate the ketchup and increase the amount of salsa to 1 cup.
—*Leticia Lewis, Kennewick, WA*

PREP: 20 min. • COOK: 15 min.
MAKES: 6 servings

  ½   cup chopped onion
  ½   cup diced celery
  1   garlic clove, minced
  1   Tbsp. butter
  ½   cup salsa
  ½   cup ketchup
  2   Tbsp. brown sugar
  2   Tbsp. cider vinegar
  1   Tbsp. Worcestershire sauce
  ½   tsp. chili powder
  ¼   tsp. salt
  ⅛   tsp. pepper

  2   cups shredded cooked chicken
  6   hamburger buns, split and toasted
       Dill pickle slices, optional

1. In a large saucepan, saute the onion, celery and garlic in butter until tender. Stir in the salsa, ketchup, brown sugar, vinegar, Worcestershire sauce, chili powder, salt and pepper.
2. Stir in chicken. Bring to a boil. Reduce heat; cover and simmer for 15 minutes. Serve about ⅓ cup chicken mixture on each bun.
Freeze option: Freeze cooled meat mixture in freezer containers. To use, partially thaw in refrigerator overnight. Heat the meat through in a saucepan, stirring occasionally; add water if necessary. Serve in buns; if desired, add pickle slices.
1 sandwich: 284 cal., 8g fat (3g sat. fat), 47mg chol., 770mg sod., 35g carb. (12g sugars, 3g fiber), 18g pro.

ITALIAN SAUSAGE SANDWICHES

My wife and I serve these hot sandwiches when we have friends over. The recipe is convenient because we can prepare the sandwiches the day before and reheat them the next day.
—*Mike Yaeger, Brookings, SD*

PREP: 30 min. • **COOK:** 30 min.
MAKES: 20 servings

- 20 Italian sausages
- 4 large green peppers, thinly sliced
- ½ cup chopped onion
- 1 can (12 oz.) tomato paste
- 1 can (15 oz.) tomato sauce
- 2 cups water
- 1 Tbsp. sugar
- 4 garlic cloves, minced
- 2 tsp. dried basil
- 1 tsp. dried oregano
- 1 tsp. salt
- 20 sandwich buns
    Shredded mozzarella cheese, optional

1. In a large Dutch oven, brown sausages a few at a time; discard all but 2 Tbsp. drippings. Saute peppers and onion in drippings until crisp-tender; drain.
2. In the same pan, combine the tomato paste, tomato sauce, water, sugar, garlic, basil, oregano and salt. Add the sausages; bring to a boil. Reduce the heat; cover and simmer for 30 minutes or until heated through. Serve on buns. Top with cheese if desired.

1 sandwich: 430 cal., 19g fat (8g sat. fat), 45mg chol., 1107mg sod., 44g carb. (11g sugars, 4g fiber), 20g pro.

ITALIAN SAUSAGE SANDWICHES

SLOPPY JOE SLIDER BAKE

2. In a large skillet, cook beef and onion over medium heat until beef is no longer pink and onion is tender, 6-8 minutes, break up beef into crumbles; drain. Stir in sloppy joe sauce, brown sugar, soy sauce and pepper. Cook and stir until combined, 1-2 minutes. Spoon beef mixture evenly over rolls; top with remaining cheese. Replace top halves of rolls.

3. For glaze, stir together butter, brown sugar, mustard, soy sauce and garlic powder. Brush over rolls; sprinkle with sesame seeds and minced onion. Bake, uncovered, until tops are golden and cheese is melted, 15-20 minutes. If desired, top with pickle slices.

Freeze option: Cover and freeze unbaked sandwiches; prepare and freeze glaze. To use, partially thaw in the refrigerator overnight. Remove from the refrigerator 30 minutes before baking. Preheat oven to 350°. Pour glaze over buns and sprinkle with sesame seeds and minced onion. Bake sandwiches as directed, increasing time by 10-15 minutes, until cheese is melted and a thermometer inserted in center reads 165°.

1 slider: 392 cal., 19g fat (10g sat. fat), 91mg chol., 668mg sod., 32g carb. (15g sugars, 2g fiber), 23g pro.

TEST KITCHEN TIP
You can also use "everything" seasoning to sprinkle on top of the rolls instead of sesame seeds and dried onion. If you use it, omit the soy sauce in the glaze to account for the extra salt in the seasoning.

MA SLOPPY JOE SLIDER BAKE

Ground beef is turned up a notch in these easy party sliders that are sure to please!
—*Rashanda Cobbins, Milwaukee, WI*

PREP: 20 min. • BAKE: 15 min.
MAKES: 1 dozen

- 1 pkg. (18 oz.) Hawaiian sweet rolls
- 12 slices cheddar cheese
- 1½ lbs. lean ground beef (90% lean)
- ½ cup chopped onion
- 1 can (15½ oz.) sloppy joe sauce
- 1 Tbsp. packed brown sugar
- 1 Tbsp. soy sauce
- ¾ tsp. pepper

GLAZE
- ¼ cup butter, melted
- 1 Tbsp. packed brown sugar
- 1 Tbsp. Dijon mustard
- 1 tsp. soy sauce
- ½ tsp. garlic powder
- 1 tsp. sesame seeds
- 1 tsp. black sesame seeds
- 1 tsp. dried minced onion
  Dill pickle slices, optional

1. Preheat the oven to 350°. Without separating the rolls, cut them in half horizontally; arrange bottom halves in a greased 13x9-in. baking pan. Top with half of cheese slices.

HERBED SEAFOOD CASSEROLE

When I wanted a seafood dish for my Christmas Eve buffet, my friend gave me the recipe for this rich, creamy casserole loaded with shrimp, scallops and crab.
—Donna Schmuland, Wetaskiwin, AB

PREP: 40 min. • **BAKE:** 50 min. + standing
MAKES: 12 servings

- 1½ cups uncooked long grain rice
- 2 Tbsp. butter
- 3 celery ribs, thinly sliced
- 1 medium onion, finely chopped
- 1 medium carrot, shredded
- 3 garlic cloves, minced
- ½ tsp. salt
- ¼ tsp. pepper
- 2 Tbsp. minced fresh parsley
- 1½ tsp. snipped fresh dill or ½ tsp. dill weed

SEAFOOD
- 1 lb. uncooked shrimp (31-40 per lb.), peeled and deveined
- 1 lb. bay scallops
- 1 can (16 oz.) crabmeat, drained, flaked and cartilage removed
- 5 Tbsp. butter, cubed
- ¼ cup all-purpose flour
- 1½ cups half-and-half cream
- 1 pkg. (8 oz.) cream cheese, cubed
- 1½ tsp. snipped fresh dill or ½ tsp. dill weed
- ½ tsp. salt
- ¼ tsp. pepper
- ¼ tsp. dried thyme

TOPPING
- 1½ cups soft bread crumbs
- 2 Tbsp. butter, melted

HERBED SEAFOOD CASSEROLE

1. Preheat oven to 325°. Cook the rice according to the package directions. Meanwhile, in a large skillet, heat butter over medium-high heat. Add celery, onion and carrot; cook and stir until vegetables are crisp-tender. Add the garlic, salt and pepper; cook 1 minute longer.
2. Add to cooked rice. Stir in parsley and dill. Transfer mixture to a greased 13x9-in. baking dish.
3. Fill a large saucepan two-thirds full with water; bring to a boil. Reduce heat to medium. Add shrimp; simmer, uncovered, 30 seconds. Add scallops; simmer just until shrimp turn pink and scallops are firm and opaque, 2-3 minutes longer. Drain, reserving 1 cup cooking liquid. Place seafood in a large bowl; stir in crab.
4. In a small saucepan, melt butter over medium heat. Stir in flour until blended; gradually stir in the cream and reserved cooking liquid. Bring to a boil; cook and stir until mixture is thickened and bubbly, about 2 minutes. Reduce heat. Stir in cream cheese, dill and seasonings until smooth. Stir into seafood mixture.
5. Pour over rice mixture. Toss bread crumbs with melted butter; sprinkle over top. Bake, uncovered, until golden brown, 50-55 minutes. Let stand for 10 minutes before serving.
1 cup: 404 cal., 20g fat (12g sat. fat), 150mg chol., 616mg sod., 29g carb. (3g sugars, 1g fiber), 26g pro.

ACAPULCO DELIGHT

This dish always delights family and
friends at potlucks and gatherings
when I bring it to share.
—*Margene Skaggs, Guinda, CA*

PREP: 25 min. • **BAKE:** 25 min.
MAKES: 10 servings

2	lbs. ground beef
1	envelope (1¼ oz.) taco seasoning
¾	cup water
1	bottle (15 oz.) mild green taco sauce
9	flour tortillas (6 in.)
2	cups shredded cheddar cheese
1	can (16 oz.) refried beans
2	cups sour cream
4	green onions, chopped
1	can (2¼ oz.) sliced ripe olives, drained
	Optional: Chopped tomatoes and chopped avocados

1. Preheat oven to 350°. In a large skillet,
cook and crumble beef over medium heat
until no longer pink; drain. Stir in the taco
seasoning and water. Add the taco sauce;
simmer until liquid is slightly thickened,
5-10 minutes.
2. Cover the bottom of a 13x9-in. baking
dish with 3 tortillas, tearing them into
pieces as necessary. Layer half the meat
mixture over tortillas; sprinkle with half
the cheese. Layer with 3 more tortillas;
spread with refried beans. Cover with sour
cream; sprinkle with green onions and
olives. Layer remaining tortillas over top;
cover with the remaining meat mixture
and cheese.
3. Bake until casserole is heated through,
25-30 minutes. Let stand a few minutes
before serving. If desired, serve with
chopped tomatoes and avocados.
1 piece: 468 cal., 27g fat (14g sat. fat),
104mg chol., 1064mg sod., 26g carb. (3g
sugars, 3g fiber), 28g pro.

**ACAPULCO
DELIGHT**

CHICKEN SALAD PARTY SANDWICHES

My famous chicken salad arrives at the party chilled in a container. When it's time to set out the food, I stir in the pecans and assemble the sandwiches. They're a hit at buffet-style potlucks.
—Trisha Kruse, Eagle, ID

TAKES: 25 min. • **MAKES:** 16 servings

- 4 cups cubed cooked chicken breast
- 1½ cups dried cranberries
- 2 celery ribs, finely chopped
- 2 green onions, thinly sliced
- ¼ cup chopped sweet pickles
- 1 cup fat-free mayonnaise
- ½ tsp. curry powder
- ¼ tsp. coarsely ground pepper
- ½ cup chopped pecans, toasted
- 16 whole wheat dinner rolls
  Leaf lettuce

1. In a large bowl, combine the first 5 ingredients. Mix mayonnaise, curry powder and pepper; stir into chicken mixture. Refrigerate until serving.
2. To serve, stir in pecans. Spoon onto lettuce-lined rolls.
1 sandwich: 235 cal., 6g fat (1g sat. fat), 30mg chol., 361mg sod., 33g carb. (13g sugars, 4g fiber), 14g pro.

ONION LOOSE-MEAT SANDWICHES

Made with French onion soup, these sandwiches don't have the typical flavor of most sloppy joes. My sisters and I rely on this recipe from Mom on days when there's little time to cook.
—Kathy Petorsky, Belle Vernon, PA

TAKES: 25 min. • **MAKES:** 8 servings

- 1½ lbs. ground beef
- 2 Tbsp. all-purpose flour
  Salt and pepper to taste
- 1 can (10½ oz.) condensed French onion soup, undiluted
- 6 to 8 hamburger buns, split
  Optional: Sliced cheddar cheese and dill pickles

1. In a large skillet, cook beef over medium heat until it is no longer pink; drain. Stir in the flour, salt and pepper until blended. Gradually add soup. Bring to a boil; cook and stir for 2 minutes or until thickened.
2. Spoon onto buns; top with cheese and pickles if desired.
1 sandwich: 253 cal., 10g fat (4g sat. fat), 43mg chol., 526mg sod., 21g carb. (4g sugars, 1g fiber), 19g pro.

TEST KITCHEN TIP

For extra flavor or texture in these loose-meat sandwiches, stir in chopped peppers, onions, tomatoes or green chiles.

HOT CHICKEN SALAD PIES

HOT CHICKEN SALAD PIES

These pies come together in a snap. They are perfect for when you have leftover chicken on hand that you need to use up.
—*Shirley Gudenschwager, Orchard, NE*

PREP: 20 min. • **BAKE:** 30 min.
MAKES: 2 pies (6 servings each)

- 2 sheets refrigerated pie crust
- 3 cups diced cooked chicken
- 2 cups cooked long grain rice
- 4 hard-boiled large eggs, chopped
- 1 can (10¾ oz.) condensed cream of mushroom soup, undiluted
- 1 cup mayonnaise
- 1 medium onion, chopped
- ½ cup chopped celery
- ¼ cup lemon juice
- 1 tsp. salt
- 1½ cups crushed cornflakes
- ¼ cup butter, melted

1. Unroll crusts into 9-in. pie plates; flute edges. Refrigerate 30 minutes. Preheat oven to 400°. Line unpricked crusts with a double thickness of foil. Fill with pie weights, dried beans or uncooked rice. Bake on a lower oven rack until edges are light golden brown, 10-15 minutes. Remove foil and weights; bake until the crusts are golden brown, 3-6 minutes longer. Cool on a wire rack; reduce heat to 350°.
2. In a large bowl, combine the chicken, rice, eggs, soup, mayonnaise, onion, celery, lemon juice and salt. Spoon chicken mixture into crusts. Combine cornflakes and butter; sprinkle over tops. Bake on lowest oven rack until lightly browned, 20-25 minutes.
1 piece: 505 cal., 32g fat (10g sat. fat), 112mg chol., 771mg sod., 38g carb. (3g sugars, 1g fiber), 15g pro.

ANTIPASTO SALAD PLATTER

I used to work in a pizza shop where this salad was the most popular item on the menu. The dish is perfect for nights when it's too hot to cook.
—*Webbie Carvajal, Alpine, TX*

TAKES: 25 min. • **MAKES:** 8 servings

- 1½ cups cubed fully cooked ham
- 1 jar (10 oz.) pimiento-stuffed olives, drained and sliced
- 1 can (3.8 oz.) sliced ripe olives, drained
- 1 pkg. (3½ oz.) sliced pepperoni, quartered
- 8 cups shredded lettuce
- 10 to 12 cherry tomatoes, quartered
- 1 cup Italian salad dressing
- 1½ cups shredded part-skim mozzarella cheese

In a large bowl, combine the ham, olives and pepperoni. On a platter or individual salad plates, arrange the lettuce, olive mixture and tomatoes. Drizzle with dressing; sprinkle with cheese.

1 serving: 342 cal., 29g fat (7g sat. fat), 41mg chol., 1830mg sod., 9g carb. (3g sugars, 2g fiber), 13g pro.

ANTIPASTO SALAD PLATTER

WINNING CRANBERRY-GLAZED HAM

A friend shared the recipe for this tender ham with me. I've served it at reunions, weddings, graduations, baptisms and holiday gatherings. It's a delicious way to please a crowd.
—*Sue Seymour, Valatie, NY*

PREP: 15 min. + marinating
BAKE: 2½ hours • **MAKES:** 16 servings

- 2   cans (16 oz. each) whole-berry cranberry sauce
- 1   cup orange juice
- ⅓   cup steak sauce
- 2   Tbsp. canola oil
- 2   Tbsp. prepared mustard
- 2   Tbsp. brown sugar
- 1   fully cooked bone-in ham (7 to 9 lbs.)

1. In a large bowl, combine the cranberry sauce, orange juice, steak sauce, oil, mustard and brown sugar. Score the surface of the ham with shallow diagonal cuts, making diamond shapes.
2. Place ham in a 2-gallon resealable bag. Add half of cranberry mixture; seal bag and turn to coat. Cover and refrigerate for 8 hours or overnight, turning several times. Cover and refrigerate remaining cranberry mixture.
3. Preheat the oven to 325°. Drain the ham, discarding marinade. Place ham on a rack in a foil-lined roasting pan; cover with foil. Bake for 1¾ hours.
4. Place reserved cranberry mixture in a small saucepan; heat through. Uncover ham; brush with cranberry mixture.
5. Bake until a thermometer reads 140°, 45-60 minutes longer, brushing with cranberry mixture every 15 minutes. Warm remaining cranberry mixture; serve with ham.
4 oz. cooked ham: 264 cal., 7g fat (2g sat. fat), 87mg chol., 1164mg sod., 22g carb. (15g sugars, 1g fiber), 29g pro.

FIRE-ROASTED ZITI WITH SAUSAGE

We punch up our pasta with smoked sausage and fire-roasted tomato sauce. It's an easy recipe to adapt and make your own—use whatever type of pasta and pasta sauce are in your pantry.
—*Jean Komlos, Plymouth, MI*

TAKES: 30 min. • **MAKES:** 8 servings

- 8   oz. uncooked ziti or rigatoni (about 3 cups)
- 1   can (28 oz.) Italian diced tomatoes, drained
- 1   jar (24 oz.) fire-roasted tomato and garlic pasta sauce
- 1   pkg. (16 oz.) smoked sausage, sliced
- 2   cups shredded part-skim mozzarella cheese, divided
- 1   cup 4% cottage cheese

1. In a Dutch oven, cook ziti according to package directions for al dente. Drain; return to pot.
2. Add tomatoes, pasta sauce and sausage to ziti; heat through over medium heat, stirring occasionally. Stir in 1 cup mozzarella cheese and cottage cheese. Sprinkle with remaining mozzarella cheese. Cook, covered, 2-5 minutes or until cheese is melted.
1¼ cups: 463 cal., 23g fat (11g sat. fat), 66mg chol., 1634mg sod., 41g carb. (15g sugars, 3g fiber), 23g pro.

SMOKED SALMON PASTA

SMOKED SALMON PASTA

This pasta originally came to be from the miscellaneous ingredients in my fridge, and depending on whom I'm cooking for, it changes a little each time I make it. The recipe makes enough for a party or for leftovers, which is a bonus because it is excellent the next day whether you serve it cold or reheated.

—*Jackie Hennon, Boise, ID*

TAKES: 25 min. • **MAKES:** 8 servings

- 1 lb. uncooked spiral or penne pasta
- 2 Tbsp. olive oil
- 2 large tomatoes, diced
- 2 cups water-packed artichoke hearts, drained and chopped
- 1½ cups kalamata olives, pitted and halved
- 1 cup chopped oil-packed sun-dried tomatoes
- ¾ cup chopped onion
- 8 oz. smoked salmon fillets
- 2 Tbsp. sun-dried tomato pesto
- 2 tsp. dried basil
- ¾ tsp. crushed red pepper flakes
- ¼ cup grated Parmesan cheese
- ¼ cup crumbled feta cheese

1. In a large saucepan, cook pasta according to package directions for al dente. Meanwhile, in a Dutch oven, heat olive oil over medium-low heat. Add the next 5 ingredients. Break the salmon into bite-sized pieces; add to tomato mixture. Stir in pesto, dried basil and red pepper flakes. Cook, stirring occasionally, until the vegetables are crisp-tender, 8-10 minutes.
2. Drain pasta. Add to salmon mixture; stir to combine. Top with cheeses.
¾ cup: 433 cal., 16g fat (3g sat. fat), 11mg chol., 924mg sod., 55g carb. (4g sugars, 4g fiber), 17g pro.

HONEY CHIPOTLE RIBS

HONEY CHIPOTLE RIBS

Nothing is better than having a sauce with the perfect slather consistency. Here's one that will ensure a lip-smacking feast. Feel free to make the sauce up to a week ahead for an easier grilling experience.

—*Caitlin Hawes, Westwood, MA*

PREP: 10 min. • **GRILL:** 1½ hours
MAKES: 12 servings

- 6 lbs. pork baby back ribs
BARBECUE SAUCE
- 3 cups ketchup
- 2 bottles (11.2 oz. each) Guinness beer
- 2 cups barbecue sauce
- ⅔ cup honey
- 1 small onion, chopped
- ¼ cup Worcestershire sauce
- 2 Tbsp. Dijon mustard
- 2 Tbsp. chopped chipotle peppers in adobo sauce
- 4 tsp. ground chipotle pepper
- 1 tsp. salt
- 1 tsp. garlic powder
- ½ tsp. pepper

1. Wrap ribs in large pieces of heavy-duty foil; seal edges of foil. Grill, covered, over indirect medium heat for 1-1½ hours or until tender.
2. In a large saucepan, combine sauce ingredients; bring to a boil. Reduce heat; simmer, uncovered, for about 45 minutes or until thickened, stirring occasionally.
3. Carefully remove ribs from foil. Place over direct heat; baste with some of the sauce. Grill, covered, over medium heat for 30 minutes or until browned, turning once and basting occasionally with additional sauce. Serve with the remaining sauce.
1 serving: 515 cal., 21g fat (8g sat. fat), 81mg chol., 1674mg sod., 54g carb. (49g sugars, 1g fiber), 23g pro.

ROASTED
PUMPKIN
LASAGNA

ROASTED PUMPKIN LASAGNA

Here's a hearty meatless meal my family enjoys. You can use a butternut squash in place of the pumpkin.
—*Wendy Masters, East Garafraxa, ON*

PREP: 1 hour. • **BAKE:** 1 hour + standing
MAKES: 12 servings

- 1 medium pie pumpkin (about 3 lbs.)
- 2 Tbsp. olive oil
- 1 tsp. salt, divided
- ¼ tsp. ground nutmeg
- 12 uncooked lasagna noodles
- ½ cup butter, cubed
- 1 cup chopped onion
- 3 garlic cloves, minced
- ½ cup all-purpose flour
- 4½ cups 2% milk
- ¼ cup chopped fresh sage
- ½ cup grated Parmesan cheese
- 2 cups shredded mozzarella cheese
  Crushed red pepper flakes, optional

1. Preheat oven to 400°. Peel pumpkin; cut in half lengthwise; discard seeds or save for toasting. Cut into ¼-in. thick slices. Place in a single layer on 2 greased 15x10x1-in. baking pan. Drizzle with oil; sprinkle with ¼ tsp. salt and nutmeg. Roast until tender, 30-35 minutes. Reduce oven temperature to 350°.

2. Meanwhile, cook lasagna noodles according to package directions for al dente. In a large saucepan, melt butter over medium heat. Add onion; cook and stir until tender, 6-7 minutes. Add garlic; cook 1 minute longer. Stir in the flour and remaining ¾ tsp. salt until smooth; gradually whisk in milk and sage. Bring to a boil, stirring constantly; cook and stir until thickened, 8-10 minutes. Remove from the heat; stir in Parmesan cheese. Drain noodles.

3. Place 3 lasagna noodles in a greased 13x9-in. baking dish. Layer with ⅓ of the pumpkin, 1⅓ cups sauce and ½ cup mozzarella cheese. Repeat layers twice. Top with the remaining noodles, sauce and mozzarella cheese.

4. Bake, covered, 30 minutes. Uncover and bake until golden brown and bubbly, 30-35 minutes longer. Let lasagna stand 10-15 minutes before serving. If desired, sprinkle with red pepper flakes.

1 piece: 350 cal., 17g fat (9g sat. fat), 45mg chol., 481mg sod., 37g carb. (8g sugars, 2g fiber), 13g pro.

FAVORITE HAMBURGER STEW

A woman at our church gave me this recipe when I needed a way to use up our bounty of home-canned tomatoes. My husband loves it, and I like that it's easy to warm up for a carefree dinner in the winter months.
—*Marcia Clay, Truman, MN*

PREP: 20 min. • **COOK:** 65 min.
MAKES: 16 servings (4 qt.)

- 2 lbs. ground beef
- 2 medium onions, chopped
- 4 cans (14½ oz. each) stewed tomatoes, undrained
- 8 medium carrots, thinly sliced
- 4 celery ribs, thinly sliced
- 2 medium potatoes, peeled and cubed
- 2 cups water
- ½ cup uncooked long grain rice
- 3 tsp. salt
- 1 tsp. pepper

1. In a Dutch oven, cook beef and onions over medium heat until meat is no longer pink, breaking it into crumbles; drain. Add the tomatoes, carrots, celery, potatoes, water, rice, salt and pepper; bring to a boil. Reduce the heat; cover and simmer for 30 minutes or until vegetables and rice are tender.

2. Uncover; simmer 20-30 minutes longer or until thickened to desired consistency.

Freeze option: Freeze the cooled stew in freezer containers. To use, partially thaw in refrigerator overnight. Heat through in a saucepan, stirring occasionally; add water if necessary.

1 cup: 191 cal., 7g fat (3g sat. fat), 35mg chol., 689mg sod., 21g carb. (8g sugars, 2g fiber), 12g pro.

HOVER YOUR CAMERA HERE
Hosting a Holiday Party? Here's How Much Food to Serve

SOURDOUGH BREAD BOWL SANDWICH

I created this for when my husband and I go to the lake. I don't like to spend a lot of time hovering over a hot stove or grill, especially in summer, and this hearty sandwich is ready in minutes. For extra flavor, brush melted garlic and herb butter on top prior to cooking.
—Shawna Welsh-Garrison, Owasso, OK

PREP: 15 min. • **COOK:** 25 min. + standing
MAKES: 8 servings

- 1 round loaf sourdough bread (1½ lbs.)
- ½ cup honey mustard salad dressing
- 4 slices sharp cheddar cheese
- ⅓ lb. thinly sliced deli ham
- 4 slices smoked provolone cheese
- ⅓ lb. thinly sliced deli smoked turkey
- 1 Tbsp. butter, melted

1. Prepare campfire or grill for low heat. Cut a thin slice off top of bread loaf. Hollow out bottom of loaf, leaving a ½-in.-thick shell (save removed bread for another use). Spread the dressing on inside of hollowed loaf and under the bread top. Layer inside with cheddar, ham, provolone and turkey. Replace top. Place on a piece of heavy-duty foil (about 24x18 in.). Brush loaf with butter. Fold foil edges over top, crimping to seal.

2. Cook over campfire or grill until heated through, 25-30 minutes. Let bread stand 15 minutes before removing foil. Cut into sandwich into wedges.

1 wedge: 346 cal., 17g fat (6g sat. fat), 46mg chol., 865mg sod., 30g carb. (5g sugars, 1g fiber), 19g pro.

TEST KITCHEN TIP

This giant round sandwich can be tricky to slice. Cut it with a serrated knife using a gentle sawing motion. Consider inserting toothpicks through each piece prior to cutting to hold the layers together.

SOURDOUGH BREAD BOWL SANDWICH

CREAMY CHICKEN LASAGNA ROLL-UPS

1. Preheat oven to 375°. Cook lasagna noodles according to package directions.
2. Meanwhile, sprinkle the chicken with herbes de Provence, ¼ tsp. salt and ¼ tsp. pepper. In a large skillet, cook chicken in oil over medium heat for 5-7 minutes or until no longer pink; set aside.
3. In a large bowl, combine ricotta, ¼ cup Parmesan cheese, milk, parsley and the remaining salt and pepper. Add chicken.
4. Drain noodles. Spread 1 cup spaghetti sauce into a greased 13x9-in. baking dish. Spread ⅓ cup chicken mixture over each noodle; carefully roll up. Place seam side down over sauce. Top with remaining sauce and Parmesan cheese.
5. Cover and bake 30 minutes. Uncover; top with the mozzarella cheese. Bake for 15-20 minutes longer or until bubbly and cheese is melted. Top with additional parsley if desired.

1 lasagna roll-up: 378 cal., 17g fat (9g sat. fat), 63mg chol., 789mg sod., 32g carb. (11g sugars, 3g fiber), 24g pro.

TEST KITCHEN TIP

In Europe, Parmigiano-Reggiano and Parmesan are considered the same cheese. But in the United States, Parmesan is a generic ingredient that may not come from Italy's Parmigiano-Reggiano region. Using the authentic Italian cheese (in a lesser amount than the ½ cup called for here) ensures a cheesy richness with less fat and fewer calories.

CREAMY CHICKEN LASAGNA ROLL-UPS

The first time I made these roll-ups, I was at home and needed to make dinner, but I didn't want to go to the store. So I used what I had on hand. You won't believe how creamy, cheesy and delicious they are!
—Cyndy Gerken, Naples, FL

PREP: 35 min. • **BAKE:** 45 min.
MAKES: 10 servings

- 10 lasagna noodles
- ¾ lb. boneless skinless chicken breasts, cubed
- 1½ tsp. herbes de Provence
- ½ tsp. salt, divided
- ½ tsp. pepper, divided
- 1 Tbsp. olive oil
- 2 cups ricotta cheese
- ½ cup grated Parmesan cheese, divided
- ¼ cup 2% milk
- 2 Tbsp. minced fresh parsley
- 4 cups spaghetti sauce
- 8 oz. fresh mozzarella cheese, thinly sliced
  Additional minced fresh parsley, optional

GOURMET BURGERS WITH SUN-DRIED TOMATO

This recipe brings together many of the flavors my family enjoys, complete with a surprise in the center of each burger. You can use almost any cheese—Gorgonzola, feta, smoked Gouda, blue or another family favorite.

—Aaron Shields, Hamburg, NY

PREP: 40 min. • **GRILL:** 10 min.
MAKES: 8 servings

1 jar (7 oz.) oil-packed sun-dried tomatoes
3 medium onions, halved and thinly sliced
3 Tbsp. balsamic vinegar
½ cup finely chopped red onion
2 Tbsp. dried basil
2 tsp. ground cumin
2 tsp. ground chipotle pepper
½ tsp. salt
¼ tsp. pepper
3 lbs. lean ground beef (90% lean)
1 cup crumbled goat cheese
8 hamburger buns, split
Mixed salad greens, optional

1. Drain tomatoes, reserving ⅓ cup oil; set aside. In a large skillet, saute sliced onions in 3 Tbsp. reserved oil until softened. Add the vinegar. Reduce heat to medium-low; cook, stirring occasionally, until deep golden brown, 30-40 minutes.

2. Meanwhile, chop sun-dried tomatoes and transfer to a large bowl. Add the red onion, seasonings and remaining 7 tsp. of the reserved oil. Crumble the beef over mixture and mix lightly but thoroughly. Shape into 16 thin patties. Place 2 Tbsp. goat cheese on the center of 8 patties. Top with remaining patties and press edges firmly to seal.

3. Grill burgers, covered, over medium heat until a thermometer reads 160° and juices run clear, 5-7 minutes on each side.

4. Place buns, cut side down, on the grill until toasted, 1-2 minutes. Serve burgers on buns with the onions and, if desired, mixed greens.

1 burger with 2 Tbsp. onions: 596 cal., 32g fat (10g sat. fat), 123mg chol., 588mg sod., 36g carb. (7g sugars, 5g fiber), 42g pro.

TEST KITCHEN TIP

Use a gentle hand when shaping the beef into patties. Overworking the meat can result in burgers that are less tender.

GOURMET BURGERS WITH SUN-DRIED TOMATO

BAKED SPAGHETTI

BAKED SPAGHETTI

This cheesy crowd-pleasing dish puts a different spin on spaghetti. The leftovers, if there are any, freeze well for a quick future meal.
—*Ruth Koberna, Brecksville, OH*

PREP: 30 min. • BAKE: 30 min.
MAKES: 12 servings

- 1 cup chopped onion
- 1 cup chopped green pepper
- 1 Tbsp. butter
- 1 can (28 oz.) diced tomatoes, undrained
- 1 can (4 oz.) mushroom stems and pieces, drained
- 1 can (2¼ oz.) sliced ripe olives, drained
- 2 tsp. dried oregano
- 1 lb. ground beef, browned and drained, optional
- 12 oz. spaghetti, cooked and drained
- 2 cups shredded cheddar cheese
- 1 can (10¾ oz.) condensed cream of mushroom soup, undiluted
- ¼ cup water
- ¼ cup grated Parmesan cheese

1. In a large skillet, saute onion and green pepper in butter until tender. Add the tomatoes, mushrooms, olives, oregano and, if desired, ground beef. Simmer, uncovered, for 10 minutes.
2. Place half of the spaghetti in a greased 13x9-in. baking dish. Layer with half of the vegetable mixture and 1 cup cheddar cheese. Repeat layers.
3. In a small bowl, combine soup and water until smooth; pour over casserole. Sprinkle with Parmesan cheese. Bake, uncovered, at 350° until heated through, 30-35 minutes.

1 cup: 239 cal., 9g fat (5g sat. fat), 25mg chol., 500mg sod., 30g carb. (5g sugars, 3g fiber), 10g pro.

HOME-STYLE
GLAZED MEAT LOAF

HOME-STYLE GLAZED MEAT LOAF

Grated carrots and cheese add a hint of color to this down-home glazed meat loaf. We look forward to meat loaf sandwiches the next day.
—*Sandra Etelamaki, Ishpeming, MI*

PREP: 15 min. • **BAKE:** 1 hour + standing
MAKES: 12 servings

- 2 large eggs, beaten
- ⅔ cup 2% milk
- 1½ cups shredded cheddar cheese
- 1 cup crushed saltines (about 30 crackers)
- 1 cup finely shredded carrots
- ½ cup finely chopped onion
- ½ tsp. salt
- ¼ tsp. garlic powder
- ¼ tsp. pepper
- 2 lbs. lean ground beef
- ½ cup packed brown sugar
- ½ cup ketchup
- 2 Tbsp. Dijon mustard
  Minced fresh parsley, optional

1. Preheat the oven to 350°. In a large bowl, combine the eggs, milk, cheese, saltines, carrots, onion, salt, garlic powder and pepper. Crumble beef over mixture and mix lightly but thoroughly. Shape into a loaf. Place in a greased 13x9-in. baking dish. Bake, uncovered, for 50 minutes.
2. For glaze, in a small saucepan, bring the brown sugar, ketchup and mustard to a boil. Reduce heat; simmer, uncovered, for 3-5 minutes or until heated through. Spoon over meat loaf.
3. Bake 10-15 minutes longer or until meat is no longer pink and a thermometer reads 160°. Drain; let stand for 10 minutes before slicing. If desired, top the meat loaf with minced fresh parsley.
1 piece: 266 cal., 12g fat (6g sat. fat), 100mg chol., 494mg sod., 18g carb. (12g sugars, 1g fiber), 20g pro.

CAJUN RICE DISH

CAJUN RICE DISH

A variety of colorful vegetables makes this delicious rice casserole a hit with everyone. I team up generous servings with garlic bread and a tossed salad.
—*Rose Kostynuik, Calgary, AB*

PREP: 5 min. • **BAKE:** 1 hour
MAKES: 8 servings

- 5 cups beef broth
- 2 cups uncooked long grain rice
- 1 lb. ground beef
- 1 medium onion, chopped
- 1 cup sliced carrots
- ½ cup sliced celery
- ½ cup frozen corn
- ½ cup frozen peas
- ½ cup chopped sweet red pepper
- 1 tsp. salt
- 1 tsp. Cajun seasoning

1. In a roasting pan, combine the broth and rice. Cover and bake at 350° for 30 minutes.

2. Meanwhile, in a large skillet, cook beef and onion over medium heat until meat is no longer pink; drain. Add to rice. Stir in the vegetables, salt and Cajun seasoning.
3. Cover and bake 30 minutes longer or until rice is tender.
1 serving: 303 cal., 6g fat (3g sat. fat), 28mg chol., 953mg sod., 45g carb. (4g sugars, 2g fiber), 16g pro.

TEST KITCHEN TIP

If you have any leftovers of Cajun Rice Dish, allow them to cool completely, then store in a tightly covered dish or sealed container. For best quality, store leftovers in the refrigerator for up to 3 days or freeze for up to 3 months.

SPINACH & CHICKEN PHYLLO PIE

For a brunch showstopper, try this savory chicken pie with phyllo and spinach. Even our kids love it. It's good with fruit—or a minty fruit salad—on the side.
—*Katie Ferrier, Houston, TX*

PREP: 35 min. • **BAKE:** 35 min.
MAKES: 8 servings

- 2 lbs. ground chicken
- 1 large onion, chopped
- 1 tsp. pepper
- 1 tsp. dried oregano
- ¾ tsp. salt
- ½ tsp. ground nutmeg
- ¼ tsp. crushed red pepper flakes
- 3 pkg. (10 oz. each) frozen chopped spinach, thawed and squeezed dry
- 4 large eggs, lightly beaten
- 3 cups crumbled feta cheese
- 20 sheets phyllo dough (14x9-in. size)
  Cooking spray

1. Preheat oven to 375°. In a large skillet, cook chicken and onion over medium-high heat 7-9 minutes or until the chicken is no longer pink, breaking up the meat into crumbles; drain. Stir in seasonings. Add the spinach; cook and stir until liquid is evaporated. Transfer to a large bowl; cool slightly. Stir in beaten eggs and cheese.
2. Layer 10 sheets of phyllo dough in a greased 13x9-in. baking dish, spritzing each with cooking spray. (Keep the remaining phyllo covered with a damp towel to prevent it from drying out.) Spread the spinach mixture over phyllo. Top with the remaining sheets of phyllo, spritzing each with cooking spray. Cut into 8 rectangles.
3. Bake, uncovered, for 35-40 minutes or until golden brown. If necessary, recut rectangles before serving.
1 piece: 442 cal., 23g fat (8g sat. fat), 191mg chol., 921mg sod., 25g carb. (3g sugars, 6g fiber), 35g pro.

SPINACH & CHICKEN PHYLLO PIE

ROAST LEG OF LAMB WITH ROSEMARY

HAM & PINEAPPLE KABOBS

For a twist on the usual holiday fare, my family turns ham and pineapple into juicy kabobs. The marinade gets its unique zip from hoisin, teriyaki and soy sauces.
—*Chandra Lane Sirois, Kansas City, MO*

PREP: 30 min. + marinating • **BAKE:** 15 min.
MAKES: 12 servings

- ¼ cup hoisin sauce
- ¼ cup unsweetened pineapple juice
- ¼ cup teriyaki sauce
- 1 Tbsp. honey
- 1½ tsp. rice vinegar
- 1½ tsp. reduced-sodium soy sauce

KABOBS
- 2 lbs. fully cooked boneless ham, cut into 1-in. pieces
- 1 large fresh pineapple, peeled, cored and cut into 1-in. cubes (about 4 cups)

1. In a large shallow dish, combine the first 6 ingredients. Add the ham; turn to coat. Refrigerate, covered, overnight.
2. Preheat oven to 350°. Drain the ham, reserving marinade. For the glaze, pour marinade into a small saucepan; bring to a boil. Reduce the heat; simmer, uncovered, 5-7 minutes or until slightly thickened, stirring occasionally. Remove from heat.
3. Meanwhile, on 12 metal or soaked wooden skewers, alternately thread the ham and pineapple; place in a foil-lined 15x10x1-in. baking pan. Brush with glaze. Bake, uncovered, 15-20 minutes or until lightly browned.

1 kabob: 144 cal., 3g fat (1g sat. fat), 39mg chol., 1109mg sod., 15g carb. (12g sugars, 1g fiber), 15g pro.

ROAST LEG OF LAMB WITH ROSEMARY

Rubbing rosemary, garlic and onion into this delectable roast lamb takes it to a whole new level of deliciousness!
—*Suzy Horvath, Milwaukie, OR*

PREP: 10 min. • **BAKE:** 2 hours + standing
MAKES: 8 servings

- ⅓ cup olive oil
- ¼ cup minced fresh rosemary
- ¼ cup finely chopped onion
- 4 garlic cloves, minced
- ½ tsp. salt
- ¼ tsp. pepper
- 1 bone-in leg of lamb (5 to 6 lbs.), trimmed

1. Preheat oven to 325°. Combine the oil, rosemary, onion, garlic, salt and pepper; rub over lamb. Place fat side up on a rack in a shallow roasting pan.
2. Bake, uncovered, 2-2½ hours or until meat reaches desired doneness (for medium-rare, a thermometer should read 135°; medium, 140°; medium-well, 145°), basting occasionally with pan juices. Let stand 15 minutes before slicing.
5 oz. cooked lamb: 316 cal., 18g fat (5g sat. fat), 128mg chol., 206mg sod., 1g carb. (0 sugars, 0 fiber), 36g pro.

LIP-SMACKIN'
BBQ CHICKEN

EASY CHICKEN CASSEROLE

This may be a basic chicken casserole, but I never bring home leftovers when I take it it to a potluck. The classic dish has broad appeal, and I especially like that the crumb topping adds crunch to each serving. Feel free to toss in frozen veggies like broccoli florets, peas or green beans. You could even add shredded cheese, crispy fried onions or pimiento peppers.
—Faye Hintz, Springfield, MO

PREP: 15 min. • **BAKE:** 30 min.
MAKES: 10 servings

- 8 cups cubed cooked chicken
- 2 cans (10½ oz. each) condensed cream of chicken soup, undiluted
- 1 cup sour cream
- 1 cup crushed Ritz crackers (about 25 crackers)
- 2 Tbsp. butter, melted
- 1 tsp. celery seed
  Optional: Minced fresh parsley

1. Preheat oven to 350°. Combine chicken, soup and sour cream; spread mixture into a greased 13x9-in. baking dish. Combine crumbs, butter and celery seed; sprinkle over chicken mixture.
2. Bake casserole, uncovered, until bubbly, for 30-35 minutes. If desired, garnish with minced parsley.

1 cup: 386 cal., 21g fat (8g sat. fat), 116mg chol., 629mg sod., 12g carb. (2g sugars, 1g fiber), 35g pro.

TEST KITCHEN TIP

Store this chicken casserole in an airtight container in the refrigerator for up to 3 days. Pull it out of the fridge while the oven preheats and reheat the casserole at 350° for 20 minutes. This dish contains dairy—so not ideal for freezing.

LIP-SMACKIN' BBQ CHICKEN

I'm proud of this dish—the first recipe I created. It definitely lives up to its name because my kids always say "Prepare to lick your lips!" whenever I serve it.
—Sue Thomas, Moore, SC

PREP: 1¼ hours • **GRILL:** 25 min.
MAKES: 12 servings

- 2 cups ketchup
- 1 cup cider vinegar
- 1 cup water
- ¼ cup packed brown sugar
- ¼ cup reduced-sodium soy sauce
- ¼ cup molasses
- ¼ cup honey
- 2 Tbsp. prepared mustard
- 3 tsp. ground cumin
- ¼ tsp. salt
- ¼ tsp. pepper
- 6 lbs. assorted bone-in chicken pieces

1. In a large saucepan, combine the first 11 ingredients; bring to a boil. Reduce heat; simmer, uncovered, 1-1½ hours or until thickened, stirring occasionally. Remove half of the sauce; reserve for brushing chicken. Keep the remaining sauce warm for serving.
2. Grill chicken, covered, over medium heat 25-35 minutes or until juices run clear, turning occasionally and brushing with the reserved sauce during the last 10 minutes. Serve with remaining sauce.
4 oz. cooked chicken: 402 cal., 17g fat (5g sat. fat), 104mg chol., 871mg sod., 27g carb. (26g sugars, 0 fiber), 34g pro.

EASY
CHICKEN
CASSEROLE

SALADS & SIDES

Add a splash of color to your next potluck, picnic or church supper
with these deliciously different mealtime sidekicks!

P. 161

P. 180

P. 153

TEXAS PECAN RICE

BEET SALAD WITH ORANGE-WALNUT DRESSING

Light and refreshing, this beet salad pairs nicely with heavier dishes. Family and friends will also appreciate the delicious homemade dressing.
—*Marian Platt, Sequim, WA*

PREP: 20 min. • BAKE: 40 min. + cooling
MAKES: 12 servings (about 1 cup dressing)

- 1 lb. fresh beets
- 6 cups torn Bibb or Boston lettuce
- 3 medium navel oranges, peeled and sectioned
- 2 cups torn curly endive
- 2 cups watercress
- ⅔ cup chopped walnuts, toasted

DRESSING

- ½ cup canola oil
- ⅓ cup orange juice
- 3 Tbsp. white wine vinegar
- 1 green onion, finely chopped
- 1 Tbsp. lemon juice
- 1 Tbsp. Dijon mustard
- ½ tsp. salt
- ⅛ tsp. white pepper

1. Place beets in a 13x9-in. baking dish; add 1 in. water. Cover and bake at 400° for 40-45 minutes or until tender. Cool; peel and julienne.
2. In a serving bowl, combine the lettuce, oranges, endive and watercress. Add the beets and walnuts.
3. In a small bowl, whisk the oil, orange juice, vinegar, onion, lemon juice, mustard, salt and pepper. Drizzle over salad; toss gently to coat.
1½ cups: 255 cal., 14g fat (1g sat. fat), 0 chol., 274mg sod., 28g carb. (8g sugars, 18g fiber), 9g pro.

TEXAS PECAN RICE

For a special holiday side dish, I dressed up an old recipe to give it a little more Texas character. Everyone loved the savory flavor and crunchy pecans.
—*Joan Hallford, North Richland Hills, TX*

PREP: 30 min. • BAKE: 1 hour
MAKES: 10 servings

- ½ cup unsalted butter, cubed
- 1½ cups sliced fresh mushrooms
- 3 green onions, sliced
- 2 cups uncooked long grain brown rice
- 1 garlic clove, minced
- 1½ cups chopped pecans, toasted
- ½ tsp. salt
- ½ tsp. dried thyme
- ½ tsp. pepper
- ¼ tsp. ground cumin
- 3 cans (10½ oz. each) condensed beef consomme, undiluted
- 2¼ cups water
- 5 bacon strips, cooked and crumbled
  Toasted pecan halves, optional

1. Preheat oven to 400°. In a Dutch oven, heat butter over medium-high heat. Add mushrooms and green onions; cook and stir until tender, 3-5 minutes. Add rice and garlic; cook and stir 3 minutes. Stir in the pecans, salt, thyme, pepper and cumin. Add consomme and water; bring to a boil.
2. Bake, covered, until liquid is absorbed and rice is tender, 1-1¼ hours. Transfer to a serving bowl. Top with bacon and, if desired, pecan halves.
¾ cup: 372 cal., 24g fat (8g sat. fat), 29mg chol., 783mg sod., 32g carb. (2g sugars, 4g fiber), 10g pro.

7-LAYER GELATIN SALAD

7-LAYER GELATIN SALAD

My mother makes this colorful gelatin salad to accompany our Christmas dinner each year. Choose different flavors to create special color combinations for particular holidays or gatherings.
—*Jan Hemness, Stockton, MO*

PREP: 30 min. + chilling
MAKES: 20 servings

- 4½ cups boiling water, divided
- 7 pkg. (3 oz. each) assorted flavored gelatin
- 4½ cups cold water, divided
- 1 can (12 oz.) evaporated milk, divided
- 1 carton (8 oz.) frozen whipped topping, thawed
  Optional: Sliced strawberries and kiwifruit

1. In a small bowl, add ¾ cup boiling water to 1 gelatin package; stir for 2 minutes to completely dissolve. Stir in ¾ cup cold water. Pour into a 3-qt. trifle or glass bowl. Refrigerate until set but not firm, about 40 minutes.
2. In a clean bowl, dissolve another gelatin package into ½ cup boiling water. Stir in ½ cup cold water and ½ cup milk. Spoon over the first layer. Refrigerate until set but not firm.
3. Repeat 5 times, alternating plain and creamy gelatin layers. Refrigerate each layer until set but not firm before adding the next layer. Refrigerate, covered, overnight. Serve salad with whipped topping and, if desired, fruit.
Note: Recipe may also be prepared in a 13x9-in. dish coated with cooking spray; follow recipe as directed. Cut into squares before serving.
1 serving: 163 cal., 3g fat (3g sat. fat), 6mg chol., 85mg sod., 30g carb. (30g sugars, 0 fiber), 4g pro.

BOHEMIAN COLLARDS

BOHEMIAN COLLARDS

I add unconventional ingredients to make these collards unique and exquisite on both the palate and on the plate.
—*Ally Phillips, Murrells Inlet, SC*

PREP: 20 min. • **COOK:** 35 min.
MAKES: 8 servings

- 1 large bunch collard greens (about 2 lbs.)
- 6 bacon strips, chopped
- 1 Tbsp. olive oil
- ½ cup chicken broth
- 1½ cups fresh or frozen corn (about 7½ oz.)
- 1 cup chopped sweet red pepper
- ½ tsp. salt
- ¼ tsp. crushed red pepper flakes
- ¼ tsp. pepper

1. Trim thick stems from collard greens; coarsely chop leaves. In a Dutch oven, cook bacon over medium heat until crisp, stirring occasionally. Remove bacon with a slotted spoon; drain on paper towels. Cook and stir collard greens in bacon drippings and oil just until coated. Add broth; bring to a boil. Reduce heat; simmer, covered, until greens are very tender, 25-30 minutes.
2. Add corn, red pepper, salt, pepper flakes and pepper. Cook and stir until heated through. Sprinkle with bacon.
½ cup: 168 cal., 11g fat (3g sat. fat), 14mg chol., 369mg sod., 13g carb. (2g sugars, 5g fiber), 7g pro. **Diabetic exchanges:** 2 fat, 1 starch.

TEST KITCHEN TIP

Don't throw out the pot liquor. That's the liquid leftover from cooking the greens, and it's rich with flavor and nutrients. Dunking a big slice of warm cornbread in it is a great way to soak up all that tasty goodness.

CHEDDAR &
SPINACH
TWICE-BAKED
POTATOES

HOVER YOUR CAMERA HERE
How to Make
a Super Cozy
Baked Potato
Dinner Board

GARLIC KNOTS

Here's a handy bread that can be made in no time flat. Refrigerated biscuits make preparation simple. The classic Italian flavors complement a variety of meals.
—Jane Paschke, University Park, FL

TAKES: 30 min. • **MAKES:** 2½ dozen

- 1 tube (12 oz.) refrigerated buttermilk biscuits
- ¼ cup canola oil
- 3 Tbsp. grated Parmesan cheese
- 1 tsp. garlic powder
- 1 tsp. dried oregano
- 1 tsp. dried parsley flakes

1. Preheat oven to 400°. Cut each biscuit into thirds. Roll each piece into a 4-in. rope and tie into a knot; tuck ends under. Place 2 in. apart on a greased baking sheet. Bake until golden brown, 8-10 minutes.
2. In a large bowl, combine the remaining ingredients; add the warm knots and gently toss to coat.
1 roll: 46 cal., 2g fat (0 sat. fat), 0 chol., 105mg sod., 6g carb. (0 sugars, 0 fiber), 1g pro.

READER RAVES

"I've taken this recipe to family and church gatherings. It's always been a hit. No matter how much I make, I never bring any leftovers home!"

—KIMBER SKIMBER, TOH.COM

CHEDDAR & SPINACH TWICE-BAKED POTATOES

My husband is a rancher who loves a hearty potato dish, so consider these spuds cowboy approved! My hungry crew never leaves any leftovers.
—Jody Augustyn, Loup City, NE

PREP: 1¼ hours • **BAKE:** 20 min.
MAKES: 12 servings

- 6 large baking potatoes (about 12 oz. each)
- ½ cup 2% milk
- 6 Tbsp. butter, softened
- 1 pkg. (10 oz.) frozen chopped spinach, thawed and squeezed dry
- ¾ cup shredded Monterey Jack cheese
- ¾ cup shredded cheddar cheese, divided
- ¼ cup finely chopped red onion
- 1 tsp. salt
- ¼ tsp. pepper

1. Preheat oven to 375°. Scrub potatoes; pierce each several times with a fork. Place in a foil-lined 15x10x1-in. baking pan; bake 60-70 minutes or until tender.
2. When cool enough to handle, cut each potato lengthwise in half. Scoop out pulp, leaving ¼-in.-thick shells. In a large bowl, mash pulp with milk and butter, adding spinach, Monterey Jack cheese, ¼ cup cheddar cheese, onion, salt and pepper.
3. Spoon into potato shells; return to baking pan. Sprinkle with remaining cheddar cheese. Bake 20-25 minutes or until heated through and cheese is melted.
1 stuffed potato half: 261 cal., 11g fat (7g sat. fat), 30mg chol., 363mg sod., 34g carb. (2g sugars, 5g fiber), 9g pro.

GARLIC
KNOTS

GARLIC-ROSEMARY BRUSSELS SPROUTS

This is my go-to Thanksgiving side dish. It is healthy and easy, and it doesn't take much time or effort to make. I usually use rosemary for my turkey, so this lets me use some of the leftover herbs.
—*Elisabeth Larsen, Pleasant Grove, UT*

PREP: 15 min. • **BAKE:** 25 min.
MAKES: 8 servings

- ¼ cup olive oil
- 4 garlic cloves, minced
- 1 tsp. salt
- ½ tsp. pepper
- 2 lbs. Brussels sprouts (about 8 cups), trimmed and halved
- 1 cup panko bread crumbs
- 1 to 2 Tbsp. minced fresh rosemary

1. Preheat the oven to 425°. Place the first 4 ingredients in a small microwave-safe bowl; microwave on high 30 seconds.
2. Place Brussels sprouts in a 15x10x1-in. pan; toss with 3 Tbsp. oil mixture. Roast 10 minutes.
3. Toss bread crumbs with rosemary and the remaining oil mixture; sprinkle over sprouts. Bake until crumbs are browned and sprouts are tender, 12-15 minutes. Serve immediately.
¾ cup: 134 cal., 7g fat (1g sat. fat), 0 chol., 342mg sod., 15g carb. (3g sugars, 4g fiber), 5g pro. **Diabetic exchanges:** 1½ fat, 1 vegetable, ½ starch.

TEST KITCHEN TIP
When roasting vegetables, give them breathing room. If the pan is too crowded, the vegetables will steam and not get nicely browned and crispy.

**THAI NOODLE
WATERMELON
SALAD**

SWEET ONION SPOON BREAD

This unique recipe has been a family favorite for years. The layers of tangy cheese, sour cream and sweet onions in the moist cornbread taste amazing together. Add chopped green chiles for extra zip.
—Heather Thomas, Fredericksburg, VA

PREP: 15 min. • **BAKE:** 25 min.
MAKES: 9 servings

- 1⅓ cups chopped sweet onions
- 1 Tbsp. butter
- 1 can (8¼ oz.) cream-style corn
- 1 pkg. (8½ oz.) cornbread/muffin mix
- 2 large egg whites, lightly beaten
- 2 Tbsp. fat-free milk
- ½ cup reduced-fat sour cream
- ⅓ cup shredded sharp cheddar cheese

1. In a small nonstick skillet, saute onions in butter until tender; set aside.
2. Meanwhile, in a large bowl, combine the corn, muffin mix, egg whites and milk. Pour into a 9-in. square baking dish coated with cooking spray. Combine sour cream and onions; spread over batter. Sprinkle with cheese.
3. Bake cornbread, uncovered, at 350° until a toothpick inserted in the center comes out clean, 25-30 minutes.
1 piece: 191 cal., 6g fat (3g sat. fat), 18mg chol., 361mg sod., 29g carb. (10g sugars, 1g fiber), 6g pro. **Diabetic exchanges:** 2 starch, ½ fat.

THAI NOODLE WATERMELON SALAD

Our county is famous for its fabulous Green River melons. While you won't find this unique salad at the county fair, it is definitely our family's favorite way to eat watermelon all summer long!
—Carmell Childs, Orangeville, UT

PREP: 25 min. • **COOK:** 25 min.
MAKES: 10 servings

- 4½ cups cubed watermelon, divided
- ½ cup sweet chili sauce
- 3 Tbsp. fish sauce or soy sauce
- 2 Tbsp. lime juice
- ½ tsp. minced fresh gingerroot
- 7 oz. uncooked stir-fry rice noodles
- 1½ cups julienned carrots
- 1 small red onion, halved and thinly sliced
- ½ cup fresh cilantro leaves, chopped
- 3 Tbsp. minced fresh mint
- 1¼ cups salted peanuts, chopped
  Lime wedges

1. Place 2 cups watermelon in a blender; cover and puree until smooth. Press through a fine-mesh strainer into a bowl; discard pulp. Pour 1 cup juice into a small saucepan (save any remaining juice for another use). Add chili sauce, fish sauce, lime juice and ginger to saucepan. Bring to a boil; cook until liquid is slightly thickened, 20-25 minutes. Remove from the heat. Refrigerate until cooled.
2. Meanwhile, prepare noodles according to the package directions; rinse with cold water and drain well. Place the noodles in a large bowl. Add the carrots, red onion, cilantro, mint and remaining 2½ cups watermelon. Drizzle salad with dressing; toss to coat. Serve with the peanuts and lime wedges.
¾ cup: 240 cal., 10g fat (2g sat. fat), 0 chol., 721mg sod., 34g carb. (14g sugars, 3g fiber), 7g pro.

LATTICE CORN PIE

With tender diced potatoes and a fresh, sweet corn flavor, this delicious pie is full of old-fashioned goodness. Once you've tasted it, you'll never want to serve corn any other way!
—*Kathy Spang, Manheim, PA*

PREP: 25 min. • **BAKE:** 35 min.
MAKES: 8 servings

- 1 cup diced peeled potatoes
- ⅓ cup 2% milk
- 2 large eggs, room temperature
- 2 cups fresh or frozen corn, thawed
- 1 tsp. sugar
- ½ tsp. salt
- 2 sheets refrigerated pie crust

1. Preheat oven to 375°. Place potatoes in a small saucepan and cover with water. Bring to a boil. Reduce heat; cover and cook until tender, 6-8 minutes. Drain and set aside.
2. In a blender, combine the milk, eggs, corn, sugar and salt; cover and process until blended.
3. Unroll 1 sheet crust into a 9-in. pie plate. Trim crust to ½ in. beyond rim of plate; flute edge. Spoon potatoes into crust; top with corn mixture (crust will be full). Roll out remaining crust; make a lattice top with crust. Seal and flute edge.
4. Bake until crust is golden brown and filling is bubbly, 35-40 minutes.
1 piece: 308 cal., 16g fat (7g sat. fat), 57mg chol., 373mg sod., 37g carb. (5g sugars, 1g fiber), 5g pro.

MOM'S APPLE CORNBREAD STUFFING

My speedy recipe is the be-all and end-all stuffing in our family. Not surprisingly, we never have leftovers.
—*Marie Forte, Raritan, NJ*

PREP: 15 min. • **BAKE:** 35 min.
MAKES: 16 servings

- 6 large Granny Smith apples, peeled and chopped
- 1 pkg. (14 oz.) crushed cornbread stuffing
- ½ cup butter, melted
- 1 can (14½ oz.) chicken broth

1. Preheat oven to 350°. Combine apples, stuffing and melted butter. Add the broth; mix well.
2. Transfer to a greased 13x9-in. baking dish. Bake 35-40 minutes or until golden brown.
¾ cup: 183 cal., 7g fat (4g sat. fat), 16mg chol., 434mg sod., 28g carb. (8g sugars, 2g fiber), 3g pro. **Diabetic exchanges:** 2 starch, 1½ fat.

TEST KITCHEN TIP

If you really want that stuffing to shine, use homemade broth. In the end, the richer the broth, the better the stuffing—so don't be afraid to go all out.

LATTICE CORN PIE

GLORIFIED HASH BROWNS

GLORIFIED HASH BROWNS

You'll be surprised at how quick and easy it is to put together this dressed-up potato casserole. When a friend made it for a church supper, I had to have the recipe. It's ideal for potlucks and family reunions.
—*Betty Kay Sitzman, Wray, CO*

PREP: 10 min. • **BAKE:** 40 min.
MAKES: 10 servings

- 2 cans (10¾ oz. each) condensed cream of celery soup, undiluted
- 2 cartons (8 oz. each) spreadable chive and onion cream cheese
- 1 pkg. (2 lbs.) frozen cubed hash brown potatoes
- 1 cup shredded cheddar cheese

1. In a large microwave-safe bowl, combine the soup and cream cheese. Cover and cook on high for 3-4 minutes or until cream cheese is melted, stirring occasionally. Add the potatoes and stir until coated.

2. Spoon mixture into a greased 13x9-in. baking dish. Bake, uncovered, at 350° for 35-40 minutes or until the potatoes are tender. Sprinkle with cheddar cheese. Bake 3-5 minutes longer or until the cheese is melted.

Freeze option: Sprinkle cheddar cheese over unbaked casserole. Cover and freeze. To use, partially thaw in refrigerator overnight. Remove from refrigerator 30 minutes before baking. Preheat oven to 350°. Bake casserole as directed, increasing time as necessary to heat through and for a thermometer inserted in center to read 165°.

1 serving: 215 cal., 12g fat (8g sat. fat), 35mg chol., 400mg sod., 20g carb. (2g sugars, 1g fiber), 6g pro.

GRILLED ELOTE FLATBREAD

Here's a fun twist on a classic Mexican dish! Keep your kitchen cooled down during the summer by grilling this fresh flatbread outdoors.
—Amanda Phillips, Portland, OR

PREP: 20 min. • **GRILL:** 15 min.
MAKES: 12 servings

- 2 medium ears sweet corn, husked
- 3 Tbsp. olive oil, divided
- 1 lb. fresh or frozen pizza dough, thawed
- ½ cup mayonnaise
- ⅓ cup crumbled Cotija cheese, divided
- ⅓ cup chopped fresh cilantro, divided
- 1 Tbsp. lime juice
- ½ tsp. chili powder
- ⅛ tsp. pepper

1. Brush corn with 1 Tbsp. oil. Grill corn, covered, over medium heat until lightly browned and tender, 10-12 minutes, turning occasionally. Cool slightly. Cut corn from cobs; transfer to a large bowl.
2. On a lightly floured surface, roll or press dough into a 15x10-in. oval (about ¼ in. thick); place on a greased sheet of foil. Brush top with 1 Tbsp. oil.
3. Carefully invert crust onto grill rack, removing foil. Brush top with remaining 1 Tbsp. oil. Grill, covered, over medium heat until the bottom is golden brown, 2-3 minutes on each side. Remove from grill; cool slightly.
4. Add the mayonnaise, 3 Tbsp. cheese, 3 Tbsp. cilantro, lime juice, chili powder and pepper to corn; stir to combine. Spread over warm crust. Sprinkle with remaining cheese and cilantro.
1 piece: 211 cal., 13g fat (2g sat. fat), 4mg chol., 195mg sod., 20g carb. (2g sugars, 1g fiber), 5g pro.

GRILLED ELOTE FLATBREAD

RIB SHACK COPYCAT MASHED POTATOES

(PICTURED ON PAGE 142)

Idaho is known for being the potato state—even our license plates say Famous Potatoes! This is my version of the scrumptious smashers that are served at a local barbecue joint. Everyone who tries them there begs for the recipe, which the restaurant won't give out, so I made my own copycat version. These can be made ahead and kept warm in the slow cooker.
—Trisha Kruse, Eagle, ID

TAKES: 30 min. • **MAKES:** 12 servings

- 2½ lbs. potatoes, peeled and cubed
- 1 cup 2% milk, warmed
- ½ cup spreadable garlic and herb cream cheese
- 3 Tbsp. butter, softened
- 1 lb. bacon strips, cooked and crumbled
- 1 cup shredded cheddar cheese
- ½ cup shredded Parmesan cheese
- 3 green onions, chopped
- 2 Tbsp. minced fresh parsley or 2 tsp. dried parsley flakes
- ¼ tsp. salt
- ¼ tsp. pepper

Place potatoes in a Dutch oven; add water to cover. Bring to a boil. Reduce the heat; cook, uncovered, 15-20 minutes or until tender. Drain and return to pan; gently mash potatoes while gradually adding milk, cream cheese spread and butter to reach desired consistency. Stir in the remaining ingredients.

⅔ cup: 238 cal., 15g fat (8g sat. fat), 41mg chol., 477mg sod., 15g carb. (2g sugars, 1g fiber), 10g pro.

GARLIC-SESAME GREEN BEANS

Sauteed bits of garlic and shallot, plus a sprinkling of toasted sesame seeds, turn ordinary beans into something special. Keep the recipe in mind for your garden crop in summer, too.
—Deirdre Cox, Kansas City, MO

PREP: 25 min. • **COOK:** 10 min.
MAKES: 12 servings

- 3 lbs. fresh green beans, trimmed
- 1 Tbsp. sesame oil
- 1 Tbsp. canola oil
- 1 shallot, finely chopped
- 6 garlic cloves, minced
- 1½ tsp. salt
- ½ tsp. pepper
- 2 Tbsp. sesame seeds, toasted

1. In a Dutch oven, bring 10 cups water to a boil. Add green beans; cook, uncovered, 6-8 minutes or until tender.

2. Meanwhile, in a small skillet, heat oils over medium heat. Add shallot, garlic, salt and pepper; cook and stir 2-3 minutes or until tender.

3. Drain green beans and return to Dutch oven. Add shallot mixture; toss to coat. Sprinkle with sesame seeds.

1 serving: 67 cal., 3g fat (0 sat. fat), 0 chol., 305mg sod., 9g carb. (3g sugars, 4g fiber), 3g pro. **Diabetic exchanges:** 2 vegetable, ½ fat.

FOUR-CHEESE MACARONI

FOUR-CHEESE MACARONI

I adapted this recipe from one a friend gave to me. It has a distinctive blue cheese taste and is a filling side dish.
—*Darlene Marturano, West Suffield, CT*

TAKES: 20 min. • **MAKES:** 8 servings

- 1 pkg. (16 oz.) elbow macaroni
- ¼ cup butter, cubed
- ¼ cup all-purpose flour
- ½ tsp. salt
- ⅛ tsp. pepper
- 3 cups 2% milk
- 2 cups shredded cheddar cheese
- 1½ cups shredded Swiss cheese
- ½ cup crumbled blue cheese
- ½ cup grated Parmesan cheese

1. Cook macaroni according to package directions. Meanwhile, in a Dutch oven, melt butter over medium heat. Stir in flour, salt and pepper until smooth; gradually whisk in milk. Bring to a boil, stirring constantly; cook and stir until thickened, about 2 minutes.
2. Reduce heat to low; stir in cheeses until melted. Drain macaroni; add to cheese sauce and stir until coated.
1 cup: 508 cal., 23g fat (13g sat. fat), 65mg chol., 603mg sod., 51g carb. (6g sugars, 2g fiber), 26g pro.

TEST KITCHEN TIP

Panko bread crumbs are an easy and delicious topping for mac and cheese. To make them, place bread crumbs evenly on a pan and bake at a low temperature for 3-5 minutes. Keep an eye on them and shuffle them around the pan for even cooking.

BLACK-EYED PEA TOMATO SALAD

MA
BLACK-EYED PEA TOMATO SALAD

Spending time in the kitchen with my late aunt was so much fun because she was an amazing cook and teacher. This black-eyed pea salad was one of her specialties. It is easy to make and is a nice alternative to pasta or potato salad. Add cooked cubed chicken breast to make it a meal on its own.
—*Patricia Ness, La Mesa, CA*

PREP: 20 min. + chilling
MAKES: 12 servings

- 4 cans (15½ oz. each) black-eyed peas, rinsed and drained
- 3 large tomatoes, chopped
- 1 large sweet red pepper, chopped
- 1 cup diced red onion
- 4 bacon strips, cooked and crumbled
- 1 jalapeno pepper, seeded and diced
- ½ cup canola oil
- ¼ cup sugar
- ¼ cup rice vinegar
- 2 Tbsp. minced fresh parsley
- 1½ tsp. salt
- ½ tsp. pepper
- ⅛ tsp. garlic powder

1. Combine the first 6 ingredients. In another bowl, whisk together remaining ingredients. Add to bean mixture; toss to coat. Refrigerate, covered, at least 6 hours or overnight.
2. Stir just before serving.
¾ cup: 242 cal., 11g fat (1g sat. fat), 3mg chol., 602mg sod., 29g carb. (9g sugars, 5g fiber), 9g pro.

EASY PEASY
BISCUITS

 GREEK PASTA SALAD

Chock-full of tomato, red and green pepper, and tricolor spirals, this full-flavored Greek pasta salad is as attractive as it is delicious. I add feta cheese and black olives to the medley before coating it with a speedy homemade dressing.
—*Dawna Waggoner, Minong, WI*

PREP: 15 min. + chilling
MAKES: 10 servings

　3　cups uncooked tricolor spiral pasta
　1　medium tomato, cut into wedges
　1　small sweet red pepper, julienned
　1　small green pepper, julienned
　4　oz. crumbled feta cheese
　½　cup sliced ripe olives
DRESSING
　⅔　cup olive oil
　¼　cup minced fresh basil
　3　Tbsp. white vinegar
　2　Tbsp. chopped green onions
　2　Tbsp. grated Parmesan cheese
　½　tsp. salt
　¼　tsp. pepper
　¼　tsp. dried oregano

1. Cook the pasta according to package directions. Rinse in cold water and drain. Place in a large serving bowl; add the tomato, peppers, feta cheese and olives.
2. In a blender, combine the dressing ingredients; cover and process until smooth. Pour over salad; toss to coat. Cover and refrigerate for 2 hours or overnight. Toss before serving.
¾ cup: 268 cal., 18g fat (4g sat. fat), 7mg chol., 298mg sod., 21g carb. (2g sugars, 2g fiber), 6g pro.

EASY PEASY BISCUITS

When I make these biscuits, I have enough left over to freeze for a future meal. They are divine with homemade preserves.
—*Amanda West, Shelbyville, TN*

PREP: 25 min. • **BAKE:** 10 min.
MAKES: 2 dozen

　4　cups all-purpose flour
　4　Tbsp. baking powder
　1　Tbsp. sugar
　1　Tbsp. ground flaxseed
　1　tsp. sea salt
　1　cup solid coconut oil
　1½　cups 2% milk

1. Preheat oven to 450°. In a large bowl, whisk the flour, baking powder, sugar, flaxseed and salt. Add coconut oil and cut in with a pastry blender until the mixture resembles coarse crumbs. Add milk; stir just until moistened.

2. Turn onto a lightly floured surface; knead gently 8-10 times. Pat or roll dough into a rectangle ½ in. thick; fold dough into thirds (as you would a letter). Pat or roll dough again into a rectangle ½ in. thick; cut with a pizza cutter or knife into 24 biscuits, each about 2½ in. square. Place 1½ in. apart on ungreased baking sheets. Bake until light brown, 8-10 minutes. Serve biscuits warm.
Freeze option: Freeze cut biscuit dough on waxed paper-lined baking sheets until firm. Transfer to airtight containers; return to freezer. To use, bake the biscuits in a preheated 350° oven until light brown, 15-20 minutes.
1 biscuit: 167 cal., 10g fat (8g sat. fat), 1mg chol., 328mg sod., 17g carb. (1g sugars, 1g fiber), 3g pro.

GREEK PASTA SALAD

FLAMBOYANT FLAMENCO SUMMER SALAD

I came up with this salad simply by choosing the best-looking vegetables at a local farmers market—the colors are so beautiful! Turn it into a full vegetarian meal by adding roasted garbanzo beans or cooked white beans as protein.
—*Crystal Schlueter, Northglenn, CO*

TAKES: 25 min. • **MAKES:** 8 servings

- 3 medium rainbow carrots
- 4 medium blood oranges, peeled and segmented
- ½ small red onion, thinly sliced
- ½ medium fresh beet, thinly sliced
- ½ medium watermelon radish, thinly sliced
- 2 radishes, thinly sliced
- 2 Tbsp. chopped pistachios, toasted
- 2 Tbsp. chopped oil-packed sun-dried tomatoes
- 1 Tbsp. capers, drained
- ¼ tsp. salt
- ¼ tsp. pepper
- ¼ cup white balsamic vinaigrette
- 4 cups torn leaf lettuce
- ¼ cup shaved Manchego or Parmesan cheese

Using a vegetable peeler, shave carrots lengthwise into very thin slices; place in a large bowl. Add oranges, red onion, beet, radishes, pistachios, tomatoes, capers, salt and pepper. Drizzle with vinaigrette; lightly toss to coat. Arrange lettuce on a platter; top with the vegetable mixture. Top with shaved cheese.

1 cup: 103 cal., 6g fat (1g sat. fat), 4mg chol., 203mg sod., 12g carb. (8g sugars, 3g fiber), 2g pro.

TEST KITCHEN TIP

This is a versatile salad, so go ahead and substitute your favorite veggies or whatever good stuff your garden is currently producing.

FLAMBOYANT FLAMENCO SUMMER SALAD

STOLLEN BUTTER ROLLS

into the dough (knead in more flour if necessary). Divide and shape into 24 balls; flatten slightly. Place 1 tsp. cold butter in center of each circle. Fold circles in half over butter; press edges to seal. Place in a greased 15x10x1-in. baking pan. Cover and let rise in a warm place until doubled, about 45 minutes.

4. Preheat oven to 375°. Bake until golden brown, 15-20 minutes. Cool in the pan for 5 minutes; serve warm.

Freeze option: Freeze cooled rolls in airtight containers. To use, microwave each roll on high for 30-45 seconds or until warmed.

1 roll: 198 cal., 9g fat (5g sat. fat), 37mg chol., 178mg sod., 28g carb. (9g sugars, 1g fiber), 4g pro.

KALE CAESAR SALAD

I love Caesar salads, so I created this blend of kale and romaine lettuces with a creamy Caesar dressing. It's perfect paired with chicken or steak for a light weeknight meal.
—*Rashanda Cobbins, Milwaukee, WI*

TAKES: 15 min. • **MAKES:** 8 servings

- 4 cups chopped fresh kale
- 4 cups torn romaine
- 1 cup Caesar salad croutons
- ½ cup shredded Parmesan cheese
- ½ cup mayonnaise
- 2 Tbsp. lemon juice
- 1 Tbsp. Worcestershire sauce
- 2 tsp. Dijon mustard
- 2 tsp. anchovy paste
- 1 garlic clove, minced
- ¼ tsp. salt
- ¼ tsp. pepper

In a large salad bowl, toss kale, romaine, croutons and cheese. For the dressing, combine remaining ingredients in a small bowl; pour over the salad and toss to coat. Serve immediately.

1 cup: 148 cal., 13g fat (3g sat. fat), 10mg chol., 417mg sod., 6g carb. (1g sugars, 1g fiber), 3g pro. **Diabetic exchanges:** 2½ fat, 1 vegetable.

MA

STOLLEN BUTTER ROLLS

My family members enjoy my stollen so much and say it's just too good to be served only on holidays. I created this buttery, less-sweet dinner roll version.
—*Mindy White, Nashville, TN*

PREP: 45 min. + rising • **BAKE:** 15 min.
MAKES: 2 dozen

- 1 pkg. (¼ oz.) active dry yeast
- ¼ cup warm water (110° to 115°)
- 1 cup warm 2% milk
- 2 large eggs, room temperature
- ½ cup butter, softened
- 1 Tbsp. sugar
- 1 tsp. salt
- 4¼ to 4¾ cups all-purpose flour
- ¾ cup chopped mixed candied fruit
- ¾ cup dried currants
- ½ cup cold butter, cut into 24 pieces (1 tsp. each)

1. In a small bowl, dissolve the yeast in warm water. In a large bowl, combine the warm milk, eggs, butter, sugar, salt, yeast mixture and 3 cups flour; beat on medium speed until smooth. Stir in enough remaining flour to form a soft dough (dough will be sticky).

2. Turn dough onto a floured surface; knead 6-8 minutes or until smooth and elastic. Place in a greased bowl, turning once to grease the top. Cover and let rise in a warm place until doubled, 1 hour.

3. Punch dough down; turn onto a floured surface. Knead candied fruit and currants

MARYLAND CORN POPS

Fresh-picked sweet corn is a big thing in Maryland. Here's my homespun version of Mexican street corn that brings in local bay flavors.
—Kristie Schley, Severna Park, MD

PREP: 25 min. • **GRILL:** 10 min.
MAKES: 2 dozen

- 8 medium ears sweet corn, husked
- 2 Tbsp. canola oil
- 1½ cups mayonnaise
- 1½ tsp. garlic powder
- ¼ tsp. freshly ground pepper
- 24 corncob holders
- 2 cups crumbled feta cheese
- 2 Tbsp. seafood seasoning
- ¼ cup minced fresh cilantro
  Lime wedges, optional

1. Brush all sides of corn with oil. Grill, covered, over medium heat until tender and lightly browned, 10-12 minutes, turning occasionally. Remove corn from the grill; cool slightly.
2. Meanwhile, in a small bowl, mix the mayonnaise, garlic powder and pepper. Cut each ear of corn into thirds. Insert 1 corncob holder into each piece. Spread corn with mayonnaise mixture; sprinkle with cheese, seafood seasoning and cilantro. If desired, serve corn pops with lime wedges.

1 corn pop: 164 cal., 14g fat (3g sat. fat), 10mg chol., 336mg sod., 7g carb. (2g sugars, 1g fiber), 3g pro.

CREAMY PINEAPPLE FLUFF SALAD

Guests will love this classic fluff salad, chock-full of pineapple, marshmallows and cherry bits.
—Janice Hensley, Owingsville, KY

TAKES: 25 min. • **MAKES:** 16 servings

- 1 pkg. (8 oz.) cream cheese, softened
- 1 can (14 oz.) sweetened condensed milk
- ¼ cup lemon juice
- 2 cans (20 oz.) pineapple tidbits, drained
- 1½ cups multicolored miniature marshmallows, divided
- 1 carton (8 oz.) frozen whipped topping, thawed
- ½ cup chopped nuts
- ⅓ cup maraschino cherries, chopped

In a large bowl, beat the cream cheese, milk and lemon juice until smooth. Add pineapple and 1 cup marshmallows; fold in whipped topping. Sprinkle with the nuts, cherries and remaining marshmallows. Refrigerate leftovers.

½ cup: 161 cal., 10g fat (6g sat. fat), 16mg chol., 50mg sod., 17g carb. (12g sugars, 1g fiber), 2g pro.

MARYLAND CORN POPS

BEST EVER BEANS & SAUSAGE

My wife cooked up this bean dish, which is popular with our friends and family. When she asks what she should bring, the reply is always: your beans and sausage—and a few copies of the recipe!
—*Robert Saulnier, Clarksburg, MA*

PREP: 15 min. • **BAKE:** 1 hour 20 min.
MAKES: 16 servings

- 1½ lbs. bulk spicy pork sausage
- 1 medium green pepper, chopped
- 1 medium onion, chopped
- 1 can (31 oz.) pork and beans
- 1 can (16 oz.) kidney beans, rinsed and drained
- 1 can (15½ oz.) great northern beans, rinsed and drained
- 1 can (15½ oz.) black-eyed peas, rinsed and drained
- 1 can (15 oz.) pinto beans, rinsed and drained
- 1 can (15 oz.) chickpeas, rinsed and drained
- 1½ cups ketchup
- ¾ cup packed brown sugar
- 2 tsp. ground mustard

1. In a large skillet, cook and crumble the sausage over medium heat until no longer pink; drain. Add the green pepper and onion; saute until tender. Drain. Add the remaining ingredients.
2. Pour into a greased 13x9-in. baking dish. Cover and bake at 325° for 1 hour. Uncover; bake 20-30 minutes longer or until bubbly.
¾ cup: 316 cal., 9g fat (3g sat. fat), 15mg chol., 857mg sod., 48g carb. (19g sugars, 9g fiber), 13g pro.

BEST EVER BEANS & SAUSAGE

MA

PATRIOTIC GELATIN SALAD

This lovely salad makes quite a bang at patriotic celebrations. It takes time to prepare since each layer must be set before the next is added, but folks love its cool, fruity and creamy appeal.
—Sue Gronholz, Beaver Dam, WI

PATRIOTIC
GELATIN
SALAD

PREP: 20 min. + chilling
MAKES: 16 servings

- 2 pkg. (3 oz. each) berry blue gelatin
- 2 pkg. (3 oz. each) strawberry gelatin
- 4 cups boiling water, divided
- 2½ cups cold water, divided
- 2 envelopes unflavored gelatin
- 2 cups 2% milk
- 1 cup sugar
- 2 cups (16 oz.) sour cream
- 2 tsp. vanilla extract

1. In 4 separate bowls, dissolve each package of gelatin in 1 cup boiling water. Add ½ cup cold water to each and stir. Pour 1 bowl of the blue gelatin into a 10-in. fluted tube pan coated with cooking spray; chill until almost set, about 30 minutes.
2. Set the other 3 bowls of gelatin aside at room temperature. Soften the unflavored gelatin in remaining cold water; let stand 5 minutes.
3. Heat milk in a saucepan over medium heat just below boiling. Stir in softened gelatin and sugar until sugar is dissolved. Remove from heat; stir in sour cream and vanilla until smooth. When blue gelatin in pan is almost set, carefully spoon 1½ cups sour cream mixture over it. Chill until it is almost set, about 30 minutes.
4. Carefully spoon 1 bowl of strawberry gelatin over cream layer. Chill until almost set. Carefully spoon 1½ cups cream mixture over the strawberry layer. Chill until almost set. Repeat steps, adding layers of blue gelatin, cream mixture and strawberry gelatin, chilling in between each. Chill several hours or overnight.
1 piece: 206 cal., 7g fat (4g sat. fat), 23mg chol., 75mg sod., 34g carb. (33g sugars, 0 fiber), 5g pro.

BARBECUED BEAN SALAD

This tangy, hearty salad is ideal for spring and summer picnics. Mild spices blend nicely with the beans and fresh garden ingredients. Be prepared to bring home an empty bowl.
—*Linda Ault, Newberry, IN*

PREP: 40 min. + standing
COOK: 1½ hours + chilling
MAKES: 20 servings

- 1 pkg. (16 oz.) dried pinto beans, rinsed
- 1 medium onion, chopped
- 1 medium green pepper, diced
- 1 medium sweet red pepper, diced
- 1 can (15¼ oz.) whole kernel corn, drained

DRESSING

- ¼ cup ketchup
- ¼ cup cider vinegar
- ¼ cup olive oil
- 3 Tbsp. brown sugar
- 1 Tbsp. Worcestershire sauce
- 1 Tbsp. chili powder
- 5 tsp. Dijon mustard
- 1 tsp. ground cumin
- 1 tsp. salt
- ¼ tsp. pepper

1. In a large kettle, cover beans with water; bring to a boil. Boil for 2 minutes. Remove from the heat and let stand 1 hour. Drain and rinse beans; return to the kettle. Cover with water again and bring to a boil. Reduce the heat; cover and simmer for 1½ hours or until beans are tender.

2. Drain and rinse beans; place in a large bowl and cool to room temperature. Add the onion, peppers and corn; toss.

3. In a saucepan, combine all dressing ingredients; simmer for 10 minutes. Pour over the vegetables and mix well. Cover and chill.

¾ cup: 138 cal., 3g fat (0 sat. fat), 0 chol., 260mg sod., 22g carb. (5g sugars, 6g fiber), 5g pro.

ROMAINE & CHERRY TOMATO SALAD

My mother made this tasty salad for me as a child, and it was my favorite. Now we serve it as a sunny appetizer or entree.
—*Blythe Twiggs, Buford, GA*

TAKES: 20 min. • MAKES: 8 servings

- 1 small bunch romaine, torn
- 2 cups grape tomatoes, halved
- 1 pkg. (12 oz.) frozen peas, thawed
- 1 small red onion, thinly sliced
- 1½ cups reduced-fat mayonnaise
- 1 cup shredded Parmesan cheese
- 8 bacon strips, cooked and crumbled

In a 3-qt. trifle bowl or glass bowl, layer romaine, tomatoes, peas and onion. Spread mayonnaise over onion. Sprinkle with cheese and bacon. Refrigerate salad until serving.

1 cup: 284 cal., 21g fat (5g sat. fat), 31mg chol., 729mg sod., 14g carb. (6g sugars, 3g fiber), 10g pro.

HOVER YOUR CAMERA HERE
How to Host the Most Spectacular 4th of July Party

STRAWBERRY SPINACH SALAD WITH CANDIED WALNUTS

(PICTURED ON COVER)

This classic salad goes with just about anything you're serving. The juicy berries add a pop of color to the greens, and the sweet, crunchy nuts are good enough to eat all on their own!
—Susan Howell, Royal Oak, MI

TAKES: 20 min. • **MAKES:** 10 servings

- ½   cup sugar
- ¼   cup water
- ½   tsp. ground cinnamon
- ½   tsp. chili powder
- ¼   tsp. curry powder
- 2   cups walnut halves

SALAD
- 1   pkg. (9 oz.) fresh baby spinach
- 2   cups sliced fresh strawberries (about 1 lb.)
- 1   medium cucumber, halved and sliced

VINAIGRETTE
- ¼   cup olive oil
- 2   Tbsp. balsamic vinegar
- 2   Tbsp. seedless raspberry jam
- 1   tsp. lemon juice
- ¼   tsp. salt
- ⅛   tsp. pepper
- ⅓   cup grated Parmesan cheese

1. In a small heavy saucepan, combine the first 5 ingredients; stir gently to moisten all the sugar. Cook over medium-low heat, gently swirling pan occasionally, until sugar is dissolved. Cover; bring to a boil over medium heat. Cook 1 minute. Uncover pan; continue to boil and gently swirl pan for 2-3 minutes or until syrup turns a deep amber color. Immediately remove from heat and carefully stir in walnuts until evenly coated. Spread onto foil to cool completely. Break into pieces.

2. In a large bowl, combine spinach, strawberries and cucumber. In a small bowl, whisk the first 6 vinaigrette ingredients. Drizzle over salad; toss to coat. Sprinkle with cheese and walnuts. Serve immediately.

1 cup: 262 cal., 19g fat (2g sat. fat), 2mg chol., 132mg sod., 21g carb. (16g sugars, 3g fiber), 5g pro.

BRING IT

When transporting salads, casseroles and other dishes, place the pan or container on the flattest possible surface (such as the floor of the back seat or the trunk) to make sure the dish stays steady and doesn't slide while the vehicle is in transit.

PINEAPPLE SWEET POTATO CASSEROLE WITH MARSHMALLOWS

PINEAPPLE SWEET POTATO CASSEROLE WITH MARSHMALLOWS

Pineapple, sugar and marshmallows lend a super sweetness to sweet potatoes. I've been making the casserole for years, both for special occasions and casual dinners.
—*Ruth Leach, Shreveport, LA*

PREP: 45 min. • **BAKE:** 40 min.
MAKES: 8 servings

- 6 medium sweet potatoes
- ½ cup butter, cubed
- ¾ cup sugar
- 1 can (20 oz.) crushed pineapple, drained
- 2 large eggs, beaten
- 1 tsp. vanilla extract
- ½ tsp. ground nutmeg
- ½ tsp. salt
- 15 large marshmallows

1. Place sweet potatoes in a large kettle and cover with water; bring to a boil. Boil gently until the potatoes can easily be pierced with the tip of a sharp knife, 30-45 minutes. Drain; cool slightly.
2. Preheat oven to 350°. Peel the potatoes and place in a large bowl with butter and sugar; mash. Add pineapple, eggs, vanilla, nutmeg and salt; stir to combine.
3. Spoon into a greased 2-qt. baking dish. Top with marshmallows. Bake, uncovered, until a knife inserted in the center comes out clean, 40-45 minutes.
1 cup: 367 cal., 13g fat (8g sat. fat), 84mg chol., 295mg sod., 62g carb. (43g sugars, 3g fiber), 4g pro.

READER RAVES
"I have been making this exact recipe since the '80s. Always a hit!"

—LST1950, TASTEOFHOME.COM

CRANBERRY RICOTTA
GNOCCHI WITH BROWN
BUTTER SAUCE

CRANBERRY RICOTTA GNOCCHI WITH BROWN BUTTER SAUCE

To make light and airy gnocchi, work quickly and handle the dough as little as possible. You'll be pleased with the resulting pillowy dumplings.
—*Sally Sibthorpe, Shelby Township, MI*

PREP: 30 min. + standing • **COOK:** 15 min.
MAKES: 8 servings

- ¾ cup dried cranberries, divided
- 2 cups ricotta cheese
- 1 cup all-purpose flour
- ½ cup grated Parmesan cheese
- 1 large egg, lightly beaten
- ¾ tsp. salt, divided
- ¾ cup butter, cubed
- 2 Tbsp. minced fresh sage
- ½ cup chopped walnuts, toasted
- ⅛ tsp. white pepper

1. Finely chop ¼ cup cranberries. In a large bowl, combine the ricotta cheese, flour, Parmesan cheese, egg, ½ tsp. salt and chopped cranberries; mix until blended. On a lightly floured surface, knead 10-12 times, forming a soft dough. Cover and let rest for 10 minutes.
2. Divide dough into 4 portions. On a floured surface, roll each portion into a ¾-in.-thick rope; cut into ¾-in. pieces. Press and roll each piece with a lightly floured fork.
3. In a Dutch oven, bring 4 qt. water to a boil. Cook the gnocchi in batches until they float, 30-60 seconds. Remove with a slotted spoon; keep warm.
4. In a large heavy saucepan, cook butter over medium heat 5 minutes. Add sage; cook 3-5 minutes longer or until butter is golden brown, stirring occasionally. Stir in walnuts, white pepper, and the remaining cranberries and salt. Add gnocchi; stir gently to coat.
¾ cup: 411 cal., 30g fat (16g sat. fat), 101mg chol., 503mg sod., 26g carb. (11g sugars, 1g fiber), 13g pro.

OVERNIGHT LAYERED LETTUCE SALAD

MA
OVERNIGHT LAYERED LETTUCE SALAD

This layered salad is a family favorite from a church cookbook I've had for 40 years. The bacon adds a nice crunch.
—*Mary Brehm, Cape Coral, FL*

PREP: 20 min. + chilling
MAKES: 16 servings

- 1 medium head iceberg lettuce, torn
- 1 medium green pepper, chopped
- 1 small sweet red pepper, chopped
- 1 medium onion, sliced and separated into rings
- 2 cups frozen peas (about 10 oz.)
- 1 cup mayonnaise
- 2 Tbsp. sugar
- 1 cup shredded cheddar cheese
- 12 bacon strips, cooked and crumbled
- ¾ cup dried cranberries

1. In a 4-qt. or 13x9-in. glass dish, layer the first 5 ingredients. In a small bowl, mix mayonnaise and sugar; spoon over salad, spreading to cover.
2. Sprinkle the top of salad with cheese, bacon and cranberries. Refrigerate salad, covered, overnight.
1 cup: 206 cal., 16g fat (4g sat. fat), 19mg chol., 250mg sod., 11g carb. (7g sugars, 2g fiber), 5g pro.

TEST KITCHEN TIP

This salad is ideal for making ahead. The ingredients all hold up well to the moisture in the mayo, and they even soak in some flavor while you sleep.

BAKED PARMESAN BROCCOLI

FRESH CORN SALAD

People who like food with some tang find this corn salad particularly appealing. It's a pretty dish, too—and economical. If you are like me and enjoy growing your own ingredients, you won't have to pick up too much at the store.

—*Carol Shaffer, Cape Girardeau, MO*

PREP: 20 min. + chilling
MAKES: 10 servings

- 8 ears fresh corn, husked and cleaned
- ½ cup canola oil
- ¼ cup cider vinegar
- 1½ tsp. lemon juice
- ¼ cup minced fresh parsley
- 2 tsp. sugar
- 1 tsp. salt
- ½ tsp. dried basil
- ⅛ to ¼ tsp. cayenne pepper
- 2 large tomatoes, seeded and coarsely chopped
- ½ cup chopped onion
- ⅓ cup chopped green pepper
- ⅓ cup chopped sweet red pepper

1. In a large saucepan, cook the corn in enough boiling water to cover until tender, 5-7 minutes. Drain, cool and set aside.
2. In a large bowl, mix the oil, vinegar, lemon juice, parsley, sugar, salt if desired, basil and cayenne pepper. Cut cooled corn off the cob (should measure 4 cups).
3. Add the corn, tomatoes, onion and peppers to the oil mixture. Mix well. Cover and chill for several hours or overnight.
½ cup: 102 cal., 2g fat (0 sat. fat), 0 chol., 251mg sod., 21g carb. (0 sugars, 0 fiber), 3g pro. **Diabetic exchanges:** 1 starch, ½ vegetable, ½ fat.

TEST KITCHEN TIP

When fresh corn isn't available, you can use frozen corn with good results.

BAKED PARMESAN BROCCOLI

I began making this creamy side dish years ago as a way to get my kids to eat broccoli. They've since grown up but still request this satisfying casserole. It's truly a family favorite.

—*Barbara Uhl, Wesley Chapel, FL*

PREP: 30 min. • **BAKE:** 15 min.
MAKES: 12 servings

- 4 bunches broccoli, cut into florets
- 6 Tbsp. butter, divided
- 1 small onion, finely chopped
- 1 garlic clove, minced
- ¼ cup all-purpose flour
- 2 cups 2% milk
- 1 large egg yolk, beaten
- 1 cup grated Parmesan cheese
- ½ tsp. salt
- ⅛ tsp. pepper
- ½ cup seasoned bread crumbs

1. Preheat oven to 400°. Place half broccoli in a steamer basket; place the basket in a large saucepan over 1 in. water. Bring to a boil; cover and steam for 3-4 minutes or until crisp-tender. Place in a greased 13x9-in. baking dish; repeat with the remaining broccoli.
2. Meanwhile, in a small saucepan over medium heat, melt 4 Tbsp. butter. Add onion; cook and stir until tender. Add garlic; cook 1 minute longer.
3. Stir in flour until blended; gradually add milk. Bring to a boil; cook and stir 2 minutes or until thickened. Stir a small amount of hot mixture into the egg yolk; return all to the pan, stirring constantly. Cook and stir 1 minute longer. Remove from heat; stir in the cheese, salt and pepper. Pour over broccoli.
4. In a small skillet, cook bread crumbs in remaining butter until golden brown; sprinkle over the top.
5. Bake, uncovered, 15-18 minutes or until heated through.
¾ cup: 191 cal., 10g fat (5g sat. fat), 41mg chol., 388mg sod., 19g carb. (7g sugars, 6g fiber), 11g pro.

**FRESH CORN
SALAD**

CHESTNUT DRESSING

I enjoyed this stuffing when I spent my first Thanksgiving with my husband, Mike. It's a family recipe his mother has been making for years. Italian seasoning and chestnuts add flavor and texture.
—*Sharon Brunner, Mohnton, PA*

PREP: 25 min. • **BAKE:** 20 min.
MAKES: 18 servings

- 4 celery ribs, chopped
- 1 large onion, chopped
- 1½ cups butter, cubed
- 3 cups chestnuts, shelled and coarsely chopped
- 3 Tbsp. Italian seasoning
- 10 slices Italian bread (¾ in. thick), cubed

1. Preheat oven to 350°. In a large skillet, saute the celery and onion in butter over medium-high heat for 2-3 minutes or until tender. Add the chestnuts and Italian seasoning. Bring to a boil. Reduce heat; simmer, uncovered, 10 minutes. Add the bread cubes and stir to coat.

2. Transfer mixture to an ungreased 13x9-in. baking dish. Bake, uncovered, until golden brown, 20-25 minutes.

½ cup: 223 cal., 16g fat (10g sat. fat), 40mg chol., 213mg sod., 18g carb. (3g sugars, 2g fiber), 2g pro.

CHESTNUT DRESSING

HEIRLOOM TOMATO PIE

HEIRLOOM TOMATO PIE

My green-thumbed neighbors like to share their garden produce with me. I return the favor by baking delicious tomato pies for all.
—*Angela Benedict, Dunbar, WV*

PREP: 45 min. • **BAKE:** 35 min. + cooling
MAKES: 8 servings

- 1¼ lbs. heirloom tomatoes (about 4 medium), cut into ¼-in. slices
- ¾ tsp. salt, divided
- 1½ cups shredded extra-sharp cheddar cheese
- ¾ cup all-purpose flour
- ¼ cup cold butter, cubed
- 1 to 2 Tbsp. half-and-half cream
- 5 bacon strips, cooked and crumbled

FILLING
- 1 pkg. (8 oz.) cream cheese, softened
- ½ cup loosely packed basil leaves, thinly sliced
- 2 Tbsp. minced fresh marjoram
- 1½ tsp. minced fresh thyme
- ½ tsp. garlic powder
- ⅛ tsp. coarsely ground pepper

1. Preheat oven to 350°. Place tomato slices in a single layer on paper towels; sprinkle with ½ tsp. salt. Let stand for 45 minutes. Pat dry.
2. Meanwhile, place cheese, flour and remaining salt in a food processor; pulse until blended. Add the butter; pulse until butter is the size of peas. While pulsing, add just enough cream to form moist crumbs. Press dough onto bottom and up side of an ungreased 9-in. fluted tart pan with removable bottom. Gently press the bacon into dough. Bake 20-22 minutes or until light brown. Cool on a wire rack.
3. In a large bowl, beat cream cheese, herbs and garlic powder until blended. Spread over crust. Top with tomato slices; sprinkle with pepper. Bake 35-40 minutes longer or until edge is golden brown and tomatoes are softened. Cool on a wire rack. Refrigerate leftovers.
1 piece: 320 cal., 25g fat (14g sat. fat), 74mg chol., 603mg sod., 14g carb. (3g sugars, 1g fiber), 11g pro.

FRESH TOMATO FLATBREAD

Looking for an easy appetizer or side? All you need are fresh tomatoes, a can of refrigerated crescent rolls, olive oil, and a sprinkling of cheese and seasonings.
—*Marlene Mohr, Cincinnati, OH*

TAKES: 25 min. • **MAKES:** 12 servings

- 2 plum tomatoes
- 1 tube (8 oz.) refrigerated crescent rolls
- 1 small onion, thinly sliced
- 2 Tbsp. olive oil
- 1 tsp. Italian seasoning
- 1 garlic clove, minced
- ¼ tsp. salt
- ⅛ tsp. pepper
- 1 Tbsp. grated Parmesan cheese

1. Thinly slice the tomatoes; place on paper towels to drain. Unroll crescent dough; place on an ungreased baking sheet. Roll into a 14x10-in. rectangle; seal seams and perforations.
2. Arrange tomatoes and onion over crust. In a small bowl, combine the oil, Italian seasoning, garlic, salt and pepper; brush over top. Sprinkle with cheese.
3. Bake at 375° for 10-14 minutes or until lightly browned. Cut into squares.
1 piece: 101 cal., 6g fat (1g sat. fat), 0 chol., 205mg sod., 9g carb. (2g sugars, 0 fiber), 2g pro.

FIRE & ICE TOMATOES

You won't miss the salt in this refreshing tomato salad. It's well-seasoned but not the least bit spicy.
—*Nan Rickey, Yuma, AZ*

PREP: 10 min. • **COOK:** 5 min. + chilling
MAKES: 8 servings

- 5 large tomatoes, cut into wedges
- 1 medium onion, sliced
- ¾ cup white vinegar
- 6 Tbsp. sugar
- ¼ cup water
- 3 tsp. mustard seed
- ¼ tsp. cayenne pepper
- 1 large cucumber, sliced

1. Place tomatoes and onion in a large heatproof nonreactive bowl. In a small saucepan, combine vinegar, sugar, water, mustard seed and cayenne; bring to a boil. Cook 1 minute, stirring to dissolve sugar; pour carefully over the tomato mixture. Cool completely.
2. Stir in cucumber. Refrigerate salad, covered, overnight.
¾ cup: 72 cal., 1g fat (0 sat. fat), 0 chol., 7mg sod., 17g carb. (14g sugars, 2g fiber), 2g pro. **Diabetic exchanges:** 1 vegetable, ½ starch.

BAKING POWDER DROP BISCUITS

One day I had company coming and realized I had run out of biscuit mix. I'd never made biscuits from scratch before, but I decided to give this recipe a try. Now this is the only way I make them!
—*Sharon Evans, Clear Lake, IA*

TAKES: 20 min. • **MAKES:** 1 dozen

- 2 cups all-purpose flour
- 2 Tbsp. sugar
- 4 tsp. baking powder
- ½ tsp. cream of tartar
- ½ tsp. salt
- ½ cup shortening
- ⅔ cup 2% milk
- 1 large egg, room temperature

1. Preheat oven to 450°. In a large bowl, combine the first 5 ingredients. Cut in shortening until the mixture resembles coarse crumbs. In a small bowl, whisk milk and egg. Stir into crumb mixture just until moistened.
2. Drop by ¼ cupfuls 2 in. apart onto an ungreased baking sheet. Bake until golden brown, 10-12 minutes. Serve warm.
1 biscuit: 170 cal., 9g fat (2g sat. fat), 17mg chol., 271mg sod., 19g carb. (3g sugars, 1g fiber), 3g pro.

FIRE & ICE TOMATOES

CLASSIC MACARONI SALAD

Here's a light take on an all-time favorite. It's perfect for picnics and barbecues but you can also serve it as part of a quick weeknight dinner
—Dorothy Bayes, Sardis, OH

TAKES: 30 min. • **MAKES:** 8 servings

- 2 cups uncooked elbow macaroni
- 1 cup fat-free mayonnaise
- 2 Tbsp. sweet pickle relish
- 2 tsp. sugar
- ¾ tsp. ground mustard
- ¼ tsp. salt
- ⅛ tsp. pepper
- ½ cup chopped celery
- ⅓ cup chopped carrot
- ¼ cup chopped onion
- 1 hard-boiled large egg, chopped
  Dash paprika

1. Cook macaroni according to package directions; drain and rinse with cold water. Cool completely.
2. For dressing, in a small bowl, combine the mayonnaise, pickle relish, sugar, mustard, salt and pepper. In a large bowl, combine the macaroni, celery, carrot and onion. Add the dressing and toss gently to coat.
3. Refrigerate until serving. Garnish with egg and paprika.
¾ cup: 115 cal., 2g fat (0 sat. fat), 27mg chol., 362mg sod., 21g carb. (6g sugars, 2g fiber), 4g pro. **Diabetic exchanges:** 1½ starch.

READER RAVES
"Great combination of flavors with a little bit of crunch. Loved it!"

—ROSOMALLEY, TASTEOFHOME.COM

CLASSIC
MACARONI
SALAD

FIESTA CORN

Corn with tomatoes and jalapenos is one of the first dishes I cooked for my husband. Don't like heat? Use green bell peppers instead of jalapenos.
—*Cassandra Ramirez, Bardstown, KY*

TAKES: 25 min. • **MAKES:** 8 servings

- ¼ cup butter, cubed
- 1 small onion, chopped
- 2 to 3 jalapeno peppers, seeded and chopped
- 6 plum tomatoes, seeded and chopped
- 5 cups fresh or frozen corn
- 1½ tsp. salt
   Lime wedges, optional

1. In a 6-qt. stockpot, heat butter over medium heat. Add onion and jalapenos; cook and stir until onion is crisp-tender, 3-4 minutes. Stir in the tomatoes; cook 3 minutes longer.
2. Add corn; cook, uncovered, until tender, stirring occasionally, 8-10 minutes. Stir in salt. If desired, serve with lime wedges.
Note: Wear disposable gloves when cutting hot peppers; the oils can burn skin. Avoid touching your face.
¾ cup: 142 cal., 7g fat (4g sat. fat), 15mg chol., 505mg sod., 20g carb. (7g sugars, 3g fiber), 4g pro.

SUPER ITALIAN CHOPPED SALAD

Antipasto ingredients are sliced and diced to make this substantial salad. I like to buy sliced meat from the deli and chop it all so we can get a bit of everything in each bite.
—*Kim Molina, Duarte, CA*

TAKES: 25 min. • **MAKES:** 10 servings

- 3 cups torn romaine
- 1 can (15 oz.) garbanzo beans or chickpeas, rinsed and drained
- 1 jar (6½ oz.) marinated artichoke hearts, drained and chopped
- 1 medium green pepper, chopped
- 2 medium tomatoes, chopped
- 1 can (2¼ oz.) sliced ripe olives, drained
- 5 slices deli ham, chopped
- 5 thin slices hard salami, chopped
- 5 slices pepperoni, chopped
- 3 slices provolone cheese, chopped
- 2 green onions, chopped
- ¼ cup olive oil
- 2 Tbsp. red wine vinegar
- ¼ tsp. salt
- ⅛ tsp. pepper
- 2 Tbsp. grated Parmesan cheese
   Pepperoncini, optional

In a large bowl, combine the first 11 ingredients. For dressing, in a small bowl, whisk the oil, vinegar, salt and pepper. Pour over salad; toss to coat. Sprinkle with cheese. Top with pepperoncini, if desired.
¾ cup: 185 cal., 13g fat (3g sat. fat), 12mg chol., 444mg sod., 11g carb. (3g sugars, 3g fiber), 7g pro.

CLASSIC MAKE-AHEAD MASHED POTATOES

CLASSIC MAKE-AHEAD MASHED POTATOES

This side dish staple saves time on busy holidays. No more frantically whipping the potatoes while hungry family and guests hang around the kitchen!
—*Marty Rummel, Trout Lake, WA*

PREP: 40 min. + chilling • **BAKE:** 55 min.
MAKES: 12 servings

- 5 lbs. potatoes, peeled and cut into wedges
- 1 pkg. (8 oz.) reduced-fat cream cheese, cubed
- 2 large egg whites, beaten
- 1 cup reduced-fat sour cream
- 2 tsp. onion powder
- 1 tsp. salt
- ½ tsp. pepper
- 1 Tbsp. butter, melted

1. Place potatoes in a Dutch oven and cover with water. Bring to a boil. Reduce heat; cover and cook for 15-20 minutes or until tender. Drain.

2. In a large bowl, mash potatoes with cream cheese. Combine the egg whites, sour cream, onion powder, salt and pepper; stir into potatoes until blended. Transfer mixture to a greased 3-qt. baking dish. Drizzle with butter. Cover potatoes and refrigerate overnight.

3. Remove from refrigerator 30 minutes before baking. Preheat the oven to 350°. Cover and bake 50 minutes. Uncover; bake 5-10 minutes longer or until a thermometer reads 160°.

Note: For best results, use a starchy potato, like a russet or Yukon Gold.

¾ cup: 220 cal., 7g fat (4g sat. fat), 22mg chol., 316mg sod., 32g carb. (4g sugars, 3g fiber), 7g pro.

VEGAN GREEN GODDESS POTATO SALAD

Don't be fooled by the green color—this salad is delicious! It's perfect for potlucks and for those with dietary restrictions.
—*Laura Wilhelm, West Hollywood, CA*

PREP: 30 min. + chilling
MAKES: 8 servings

- 2 lbs. baby red potatoes, halved
- 4 green onions
- 2 medium ripe avocados, peeled and pitted
- ½ cup sprigs fresh parsley, stems removed
- ½ cup vegan mayonnaise
- 3 tarragon sprigs, stems removed
- 2 tsp. capers, drained
- 1 tsp. seasoned salt
- 1 celery rib, finely chopped
  Sliced radishes

Place potatoes in a large saucepan; add water to cover. Bring to a boil. Reduce heat; cook, uncovered, 8-10 minutes or until tender. Meanwhile, chop green onions, reserving the white portions for salad. Add green portions to a blender. Add the avocados, parsley, mayonnaise, tarragon, capers and seasoned salt. Cover and process until blended, scraping down sides as needed. Drain potatoes; transfer to a large bowl. Add celery, white portions of green onions, and dressing; toss to coat. Refrigerate, covered, at least 1 hour. Top with radishes and additional parsley.

¾ cup: 235 cal., 15g fat (2g sat. fat), 0 chol., 295mg sod., 24g carb. (1g sugars, 4g fiber), 3g pro. **Diabetic exchanges:** 3 fat, 1½ starch.

VEGAN GREEN GODDESS POTATO SALAD

HOVER YOUR CAMERA HERE
13 Potluck Etiquette Rules to Memorize Before Your Next Party

TABBOULEH

Tabbouleh, also known as tabouleh, is a classic Middle Eastern salad. The fresh veggies and mint leaves make it light and invigorating on a hot day.
—*Michael & Mathil Chebat, Lake Ridge, VA*

TAKES: 30 min. • **MAKES:** 8 servings

- ¼ cup bulgur
- 3 bunches fresh parsley, minced (about 2 cups)
- 3 large tomatoes, finely chopped
- 1 small onion, finely chopped
- ¼ cup lemon juice
- ¼ cup olive oil
- 5 fresh mint leaves, minced
- ½ tsp. salt
- ½ tsp. pepper
- ¼ tsp. cayenne pepper

Prepare bulgur according to package directions; cool. Transfer to a large bowl. Stir in remaining ingredients. If desired, chill before serving.

⅔ cup: 100 cal., 7g fat (1g sat. fat), 0 chol., 164mg sod., 9g carb. (3g sugars, 2g fiber), 2g pro. **Diabetic exchanges:** 1½ fat, ½ starch.

READER RAVES
"Delicious! Enjoyed the small amount of grain in the mix...so vibrant and fresh."

—**ANNRMS, TASTEOFHOME.COM**

SWEET CORN MUFFINS

I love to make cornbread and corn muffins, but often the results are not moist or sweet enough for my taste. I experimented until I came up with these light, pleasantly sweet muffins. They ended up winning a blue ribbon at our county fair.
—*Patty Bourne, Owings, MD*

PREP: 10 min. • **BAKE:** 25 min.
MAKES: 1 dozen

- 1½ cups all-purpose flour
- 1 cup sugar
- ¾ cup cornmeal
- 1 Tbsp. baking powder
- ½ tsp. salt
- 2 large eggs, room temperature
- ½ cup shortening
- 1 cup 2% milk, divided

In a bowl, combine the dry ingredients. Add eggs, shortening and ½ cup milk; beat for 1 minute. Add remaining milk; beat just until blended. Fill 12 paper-lined muffin cups three-fourths full. Bake at 350° until a toothpick inserted in muffin comes out clean, 25-30 minutes.

1 muffin: 254 cal., 10g fat (3g sat. fat), 33mg chol., 241mg sod., 38g carb. (18g sugars, 1g fiber), 4g pro.

HAM, BROCCOLI
& ORZO CASSEROLE

HAM, BROCCOLI & ORZO CASSEROLE

A kid-pleaser and perfect comfort food, this hot, gooey casserole is a complete meal in one. For an extra homey touch, I make mine in my favorite hand-me-down casserole dish from my dear Grandma Laverne.
—Heather Arndt Anderson, Portland, OR

PREP: 30 min. • **BAKE:** 20 min.
MAKES: 8 servings

- 4 cups chicken stock
- 2 cups uncooked orzo pasta
- 3 Tbsp. butter
- ¼ cup all-purpose flour
- 2 cups 2% milk
- ½ tsp. salt
- ½ tsp. pepper
- 2 cups shredded sharp cheddar cheese, divided
- 1½ cups cubed fully cooked ham
- 2 cups chopped fresh broccoli
- 2 cups chopped fresh kale
- 1 cup french-fried onions

1. Preheat the oven to 350°. In a large saucepan, bring stock to a boil; stir in orzo. Cook, uncovered, until orzo is al dente and broth is absorbed, 8-10 minutes .
2. Meanwhile, in a large saucepan, heat butter over medium heat. Stir in flour until blended; cook and stir until lightly browned, 4-5 minutes. Gradually whisk in milk, salt and pepper. Bring to a boil, stirring constantly; cook and stir until thickened, 1-2 minutes. Stir in 1½ cups cheese; cook until cheese is melted.
3. Add orzo, ham, broccoli and kale. Transfer to a greased 13x9-in. baking dish; sprinkle with onions and the remaining cheese. Bake, uncovered, until bubbly, 20-25 minutes.
1 cup: 637 cal., 27g fat (14g sat. fat), 80mg chol., 1386mg sod., 66g carb. (8g sugars, 3g fiber), 32g pro.

FRESH GREEN BEAN SALAD

FRESH GREEN BEAN SALAD

I had a green bean salad at a local deli and enjoyed it so much that I tried to re-create it at home. The result was yummy! It lasts for several days in the fridge, and the taste keeps getting better.
—Allison Brooks, Fort Collins, CO

PREP: 35 min. • **MAKES:** 12 servings

- 4 cups fresh green beans, trimmed and halved
- 2 cups cherry tomatoes, halved
- 1 large English cucumber, seeded and chopped
- 1 cup fresh baby carrots, cut in half lengthwise
- 1 cup coarsely chopped fresh parsley

DRESSING
- ½ cup olive oil
- 2 Tbsp. lemon juice
- 1 Tbsp. white wine vinegar
- 1 Tbsp. grated lemon zest
- 1 tsp. Dijon mustard
- 1 garlic clove, minced
- ½ tsp. salt
- ½ tsp. ground mustard
- ¼ tsp. pepper

1. In a large saucepan, bring 4 cups water to a boil. Add beans; cook, uncovered, for 3 minutes. Drain and immediately place beans in ice water. Drain and pat dry.
2. In a large bowl, combine the beans, tomatoes, cucumber, carrots and parsley. In a small bowl, whisk the dressing ingredients. Pour over salad; toss to coat. Refrigerate until serving. Serve with a slotted spoon.
To make ahead: Green beans can be boiled, chilled in ice water and drained as directed a day in advance. Store in the refrigerator.
¾ cup: 106 cal., 9g fat (1g sat. fat), 0 chol., 124mg sod., 6g carb. (3g sugars, 2g fiber), 1g pro. **Diabetic exchanges:** 2 fat, 1 vegetable.

GOLDEN MASHED POTATOES

SPINACH SALAD WITH GOAT CHEESE & BEETS

Here's an easy salad that looks and tastes festive for the holiday season. Vinaigrette dressing coats the greens nicely.
—*Nancy Latulippe, Simcoe, ON*

PREP: 45 min. + cooling
MAKES: 10 servings

- 1¼ lbs. fresh beets
- 1 Tbsp. balsamic vinegar
- 1½ tsp. honey
- 1½ tsp. Dijon mustard
- ¼ tsp. salt
- ¼ tsp. pepper
- ¼ cup olive oil
- 5 cups fresh baby spinach
- 2 oz. fresh goat cheese, crumbled
- ½ cup chopped walnuts, toasted

1. Scrub beets and trim tops to 1 in. Place in a Dutch oven and cover with water. Bring to a boil. Reduce heat; cover and simmer until tender, 30-60 minutes. Remove from the water; cool. Peel beets and cut into 1-in. pieces.
2. In a small bowl, whisk the vinegar, honey, mustard, salt and pepper. Slowly whisk in oil until blended.
3. Place spinach in salad bowl. Drizzle with dressing; toss to coat. Top with beets, goat cheese and walnuts. If desired, sprinkle with additional pepper.
¾ cup: 113 cal., 10g fat (2g sat. fat), 4mg chol., 128mg sod., 5g carb. (3g sugars, 1g fiber), 2g pro.

MA
GOLDEN MASHED POTATOES

When there's no gravy with the meat, this side dish is fabulous to serve in place of regular mashed potatoes. I make it often to take to picnics and church socials. My husband even made it for his family's reunion one year when I couldn't go!
—*Cindy Stith, Wickliffe, KY*

PREP: 40 min. • **BAKE:** 30 min.
MAKES: 12 servings

- 9 large potatoes (about 4 lbs.), peeled and cubed
- 1 lb. carrots, cut into ½-in. chunks
- 8 green onions, thinly sliced
- ½ cup butter
- 1 cup sour cream
- 1½ tsp. salt
- ⅛ tsp. pepper
- ¾ cup shredded cheddar cheese

1. In a soup kettle or Dutch oven, cook the potatoes and carrots in boiling salted water until tender; drain. Place in a bowl; mash and set aside.
2. In a skillet, saute onions in butter until tender. Add to potato mixture. Add sour cream, salt and pepper; mix until blended.
3. Transfer mixture to a greased 13x9-in. baking dish. Sprinkle with cheese. Bake, uncovered, at 350° until heated through, 30-40 minutes.
Freeze option: Cool unbaked casserole; cover and freeze. To use, partially thaw in refrigerator overnight. Remove from refrigerator 30 minutes before baking. Preheat oven to 350°. Bake casserole as directed, increasing time as necessary to heat through and for a thermometer inserted in center to read 165°.
¾ cup: 370 cal., 13g fat (9g sat. fat), 41mg chol., 456mg sod., 55g carb. (8g sugars, 6g fiber), 9g pro.

SPINACH SALAD WITH
GOAT CHEESE & BEETS

**HOVER YOUR
CAMERA HERE**
You Can Use a
Twin Fitted Sheet
as a Tablecloth
and It's a Genius
Party Hack

TUSCAN-STYLE ROASTED ASPARAGUS

This is especially wonderful when locally grown asparagus is in season. It's so easy for celebrations because you can serve it hot or cold.

—*Jannine Fisk, Malden, MA*

PREP: 20 min. • **BAKE:** 15 min.
MAKES: 8 servings

- 1½ lbs. fresh asparagus, trimmed
- 1½ cups grape tomatoes, halved
- 3 Tbsp. pine nuts
- 3 Tbsp. olive oil, divided
- 2 garlic cloves, minced
- 1 tsp. kosher salt
- ½ tsp. pepper
- 1 Tbsp. lemon juice
- ⅓ cup grated Parmesan cheese
- 1 tsp. grated lemon zest

1. Preheat the oven to 400°. Place the asparagus, tomatoes and pine nuts on a foil-lined 15x10x1-in. baking pan. Mix 2 Tbsp. oil, garlic, salt and pepper; add to asparagus and toss to coat.

2. Bake for 15-20 minutes or just until the asparagus is tender. Drizzle with the remaining oil and lemon juice; sprinkle with Parmesan cheese and lemon zest. Toss to combine.

1 serving: 95 cal., 8g fat (2g sat. fat), 3mg chol., 294mg sod., 4g carb. (2g sugars, 1g fiber), 3g pro. **Diabetic exchanges:** 1½ fat, 1 vegetable.

TEST KITCHEN TIP

Asparagus sizes vary and will take less or more time to cook based on the thickness. To avoid mushy asparagus, be sure to test your asparagus toward the end of the roasting time. If you overcook your asparagus, it'll end up soft and mushy.

TUSCAN-STYLE ROASTED ASPARAGUS

TROPICAL GINGER RICE

IRISH SODA BREAD MUFFINS

Irish soda bread is traditionally prepared in a loaf shape, but these muffins have the same terrific flavor.
—*Lorraine Ballsieper, Deep River, CT*

TAKES: 30 min. • MAKES: 1 dozen

- 2¼ cups all-purpose flour
- ½ cup plus 1 Tbsp. sugar, divided
- 2 tsp. baking powder
- ½ tsp. salt
- ¼ tsp. baking soda
- 1 tsp. caraway seeds
- 1 large egg, room temperature
- 1 cup buttermilk
- ¼ cup butter, melted
- ¼ cup canola oil
- ¾ cup dried currants or raisins

1. In a large bowl, combine the flour, ½ cup sugar, baking powder, salt, baking soda and caraway seeds. In another bowl, beat the egg, buttermilk, butter and oil. Stir into dry ingredients just until moistened. Fold in currants.

2. Fill greased muffin cups three-fourths full. Sprinkle with remaining sugar. Bake at 400° for 15 minutes or until a toothpick inserted in the center comes out clean. Cool for 5 minutes before removing from pan to wire rack. Serve warm.

1 muffin: 235 cal., 9g fat (3g sat. fat), 28mg chol., 247mg sod., 35g carb. (17g sugars, 1g fiber), 4g pro.

TROPICAL GINGER RICE

This change-of-pace side dish comes together in moments and rounds out any family meal with a burst of sweet-tart flavor. Try it with dried cherries, too!
—*Charlene Chambers, Ormond Beach, FL*

TAKES: 25 min. • MAKES: 8 servings

- 2 cups uncooked long grain rice
- 1 Tbsp. minced fresh gingerroot
- 4 cups chicken broth
- ⅔ cup dried tropical fruit
- ⅔ cup chopped pecans, toasted

In a large saucepan, combine rice, ginger and broth; bring to a boil. Reduce heat; simmer, covered, 18-22 minutes or until liquid is absorbed and rice is tender. Stir in dried fruit and pecans.

1 cup: 186 cal., 5g fat (0 sat. fat), 2mg chol., 408mg sod., 32g carb. (5g sugars, 1g fiber), 4g pro.

TEST KITCHEN TIP

The hotter you cook your rice, the more quickly the liquid will evaporate. On the stovetop, after your rice reaches its initial boil, turn it down to a low simmer to keep evaporation at a minimum. A rice cooker or pressure cooker will automatically do this.

CAULIFLOWER
AU GRATIN

CAULIFLOWER AU GRATIN

Here's a lower-carb side dish that pairs well with pork, ham or beef. It's so creamy and delicious that even the kids will ask for seconds! If you like a little crunch, sprinkle buttered bread crumbs over the top for the last five minutes in the oven.
—*Mary Zinchiak, Boardman, OH*

PREP: 25 min. • **BAKE:** 45 min.
MAKES: 8 servings

- 1 large head cauliflower, cut into florets
- 2 Tbsp. olive oil
- 1 tsp. salt, divided
- 1 tsp. pepper, divided
- 4 Tbsp. butter, cubed
- 3 Tbsp. all-purpose flour
- 2 cups 2% milk
- 1 cup shredded Swiss cheese
- ½ cup grated Parmesan cheese
- ½ tsp. onion powder
- ½ tsp. ground mustard
- ½ tsp. Worcestershire sauce
- ⅛ tsp. cayenne pepper
  Chopped fresh thyme, optional

1. Preheat oven to 375°. Place cauliflower on a rimmed baking sheet. Drizzle with oil; sprinkle with ½ tsp. salt and ½ tsp. pepper. Toss to coat. Bake 8 minutes. Stir; bake until crisp-tender and lightly browned, 7-8 minutes longer.
2. In a large saucepan, melt butter over medium heat. Stir in flour until smooth; gradually whisk in milk. Bring to a simmer, stirring constantly; cook and stir until thickened, 2-3 minutes. Remove from the heat. Stir in the next 6 ingredients and the remaining ½ tsp. salt and ½ tsp. pepper until smooth.
3. Pour ¾ cup cheese sauce into a greased 2-qt. baking dish. Top with cauliflower and remaining cheese sauce. Bake, uncovered, 30-35 minutes or until bubbly and lightly browned. If desired, top cauliflower with chopped fresh thyme.
¾ cup: 196 cal., 14g fat (7g sat. fat), 34mg chol., 291mg sod., 11g carb. (5g sugars, 2g fiber), 9g pro.

COLESLAW WALDORF SALAD

COLESLAW WALDORF SALAD

Potlucks tend to have a lot of heavy dishes, so a bright, fresh salad is a welcome addition. I came up with this recipe as a way to serve something crunchy and fruity with a touch of sweetness. Sometimes I add shredded coconut and use toasted pecans instead of walnuts.
—*Trisha Kruse, Eagle, ID*

TAKES: 20 min. • **MAKES:** 18 servings

- 8 cups shredded cabbage
- 1 cup vanilla yogurt
- ½ cup mayonnaise
- ¼ cup orange juice
- 2 Tbsp. cider vinegar
- 2 large red apples, chopped
- 2 cups green grapes, halved
- 2 celery ribs, thinly sliced
- ¾ cup chopped walnuts, toasted
- ½ cup golden raisins
- ½ cup chopped dried apricots

Place cabbage in a large bowl. In another bowl, whisk yogurt, mayonnaise, orange juice and vinegar until combined. Pour over cabbage; toss to coat. Stir in the remaining ingredients. Refrigerate salad until serving.
¾ cup: 139 cal., 8g fat (1g sat. fat), 1mg chol., 55mg sod., 17g carb. (12g sugars, 2g fiber), 2g pro. **Diabetic exchanges:** 1½ fat, 1 starch.

MOJITO MARINATED FRUIT

All the flavors of the popular mojito cocktail are featured in this fantastic salad. After you eat the fruit, you'll want to sip the luscious syrup!
—*Marcy Griffith, Excelsior, MN*

PREP: 20 min. + chilling
MAKES: 8 servings

- ⅔ cup sugar
- ⅓ cup water
- ½ cup light rum
- 2 Tbsp. lime juice
- 1 tsp. grated lime zest
- 2 cups each cantaloupe, honeydew and seedless watermelon balls or chunks
- 2 cups cubed fresh pineapple
- 3 mint sprigs
  Fresh mint leaves, optional

1. In a small saucepan, combine sugar and water; cook and stir over medium heat until sugar is dissolved. Remove from heat. Stir in the rum, lime juice and zest. Cool completely.
2. In a large bowl, combine the melons, pineapple and mint sprigs. Add the rum mixture; toss to coat. Refrigerate salad, covered, overnight.
3. Discard mint sprigs. Spoon fruit with syrup into serving dishes. If desired, top with mint.
1 cup: 128 cal., 0 fat (0 sat. fat), 0 chol., 8mg sod., 26g carb. (24g sugars, 1g fiber), 1g pro.

SWEET POTATO & CARROT CASSEROLE

This tangy and sweet casserole is full of flavor. We've served it at many celebrations over the years, and it's always been a big hit.
—*Gloria Mezikofsky, Wakefield, MA*

PREP: 55 min. • **BAKE:** 25 min. + standing
MAKES: 12 servings

- ½ cup golden raisins
- 3½ lbs. medium sweet potatoes (about 6 potatoes)
- 4 large carrots, cut into 1½-in. pieces
- ¼ cup butter
- 1½ cups packed brown sugar
- ⅓ cup orange juice

1. Preheat oven to 375°. In a small bowl, cover raisins with hot water; let stand 30 minutes.
2. Meanwhile, place potatoes in a 6-qt. stockpot; add water to cover. Bring to a boil. Reduce the heat; cook, uncovered, just until tender, about 15-20 minutes. Remove the potatoes and cool slightly. Add the carrots to same pot of boiling water; cook, uncovered, until tender, 15-20 minutes; drain.
3. Peel sweet potatoes and cut crosswise into 1½-in.-thick slices. Arrange potatoes and carrots in a greased 13x9-in. baking dish, cut sides down.
4. Drain raisins. In a small saucepan, melt butter over medium heat; stir in raisins. Add brown sugar and orange juice, stirring to dissolve sugar. Pour over vegetables.
5. Bake, uncovered, until heated through and sauce is bubbly, 25-30 minutes; if desired, baste occasionally with sauce. Let stand 10 minutes; toss before serving.
¾ cup: 307 cal., 4g fat (2g sat. fat), 10mg chol., 69mg sod., 67g carb. (45g sugars, 5g fiber), 3g pro.

CHEESY CAULIFLOWER BREADSTICKS

CHEESY CAULIFLOWER BREADSTICKS

These grain-free breadsticks are made with cauliflower instead of flour. Serve with your favorite marinara sauce.
—*Nick Iverson, Denver, CO*

PREP: 20 min. • **BAKE:** 30 min.
MAKES: 12 servings

- 1 medium head cauliflower, cut into 1-in. florets (about 6 cups)
- ½ cup shredded part-skim mozzarella cheese
- ½ cup grated Parmesan cheese
- ½ cup shredded cheddar cheese
- 1 large egg
- ¼ cup chopped fresh basil
- ¼ cup chopped fresh parsley
- 1 garlic clove, minced
- 1 tsp. salt
- ½ tsp. pepper
  Marinara sauce, optional

1. Preheat oven to 425°. Process the cauliflower in batches in a food processor until finely ground. Microwave, covered, in a microwave-safe bowl on high until tender, about 8 minutes. When cauliflower is cool enough to handle, wrap in a clean kitchen towel and squeeze dry. Return to the bowl.

2. Meanwhile, in another bowl, mix the cheeses together. Stir half of the cheese mixture into the cauliflower; reserve the remaining cheese mixture. Combine next 6 ingredients; stir into cauliflower.

3. On a baking sheet lined with parchment, shape cauliflower mixture into an 11x9-in. rectangle. Bake until the edges are golden brown, 20-25 minutes. Top with reserved cheese; bake until melted and bubbly, 10-12 minutes. Cut into 12 breadsticks. If desired, serve with marinara sauce.

1 serving: 66 cal., 4g fat (2g sat. fat), 26mg chol., 340mg sod., 4g carb. (1g sugars, 1g fiber), 5g pro. **Diabetic exchanges:** 1 vegetable, 1 medium-fat meat.

GRANDMA'S CLASSIC
POTATO SALAD

Bring to a gentle boil; cook and stir for 2 minutes longer. Remove from the heat and cool completely. Gently stir in vinegar.

4. Chop and refrigerate 1 hard-boiled egg; chop the remaining 3 hard-boiled eggs. In a large bowl, combine the potatoes, celery, chopped onion and eggs; add dressing and stir until blended. Refrigerate until chilled. Garnish with reserved chopped egg and, if desired, sliced green onions.

¾ cup: 144 cal., 3g fat (1g sat. fat), 112mg chol., 402mg sod., 23g carb. (3g sugars, 2g fiber), 6g pro. **Diabetic exchanges:** 1½ starch, ½ fat.

SUMMER SQUASH SALAD

Packing a perfect crunch, this salad is a tasty alternative to coleslaw. Like most gardeners, we usually have an abundance of squash and zucchini in the summer, so this dish is a good way to use up all of our fresh produce.
—*Diane Hixon, Niceville, FL*

PREP: 15 min. + chilling
MAKES: 12 servings

    4   cups julienned zucchini
    4   cups julienned yellow squash
    2   cups sliced radishes
    1   cup canola oil
    ⅓   cup cider vinegar
    2   Tbsp. Dijon mustard
    2   Tbsp. snipped fresh parsley
    1½ tsp. salt
    1   tsp. dill weed
    ½   tsp. pepper

In a large bowl, toss the zucchini, squash and radishes. In a small bowl, whisk the remaining ingredients. Pour over the vegetables. Cover and refrigerate for at least 2 hours. If desired, top with additional snipped fresh parsley.

¾ cup: 188 cal., 19g fat (1g sat. fat), 0 chol., 368mg sod., 4g carb. (3g sugars, 1g fiber), 1g pro.

GRANDMA'S CLASSIC POTATO SALAD

When I asked my grandmother the history of this classic potato salad recipe, she told me that her mom used to make it when she was a little girl. It has definitely stood the test of time.
—*Kimberly Wallace, Dennison, OH*

PREP: 25 min. • **COOK:** 20 min. + chilling
MAKES: 10 servings

    6   medium potatoes, peeled and cubed
    ¼   cup all-purpose flour
    1   Tbsp. sugar
    1½ tsp. salt
    1   tsp. ground mustard
    1   tsp. pepper
    ¾   cup water
    2   large eggs, beaten
    ¼   cup white vinegar
    4   hard-boiled large eggs, divided use
    2   celery ribs, chopped
    1   medium onion, chopped
        Sliced green onions, optional

1. Place potatoes in a large saucepan and cover with water. Bring to a boil. Reduce the heat; cover and cook 15-20 minutes or until tender. Drain potatoes and cool to room temperature.

2. Meanwhile, in a small heavy saucepan, combine the flour, sugar, salt, mustard and pepper. Gradually stir in water until smooth. Cook and stir over medium-high heat until thickened and bubbly. Reduce heat; cook and stir 2 minutes longer.

3. Remove from the heat. Stir a small amount of hot mixture into beaten eggs; return all to the pan, stirring constantly.

SUMMER SQUASH SALAD

BIG-BATCH DISHES

Need a dish to pass? Hosting a large party? These delicious high-yield potluck favorites are perfect for all kinds of gatherings.

P. 220

P. 221

P. 210

TERIYAKI MEATBALLS

SAUCE
¼ cup canola oil
¼ cup soy sauce
3 Tbsp. honey
2 Tbsp. vinegar
¾ tsp. garlic powder
½ tsp. ground ginger
   Green onions, optional

1. Preheat the oven to 400°. Drain the pineapple, reserving ¼ cup juice; set pineapple aside. In a bowl, combine onion, peppers, bread crumbs, ginger, salt and reserved pineapple juice. Crumble beef over mixture and mix well. Shape mixture into 1-in. balls.

2. Place 6 sauce ingredients in a blender; cover and process 1 minute. Place 2 Tbsp. sauce in a greased 13x9-in. baking dish. Add meatballs. Pour remaining sauce over meatballs. Bake, uncovered, until meat is no longer pink, 18-20 minutes. Place 1 pineapple chunk on each meatball; secure with a toothpick. If desired, garnish with green onions.

1 meatball: 55 cal., 3g fat (1g sat. fat), 9mg chol., 119mg sod., 5g carb. (3g sugars, 0 fiber), 3g pro.

TEST KITCHEN TIP

Save the juice from canned pineapple by pouring it into ice cube trays and freezing it. When solid, transfer the cubes to an airtight freezer container. When a recipe calls for 1-2 Tbsp. pineapple juice, thaw 1-2 cubes and use as directed.

TERIYAKI MEATBALLS

This onetime appetizer idea was changed so many times because of my family's suggestions that it eventually became a main course. I think the homemade sauce sets these meatballs apart.
—*Evette Nowicki, Oak Harbor, WA*

PREP: 20 min. • **BAKE:** 20 min.
MAKES: 3½ dozen

2 cans (8 oz. each) pineapple chunks
1 medium onion, finely chopped
¼ cup finely chopped
   sweet yellow pepper
¼ cup finely chopped sweet red pepper
½ cup dry bread crumbs
½ tsp. ground ginger
¼ tsp. salt
1 lb. lean ground beef

**GREEN TOMATO
CHOWCHOW**

MA

PIZZA BEANS

Take this pizza-inspired dish to your next party. It makes an amazing side, or enjoy a larger serving alongside a fresh green salad for a delicious entree. It can even be made the day before and reheated.
—*Taste of Home Test Kitchen*

PREP: 20 min. • **COOK:** 6 hours
MAKES: 20 servings

- 1 lb. bulk Italian sausage
- 2 cups chopped celery
- 2 cups chopped onion
- 1 can (14½ oz.) cut green beans, drained
- 1 can (14½ oz.) cut wax beans, drained
- 1 can (16 oz.) kidney beans, rinsed and drained
- 1 can (16 oz.) butter beans, drained
- 1 can (15 oz.) pork and beans
- 3 cans (8 oz. each) pizza sauce
  Optional toppings: Grated Parmesan cheese, minced fresh oregano and crushed red pepper flakes

In a large skillet, brown sausage over medium heat until it is no longer pink, breaking it into crumbles. Transfer to a 5-qt. slow cooker with a slotted spoon. Add the celery and onion to skillet; cook until softened, about 5 minutes. Drain. Add the vegetable mixture and the next 6 ingredients to slow cooker; mix well. Cover; cook on low until bubbly, 6-8 hours. If desired, serve with toppings.

Freeze option: Freeze cooled beans in freezer containers. To use, partially thaw in refrigerator overnight. Heat through in a saucepan, stirring occasionally; add a little water or broth if necessary.
¾ cup: 142 cal., 6g fat (2g sat. fat), 12mg chol., 542mg sod., 17g carb. (4g sugars, 5g fiber), 7g pro.

GREEN TOMATO CHOWCHOW

My grandmom's cherished chowchow has Pennsylvania Dutch roots. The relish is tart and sweet with a smidge of spice.
—*Sharon Tipton, Casselberry, FL*

PREP: 20 min.
COOK: 1 hour + cooling
MAKES: 10 cups

- 3 lbs. green tomatoes (about 5 medium)
- 2 Tbsp. salt
- 1 medium head cabbage
- 1 lb. onions (about 3 medium)
- 1 lb. green and sweet red peppers (about 3 medium), seeded
- 1 jalapeno pepper, seeded and chopped, optional
- 4 cups cider vinegar
- 2¾ cups sugar
- 4 tsp. mixed pickling spices

1. Chop tomatoes. Transfer to a strainer and sprinkle with salt; let tomatoes stand 10 minutes. Meanwhile, chop the cabbage, onions, and green and red peppers. Place in a Dutch oven. Add drained tomatoes to pan and, if desired, jalapeno.
2. Stir in vinegar and sugar. Place the pickling spices on a double thickness of cheesecloth. Gather corners to enclose spices; tie securely with string. Add spice bag to pan. Bring to a boil. Reduce the heat; simmer, uncovered, until thickened, stirring occasionally, 1-1½ hours. Discard the spice bag. Cool to room temperature; refrigerate leftovers.
Note: Wear disposable gloves when cutting hot peppers; the oils can burn skin. Avoid touching your face.
¼ cup: 80 cal., 0 fat (0 sat. fat), 0 chol., 276mg sod., 19g carb. (17g sugars, 1g fiber), 1g pro.

PIZZA BEANS

BACON-WRAPPED WATER CHESTNUTS

Whenever I attend a potluck, folks always ask me to bring these bites—they've become my trademark. I especially like to prepare them for holiday gatherings.
—*Debi Jellison, Jacksonville, FL*

PREP: 20 min. • **BAKE:** 35 min.
MAKES: about 5 dozen

- 1 lb. sliced bacon
- 2 cans (8 oz. each) whole water chestnuts, rinsed and drained
- 1 cup ketchup
- ¾ cup packed brown sugar

1. Cut bacon strips into thirds; wrap a strip around each water chestnut and secure with a wooden toothpick. Place in an ungreased 15x10x1-in. baking pan. Bake at 375° until bacon is crisp, 25 minutes.

2. Meanwhile, in a small saucepan, combine ketchup and brown sugar; cook and stir over medium heat until sugar has dissolved. Remove water chestnuts to paper towels; drain. Dip in ketchup mixture; place in a lightly greased 13x9-in. baking dish. Spoon the remaining sauce over the water chestnuts. Return to the oven for 10 minutes.

1 piece: 33 cal., 1g fat (0 sat. fat), 2mg chol., 92mg sod., 5g carb. (4g sugars, 0 fiber), 1g pro.

BACON-WRAPPED WATER CHESTNUTS

PINA COLADA CUPCAKES

out clean, 18-20 minutes. Cool in pans for 10 minutes before removing to wire racks to cool completely.

3. In a large bowl, beat butter until creamy. Beat in the coconut milk and rum extract. Gradually beat in confectioners' sugar until smooth. Spread over cupcakes. If desired, garnish with coconut, cherries and pineapple wedges.

1 cupcake: 330 cal., 15g fat (7g sat. fat), 44mg chol., 189mg sod., 47g carb. (35g sugars, 0 fiber), 3g pro.

SCALLOPED POTATOES & HAM

A friend of mine served this scrumptious, hearty dish at her wedding. I liked it so much, I asked for the recipe. The potatoes and ham taste wonderful covered in a creamy cheese sauce, and the dish is excellent for a big group.
—Ruth Ann Stelfox, Raymond, AB

PREP: 30 min. • BAKE: 1 hour 20 min.
MAKES: 4 casseroles (10 servings each)

- 2 **cans (10¾ oz. each) condensed cream of mushroom soup, undiluted**
- 2 **cans (10¾ oz. each) condensed cream of celery soup, undiluted**
- 1 **can (10¾ oz.) condensed cheddar cheese soup, undiluted**
- 1 **can (12 oz.) evaporated milk**
- 10 **lbs. medium potatoes, peeled and thinly sliced**
- 5 **lbs. fully cooked ham, cubed**
- 4 **cups shredded cheddar cheese**

1. Preheat oven to 325°. In 2 large bowls, combine soups and milk. Add potatoes and ham; toss to coat. Divide the mixture among 4 greased 13x9-in. baking dishes.
2. Cover and bake 1¼ hours or until the potatoes are tender. Uncover; sprinkle with cheese. Bake 5-10 minutes longer or until cheese is melted.

1 cup: 226 cal., 10g fat (5g sat. fat), 46mg chol., 970mg sod., 20g carb. (2g sugars, 1g fiber), 15g pro.

PINA COLADA CUPCAKES

These treats are fun and colorful for picnics and potlucks. They can be served as cupcakes or cut into cubes and layered into individual dishes to make mini trifles.
—Jennifer Gilbert, Brighton, MI

PREP: 20 min.
BAKE: 20 min. + cooling
MAKES: 2 dozen

- 3 **large eggs, lightly beaten**
- ½ **cup unsweetened pineapple juice**
- ½ **cup canola oil**
- 1 **cup canned coconut milk**
- 2 **tsp. rum extract**
- 3 **cups all-purpose flour**
- 2 **cups sugar**
- 2 **tsp. baking powder**
- ½ **tsp. baking soda**
- ½ **tsp. salt**
- FROSTING
- 1 **cup butter, softened**
- 3 **Tbsp. canned coconut milk**
- 1 **tsp. rum extract**
- 3½ **cups confectioners' sugar**
  Optional: Toasted sweetened shredded coconut, maraschino cherries, pineapple wedges

1. Preheat oven to 350°. Line 24 muffin cups with foil liners. In a large bowl, whisk eggs, juice, oil, milk and extract until well blended. In another bowl, whisk flour, sugar, baking powder, baking soda and salt; gradually beat into egg mixture.
2. Fill prepared cups two-thirds full. Bake until a toothpick inserted in center comes

PHILLY CHEESESTEAK SLIDERS

(MA)

BEST EVER CRESCENT ROLLS

My daughter and I have cranked out dozens of these homemade crescent rolls for holidays and other special occasions. It's a team effort—I cut the dough into pie-shaped wedges; she rolls them up.
—*Irene Yeh, Mequon, WI*

PREP: 40 min. + chilling
BAKE: 10 min./batch • **MAKES:** 32 rolls

- 3¾ to 4¼ **cups all-purpose flour**
- 2 **pkg. (¼ oz. each) active dry yeast**
- 1 **tsp. salt**
- 1 **cup 2% milk**
- ½ **cup butter, cubed**
- ¼ **cup honey**
- 3 **large egg yolks. room temperature**
- 2 **Tbsp. butter, melted**

1. Combine 1½ cups flour, yeast and salt. In a small saucepan, heat milk, cubed butter and honey to 120°-130°. Add to the dry ingredients; beat on medium speed for 2 minutes. Add egg yolks; beat on high for 2 minutes. Stir in enough remaining flour to form a soft dough (the dough will be sticky).

2. Turn dough onto a floured surface; knead dough until smooth and elastic, 6-8 minutes. Place in a greased bowl, turning once to grease the top. Cover and let rise in a warm place until doubled, about 45 minutes.

3. Punch down the dough. Cover and refrigerate overnight.

4. Turn chilled dough onto a lightly floured surface; divide in half. Roll each portion into a 14-in. circle; cut each circle into 16 wedges. Lightly brush wedges with melted butter. Roll up from wide ends, pinching pointed ends to seal. Place 2 in. apart on parchment-lined baking sheets, point side down. Cover; let rise in a warm place until doubled, about 45 minutes.

5. Preheat oven to 375°. Bake until golden brown, 9-11 minutes. Remove from pans to wire racks; serve warm.

Freeze option: Immediately after shaping, freeze rolls on parchment-lined baking sheets until firm. Transfer to a freezer container; return to freezer. Freeze for up to 4 weeks. To use, let rise, increasing rise time to 2½-3 hours. Bake as directed.

Note: To make filled crescent rolls, sprinkle dough with filling of choice immediately after brushing with butter; shape and bake as directed.

1 unfilled roll: 104 cal., 4g fat (3g sat. fat), 28mg chol., 107mg sod., 14g carb. (3g sugars, 1g fiber), 2g pro.

Chive Crescents: Divide ⅔ cup minced fresh chives between 2 circles of dough.

Orange-Pecan Crescents: Toss 1 cup finely chopped pecans with ⅓ cup sugar and 4 tsp. grated orange zest; divide mixture between 2 circles.

Cranberry-Thyme Crescents: Toss 1 cup finely chopped dried cranberries with ⅔ cup finely chopped walnuts and 2 tsp. minced fresh thyme leaves; divide mixture between 2 circles.

PHILLY CHEESESTEAK SLIDERS

Here's a wonderful way to use leftover roast beef. Sliced roast beef from the deli also works.
—Debra Waggoner, Grand Island, NE

PREP: 20 min. + chilling • **BAKE:** 25 min.
MAKES: 2 dozen

- 2 large green peppers, sliced
- 1 large sweet onion, sliced
- 1 Tbsp. olive oil
- 2 pkg. (12 oz. each) Hawaiian sweet rolls
- 1½ lbs. sliced deli roast beef
- 12 slices provolone cheese
- ¾ cup butter
- 1½ tsp. dried minced onion
- 1½ tsp. Worcestershire sauce
- 1 tsp. garlic powder

1. In a large skillet, cook green peppers and onion in the oil over medium-high heat until tender, 8-10 minutes. Without separating rolls, cut each package in half horizontally; arrange bottom halves in a greased 13x9-in. baking pan. Layer with roast beef, pepper mixture and cheese; replace top halves of rolls.
2. In a small saucepan, melt butter; add dried onion, Worcestershire sauce and garlic powder. Drizzle over rolls. Cover and refrigerate 8 hours or overnight.
3. Preheat oven to 350°. Remove rolls from refrigerator 30 minutes before baking. Bake, uncovered, 15 minutes. Cover with foil; bake until cheese is melted, 10 minutes longer.
1 slider: 247 cal., 14g fat (8g sat. fat), 56mg chol., 413mg sod., 18g carb. (7g sugars, 1g fiber), 14g pro.

**PHILLY CHEESESTEAK
WONTON CUPS**

medium heat until heated through, about
5 minutes. Add sauteed onion and green
pepper. Place about 2 Tbsp. beef mixture
in each cup; sprinkle each with scant
1 Tbsp. cheese.

4. Bake the cups until heated through,
8-10 minutes. Serve immediately. If
desired, top with pepperoncini and
serve with steak sauce.

1 wonton: 66 cal., 2g fat (1g sat. fat),
12mg chol., 360mg sod., 6g carb.
(0 sugars, 0 fiber), 5g pro.

BAKED BEANS
WITH PINEAPPLE

This marvelous recipe is a staple at our
neighborhood's annual barbecue.
—*J. Hindson, Victoria, BC*

PREP: 25 min. • **BAKE:** 45 min.
MAKES: 30 servings

- 1 lb. bacon strips, diced
- 1 large onion, chopped
- 3 cans (two 55 oz., one 28 oz.)
  baked beans
- 2 cans (one 20 oz., one 8 oz.)
  crushed pineapple, drained
- ½ cup packed brown sugar
- ½ cup ketchup

1. In a large skillet, cook bacon over
medium heat until crisp. Remove with
a slotted spoon to paper towels. Drain
skillet, reserving 2 Tbsp. drippings.
Saute onion in drippings until tender.

2. In a very large bowl, combine beans,
pineapple, bacon and onion. Combine
brown sugar and ketchup; stir into the
bean mixture.

3. Transfer to 2 greased 3-qt. or 13x9-in.
baking dishes. Cover and bake at 350° for
20 minutes. Uncover; bake 25-35 minutes
longer or until bubbly and beans reach
desired thickness.

½ cup: 266 cal., 10g fat (3g sat. fat), 22mg
chol., 830mg sod., 37g carb. (18g sugars,
8g fiber), 12g pro.

PHILLY CHEESESTEAK
WONTON CUPS

I love the versatility of wonton wrappers.
You can fill them with any mix of flavors
or ingredients to suit your tastes. The first
batch of these cups I tried with a Mexican-
inspired filling, which was delicious. But
this fun version is a riff on the classic
Philly cheesesteak, which is one of my
favorite sandwiches.
—*Cyndy Gerken, Naples, FL*

PREP: 40 min. • **BAKE:** 10 min./batch
MAKES: 3 dozen

- 36 wonton wrappers
- 2 tsp. canola oil
- 1 large onion, chopped
- 1 medium green pepper, chopped
- 1 lb. sliced deli roast beef,
  cut into ¾-in. pieces
- ¼ cup Worcestershire sauce
- 3 tsp. Montreal steak seasoning
- ¼ tsp. pepper
- 2 cups shredded provolone cheese
  Optional: Chopped sliced
  pepperoncini and steak sauce

1. Preheat oven to 375°. Press wonton
wrappers in greased muffin cups. Bake
until golden brown, 4-5 minutes.

2. Meanwhile, in a skillet, heat the oil over
medium-high heat. Saute onion and green
pepper until tender, 3-5 minutes. Remove
from pan.

3. Toss beef with Worcestershire sauce,
steak seasoning and pepper. In the same
pan, cook and stir the beef mixture over

**BAKED BEANS
WITH PINEAPPLE**

**HOVER YOUR
CAMERA HERE**
How to Throw an
Epic Backyard
Party

HEARTY RICE DRESSING

This satisfying dressing has always been received well at church socials and family reunions. I cut back on the recipe if I'm serving a smaller group.
—*Ruth Hayward, Lake Charles, LA*

PREP: 25 min. • **BAKE:** 1 hour
MAKES: 50 servings

- 3 lbs. ground beef
- 2 lbs. ground pork
- 2 large onions, chopped
- 3 celery ribs, chopped
- 1 large green pepper, chopped
- 1 jar (4 oz.) diced pimientos, drained
- 5 cups water
- 2 cans (10¾ oz. each) condensed cream of chicken soup, undiluted
- 2 cans (10½ oz. each) condensed French onion soup
- 1 can (10¾ oz.) condensed cream of mushroom soup, undiluted
- 2 Tbsp. Creole seasoning
- 1 tsp. salt
- 1 tsp. pepper
- ½ tsp. cayenne pepper
- 4 cups uncooked long grain rice

1. Combine beef, pork and onions. Divide mixture evenly among several large Dutch ovens or stockpots. Cook over medium heat until meat is no longer pink, breaking it into crumbles; drain.
2. In a large bowl, combine the celery, green pepper and pimientos. Add water, soups and seasonings. Stir into the meat mixture, dividing vegetable-soup mixture evenly among the meat mixtures. Bring each to a boil; stir in rice.
3. Preheat the oven to 350°. Carefully transfer mixtures to 3 greased 13x9-in. baking dishes. Cover each and bake for 30 minutes; stir. Cover and bake for 30-40 minutes longer or until the rice is tender.

¾ cup: 153 cal., 6g fat (2g sat. fat), 26mg chol., 293mg sod., 14g carb. (1g sugars, 1g fiber), 10g pro.

CHIPPED BEEF CHEESE BALL

This delicious appetizer is near and dear to our family. It is a symbol of our family's Christmas and New Year's celebrations. My mom made it for more than 30 years.
—*Molly Sumner, Creve Coeur, MO*

PREP: 10 min. + chilling • **MAKES:** 2 cups

- 5 pkg. (2 oz. each) thinly sliced dried beef
- 12 oz. cream cheese, softened
- ⅓ cup finely chopped sweet onion
- 4 drops Worcestershire sauce
  Ritz crackers and assorted fresh vegetables

1. Place beef in a food processor; pulse until finely chopped. In a large bowl, beat cream cheese until smooth. Stir in ⅔ cup beef and the onion and Worcestershire sauce. Refrigerate, covered, at least 1 hour.
2. Place remaining beef in a small shallow bowl. Shape the cheese mixture into a ball; roll in the beef to coat evenly. Wrap and refrigerate at least 1 hour. Serve with crackers and vegetables.

1 Tbsp.: 47 cal., 4g fat (2g sat. fat), 16mg chol., 136mg sod., 1g carb. (0 sugars, 0 fiber), 2g pro.

HEARTY RICE DRESSING

CRANBERRY-ORANGE
VODKA SLUSH

CRANBERRY-ORANGE VODKA SLUSH

Years ago, my mother made a rosy
and refreshing party drink I've never
forgotten. The sparkle comes from fruit
juices, vodka and lemon-lime soda.
—*Melinda Strable, Ankeny, IA*

PREP: 15 min. + freezing
MAKES: 24 servings

- 9 cups water
- 2 cups sugar
- 1 can (12 oz.) frozen cranberry juice concentrate, partially thawed
- 1 can (12 oz.) frozen orange juice concentrate, partially thawed
- ¾ cup thawed lemonade concentrate
- 2 cups vodka
- 8 cups lemon-lime soda, chilled

1. In a 5-qt. bowl, mix water and sugar
until sugar is dissolved. Stir in the juice
and lemonade concentrates and the
vodka until blended. Transfer mixture to
freezer containers, allowing headspace
for expansion; freeze slush overnight.
2. To serve, place ⅔ cup slush in each
glass. Add ⅓ cup soda.
1 cup: 210 cal., 0 fat (0 sat. fat), 0 chol.,
10mg sod., 43g carb. (39g sugars,
0 fiber), 0 pro.

SOUR CREAM POUND CAKE

Because I'm our town's postmaster, I can bake only in my spare time. I especially enjoy making desserts such as this one. It tastes amazing as is, or tuck it under ice cream and chocolate syrup like a hot fudge sundae!
—*Karen Conrad, East Troy, WI*

PREP: 15 min. • **BAKE:** 1¼ hours + cooling
MAKES: 20 servings

- 1 cup butter, softened
- 3 cups sugar
- 6 large eggs, room temperature
- 3 cups all-purpose flour
- ¼ tsp. baking soda
- ¼ tsp. salt
- 1 cup sour cream
- 2 tsp. vanilla extract
  Confectioners' sugar, optional

1. In a bowl, cream the butter and sugar until light and fluffy, 5-7 minutes. Add the eggs, 1 at a time, beating well after each addition. Combine flour, baking soda and salt; add to creamed mixture alternately with sour cream and vanilla. Beat on low just until blended. Pour into a greased and floured 10-in. fluted tube pan.

2. Bake at 325° for 1¼-1½ hours or until a toothpick comes out clean. Cool in pan for 15 minutes before removing to a wire rack to cool completely. Sprinkle with confectioners' sugar if desired.

1 piece: 311 cal., 13g fat (7g sat. fat), 96mg chol., 163mg sod., 45g carb. (30g sugars, 1g fiber), 4g pro.

TEST KITCHEN TIP

Because traditional pound cake is typically a denser, buttery cake, all-purpose flour tends to do the best job. Cake flour produces a very light and tender crumb, which is lovely in many cakes but not quite right for pound cakes.

SOUR CREAM POUND CAKE

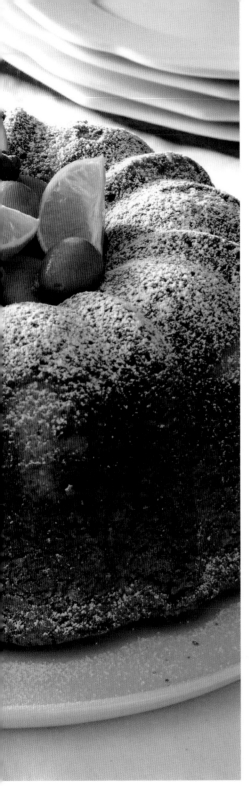

CHEESY SPAGHETTI BAKE

With the favorite ingredients of spaghetti and meat sauce, this recipe makes two hearty family-style casseroles. It's marvelous for entertaining or a potluck.
—*Sue Braunschweig, Delafield, WI*

PREP: 45 min. • **BAKE:** 40 min.
MAKES: 2 casseroles (12 servings each)

- 1 lb. uncooked spaghetti, broken into 3-in. pieces
- 4 lbs. ground beef
- 2 large onions, chopped
- 1 large green pepper, chopped
- 4 cups 2% milk
- 4 cans (10¾ oz. each) condensed tomato soup, undiluted
- 2 cans (10¾ oz. each) condensed cream of mushroom soup, undiluted
- 4 cups shredded sharp cheddar cheese, divided

1. Cook spaghetti according to package directions. Drain and place in 2 greased 13x9-in. baking dishes; set aside.
2. In each of 2 Dutch ovens or large stockpots, cook half the beef, onions and green pepper over medium heat until meat is no longer pink, breaking it into crumbles; drain. To each pot, add 2 cups milk, 2 cans tomato soup, 1 can mushroom soup and 1 cup cheese. Bring to a boil.
3. Spoon over spaghetti (spaghetti will absorb liquid during baking). Sprinkle with remaining cheese. Bake, uncovered, at 350° for 40-45 minutes or until bubbly and top is lightly browned.
1 serving: 305 cal., 14g fat (8g sat. fat), 63mg chol., 349mg sod., 21g carb. (5g sugars, 1g fiber), 22g pro.

PUNCH DELIGHT

When we celebrated my mother's 75th birthday, we wanted a punch everyone could enjoy. This delightful combination of lemonades, juice and soda was perfect and so easy to make. Our guests loved it.
—*Barbara Koehnke, Fremont, WI*

TAKES: 10 min.
MAKES: 20 servings (5 qt.)

- 1 can (12 oz.) frozen orange juice concentrate, thawed
- 1 can (12 oz.) frozen lemonade concentrate, thawed
- 1 can (12 oz.) frozen pink lemonade concentrate, thawed
- 2 liters Mello Yello soda, chilled
- 2 liters 50/50 or lemon-lime soda, chilled
  Ice cubes

In a large punch bowl, combine the 3 concentrates. Gradually stir in sodas. Add ice.
1 cup: 172 cal., 0 fat (0 sat. fat), 0 chol., 25mg sod., 44g carb. (42g sugars, 0 fiber), 1g pro.

TEST KITCHEN TIP
For best results, allow the concentrates to thaw overnight in the refrigerator.

ALWAYS-TENDER ROASTED TURKEY

HOVER YOUR CAMERA HERE
Your Holiday Handbook for Hosting Thanksgiving

ALWAYS-TENDER ROASTED TURKEY

For years I prepared my Thanksgiving turkey only to have it turn out dry. That's when I decided to try this recipe. Baking the bird in an oven bag keeps it moist and tender—and there's no basting involved.
—*Shirley Bedzis, San Diego, CA*

PREP: 30 min. • **BAKE:** 3 hours + standing
MAKES: 24 servings

- ¼ cup butter, softened
- 6 garlic cloves, minced
- 1 turkey (22 to 24 lbs.)
- 2 tsp. salt
- 2 tsp. pepper
- 1 Tbsp. all-purpose flour
- 1 turkey-size oven roasting bag
- 4 celery ribs, coarsely chopped
- 2 medium onions, sliced

1. In a small bowl, combine butter and garlic. Pat turkey dry. Carefully loosen skin of turkey; rub butter mixture under the skin. Sprinkle salt and pepper over skin of turkey and inside cavity. Skewer turkey openings; tie drumsticks together.
2. Place the flour in oven bag and shake to coat. Place oven bag in a roasting pan; add celery and onions. Place the turkey, breast side up, over vegetables. Cut six ½-in. slits in top of bag; close bag with tie provided.
3. Bake at 350° for 3-3½ hours or until a thermometer reads 180°. Let stand for 15 minutes before carving. Skim fat and thicken drippings if desired.
To make ahead: If preparing turkey the day before, pour drippings into a measuring cup; skim fat. Arrange turkey slices in an ungreased shallow roasting pan; pour drippings over turkey. Cool completely. Cover and refrigerate overnight. The next day, bake turkey at 350° for 45-65 minutes or until heated through.
8 oz. cooked turkey: 512 cal., 24g fat (8g sat. fat), 230mg chol., 375mg sod., 2g carb. (1g sugars, 0 fiber), 67g pro.

SOUR CREAM FAN ROLLS

I received this recipe from an email pen pal in Canada. The dough is so easy to work with, and it makes the lightest yeast rolls. I haven't used another white bread recipe since I started making this one.
—*Carrie Ormsby, West Jordan, UT*

PREP: 30 min. + rising
BAKE: 20 min./batch • **MAKES:** 2½ dozen

- 7 to 8 cups all-purpose flour
- ½ cup sugar
- 2 Tbsp. active dry yeast
- 1½ tsp. salt
- ¼ tsp. baking powder
- 2 cups sour cream
- 1 cup water
- 6 Tbsp. butter, cubed
- 2 large eggs, room temperature, lightly beaten

1. In a large bowl, combine 3½ cups flour, sugar, yeast, salt and baking powder. In a small saucepan, heat the sour cream, water and butter to 120°-130°; add to dry ingredients. Beat on medium speed for 2 minutes. Add eggs and ½ cup flour; beat 2 minutes longer. Stir in enough remaining flour to form a soft dough.
2. Turn onto a floured surface; knead until smooth and elastic, 6-8 minutes. Place in a greased bowl, turning once to grease top. Cover and let rise in a warm place until doubled, about 1 hour.
3. Punch dough down. Turn onto a lightly floured surface; divide in half. Roll each portion into a 23x9-in. rectangle. Cut into 1½-in. strips. Stack 5 strips together; cut into 1½-in. pieces and place cut side up in a greased muffin cup. Repeat with the remaining strips. Cover and let rise until doubled, about 20 minutes.
4. Bake at 350° for 20-25 minutes or until golden brown. Remove rolls from pans to wire racks.
1 roll: 182 cal., 6g fat (3g sat. fat), 31mg chol., 158mg sod., 27g carb. (5g sugars, 1g fiber), 4g pro.

SOUR CREAM
FAN ROLLS

GREAT-GRANDMA'S OATMEAL COOKIES

This yummy cookie—a favorite of my husband's—goes back to my great-grandmother. At Christmastime, we use colored sugar for a festive touch.
—*Mary Ann Konechne, Kimball, SD*

PREP: 35 min. • **BAKE:** 15 min./batch
MAKES: 12 dozen

- 1½ cups shortening
- 2 cups sugar
- 4 large eggs, room temperature
- 4 tsp. water
- 4 cups all-purpose flour
- 2 tsp. baking soda
- 2 tsp. ground cinnamon
- ½ tsp. salt
- 4 cups quick-cooking oats
- 2 cups chopped raisins
- 1 cup chopped walnuts
   Additional sugar or colored sugar

1. Preheat the oven to 350°. Cream the shortening and sugar until light and fluffy, 5-7 minutes. Add eggs, 1 at a time, beating well after each addition. Beat in water. In another bowl, whisk together flour, baking soda, cinnamon and salt; add to creamed mixture and mix well. Stir in oats, raisins and walnuts.

2. On a surface sprinkled with additional sugar, roll dough to ¼-in. thickness. Cut with a floured 2½-in. cookie cutter into desired shapes. Place 2 in. apart on greased baking sheets. Bake until set, 12-15 minutes. Remove cookies to wire racks to cool.

1 cookie: 63 cal., 3g fat (1g sat. fat), 5mg chol., 28mg sod., 9g carb. (4g sugars, 0 fiber), 1g pro.

TEST KITCHEN TIP

If you want to add a sweet icing to these cookies, mix 1 cup confectioners' sugar with ¼ tsp. cinnamon and 5-6 tsp. water to make a quick glaze.

GREAT-GRANDMA'S OATMEAL COOKIES

 MAKE-AHEAD MEATBALLS
My husband and I have company often. Keeping a supply of these frozen meatballs on hand means I can easily prepare a quick, satisfying meal. I start with a versatile meatball mix that makes about 12 dozen meatballs, then freeze them in batches for future use.
—*Ruth Andrewson, Leavenworth, WA*

PREP: 30 min. • **BAKE:** 10 min.
MAKES: 5 batches
(about 30 meatballs per batch)

- 4 large eggs, lightly beaten
- 2 cups dry bread crumbs
- ½ cup finely chopped onion
- 1 Tbsp. salt
- 2 tsp. Worcestershire sauce
- ½ tsp. white pepper
- 4 lbs. lean ground beef (90% lean)

1. Preheat oven to 400°. In a large bowl, combine the first 6 ingredients. Crumble beef over mixture and mix well. Shape into 1-in. balls, about 12 dozen.
2. Place meatballs on greased racks in shallow baking pans. Bake 10-15 minutes or until no longer pink, turning often; drain. Cool.
Freeze option: Freeze cooled meatballs in freezer containers. To use, partially thaw in refrigerator overnight. Reheat on a greased 15x10x1-in. baking pan in a preheated 350° oven until heated through.
5 meatballs: 134 cal., 6g fat (2g sat. fat), 62mg chol., 334mg sod., 6g carb. (1g sugars, 0 fiber), 14g pro. **Diabetic exchanges:** 2 lean meat, ½ starch.

BACON-CHEDDAR POTATO CROQUETTES

 BACON-CHEDDAR POTATO CROQUETTES
Instead of throwing out leftover mashed potatoes, use them to make croquettes. The little baked balls are yummy with ranch dressing, barbecue sauce or Dijon mayonnaise for dipping.
—*Pamela Shank, Parkersburg, WV*

PREP: 20 min. + chilling • **BAKE:** 20 min.
MAKES: about 5 dozen

- 4 cups cold mashed potatoes (with added milk and butter)
- 6 bacon strips, cooked and crumbled
- ½ cup shredded cheddar cheese
- 2 large eggs, lightly beaten
- ¼ cup sour cream
- 1 Tbsp. minced chives
- ½ tsp. salt
- ¼ tsp. pepper
- 40 Ritz crackers, crushed
- ¼ cup butter, melted
- 1 tsp. paprika
  Barbecue sauce, Dijon-mayonnaise blend or ranch salad dressing

1. In a large bowl, combine the first 8 ingredients. Shape potato mixture by tablespoonfuls into balls. Roll in cracker crumbs. Place on parchment-lined baking sheets. Cover and refrigerate for 2 hours or overnight.
2. Combine butter and paprika; drizzle over croquettes. Bake at 375° until golden brown, 18-20 minutes. Serve with dipping sauce of your choice.
Freeze option: Prepare croquettes as directed, omitting chilling step. Transfer to waxed paper-lined baking sheets. Prepare the butter mixture; drizzle over croquettes. Cover and freeze until firm. Transfer to freezer containers; return to the freezer. To use, bake the croquettes as directed, increasing time to 20-25 minutes. Serve with dipping sauce.
1 appetizer: 46 cal., 3g fat (1g sat. fat), 12mg chol., 112mg sod., 4g carb. (0 sugars, 0 fiber), 1g pro.

CALIFORNIA ROLLS

These taste as good as any restaurant or store-bought California rolls. Plus, this is one of the easiest sushi recipes to make! For the best results, use sushi rice to ensure the right sticky consistency.
—Taste of Home *Test Kitchen*

PREP: 1 hour + standing
MAKES: 64 pieces

2 cups sushi rice, rinsed and drained
2 cups water
¼ cup rice vinegar
2 Tbsp. sugar
½ tsp. salt
2 Tbsp. sesame seeds, toasted
2 Tbsp. black sesame seeds
   Bamboo sushi mat
8 nori sheets
1 small cucumber,
   seeded and julienned
3 oz. imitation crabmeat sticks,
   julienned
1 medium ripe avocado,
   peeled and julienned
   Optional: Reduced-sodium
   soy sauce, prepared wasabi
   and pickled ginger slices

1. In a large saucepan, combine rice and water; let stand for 30 minutes. Bring to a boil. Reduce heat to low; cover and simmer for 15-20 minutes or until the water is absorbed and the rice is tender. Remove from heat. Let stand, covered, for 10 minutes.

2. Meanwhile, in a small bowl, combine the vinegar, sugar and salt, stirring until sugar is dissolved.

3. Transfer rice to a large shallow bowl; drizzle with the vinegar mixture. With a wooden paddle or spoon, stir rice with a slicing motion to cool slightly. Cover with a damp cloth to keep moist. (Rice mixture may be made up to 2 hours ahead and stored at room temperature, covered with a damp towel. Do not refrigerate.)

4. Sprinkle toasted and black sesame seeds onto a plate; set aside. Place sushi mat on a work surface so mat rolls away from you; line with plastic wrap. Place ¾ cup rice on plastic. With moistened fingers, press rice into an 8-in. square. Top with 1 nori sheet.

5. Arrange a small amount of cucumber, crab and avocado about 1½ in. from bottom edge of nori sheet. Roll up rice mixture over filling, using bamboo mat to lift and compress the mixture while rolling; remove plastic wrap as you roll.

6. Remove mat; roll sushi rolls in sesame seeds. Cover with plastic wrap. Repeat with remaining ingredients to make 8 rolls. Cut each into 8 pieces. Serve with soy sauce, wasabi and ginger slices if desired.

1 piece: 35 cal., 1g fat (0 sat. fat), 0 chol., 30mg sod., 6g carb. (1g sugars, 1g fiber), 1g pro. **Diabetic exchanges:** ½ starch.

TURKEY, GOUDA & APPLE TEA SANDWICHES

 TURKEY, GOUDA & APPLE TEA SANDWICHES

These fun mini sandwiches are a tasty addition to any function. The cranberry mayo lends a unique flavor twist, and the apples add a nice crunch. These sammies will be the life of the party!
—Taste of Home *Test Kitchen*

TAKES: 25 min. • **MAKES:** 4 dozen

- ⅔ cup reduced-fat mayonnaise
- 2 Tbsp. whole-berry cranberry sauce
- 24 very thin slices wheat or white bread, crusts removed
- 12 slices deli turkey
- 2 medium apples, thinly sliced
- 12 thin slices smoked Gouda cheese
- 4 cups fresh baby spinach

1. Place the mayonnaise and cranberry sauce in a small food processor. Cover and process until blended. Spread over each bread slice.

2. Layer the turkey, apples, cheese and spinach over each of 12 bread slices; top with remaining bread. Cut each sandwich into quarters.

To make ahead: Cranberry spread can be prepared a day in advance; cover and store in the refrigerator.

1 tea sandwich: 59 cal., 3g fat (1g sat. fat), 8mg chol., 150mg sod., 5g carb. (1g sugars, 0 fiber), 3g pro.

APPLESAUCE
MUFFINS

BAKED HAM WITH PINEAPPLE

I first learned the technique for cooking ham with pineapple for a themed dinner my husband and I hosted. Since it is widely known as the symbol of hospitality, pineapple was the star ingredient on our menu and on this lovely baked ham.
—*JoAnn Fox, Johnson City, TN*

PREP: 15 min. • **BAKE:** 2 hours
MAKES: 20 servings

1 fully cooked bone-in ham (6 to 8 lbs.)
   Whole cloves
1 can (20 oz.) sliced pineapple
½ cup packed brown sugar
12 maraschino cherries

1. Place ham in a roasting pan. Score the surface with shallow diagonal cuts, making diamond shapes; insert cloves into diamonds. Cover and bake at 325° for 1½ hours. Drain pineapple, reserving ¼ cup juice. Combine brown sugar and reserved pineapple juice; pour over ham. Arrange pineapple and cherries on ham.
2. Bake, uncovered, until a thermometer reads 140° and ham is heated through, 30-45 minutes longer.
3 oz. cooked ham: 219 cal., 13g fat (5g sat. fat), 48mg chol., 924mg sod., 8g carb. (8g sugars, 0 fiber), 17g pro.

TEST KITCHEN TIP

Dark brown sugar contains more molasses than light or golden brown sugar. The types are generally interchangeable in recipes. But if you prefer a bolder flavor, choose dark brown sugar.

APPLESAUCE MUFFINS

These are such a popular item at the restaurant I own that I had the recipe printed on a card to share with guests.
—*Linda Williams, LaFayette, AL*

PREP: 10 min. • **BAKE:** 20 min.
MAKES: about 2 dozen

1 cup butter, softened
2 cups sugar
2 large eggs, room temperature
1 tsp. vanilla extract
2 cups applesauce
4 cups all-purpose flour
1 tsp. baking soda
1 tsp. ground cinnamon
1 tsp. ground allspice
¼ tsp. ground cloves
1 cup chopped walnuts, optional
   Cinnamon sugar, optional

1. Preheat oven to 350°. In a bowl, cream butter and sugar until light and fluffy, 5-7 minutes. Beat in eggs and vanilla. Stir in applesauce. Combine flour, baking soda and spices; stir into the creamed mixture. If desired, fold in nuts.
2. Fill greased or paper-lined muffin cups three-fourths full. Bake until a toothpick comes out clean, 20-25 minutes. Cool for 5 minutes before removing muffins from pans to wire racks. If desired, sprinkle with cinnamon sugar.
1 muffin: 224 cal., 8g fat (5g sat. fat), 36mg chol., 120mg sod., 35g carb. (19g sugars, 1g fiber), 3g pro. **Diabetic exchanges:** 2 starch, 1½ fat.

BAKED HAM WITH PINEAPPLE

CHEESECAKE POPS

The possibilities are endless with these cheesecake bites. Customize them for any occasion by using different toppings.
—*Evelyn Moore, Elk Grove, CA*

PREP: 2 hours + freezing
MAKES: 45 cheesecake pops

- 3 pkg. (8 oz. each) cream cheese, softened
- 1 cup sugar
- 1 cup sour cream
- 1 tsp. vanilla extract
- 3 large eggs, room temperature, lightly beaten
- 1 cup graham cracker crumbs
- 45 lollipop sticks (4 in. long)
- 3 pkg. (10 to 12 oz. each) white baking chips
- 3 Tbsp. shortening
  Toppings: Grated coconut, grated chocolate and assorted sprinkles

1. Line the bottom of a 9-in. springform pan with parchment; coat paper and side of pan with cooking spray.
2. In a large bowl, beat cream cheese and sugar until smooth. Beat in sour cream and vanilla until blended. Add eggs; beat on low speed just until combined. Pour into prepared pan.
3. Place pan on a baking sheet. Bake at 350° until the center is almost set, 45-50 minutes. Cool on a wire rack for 10 minutes. Carefully run a knife around edge of pan to loosen; cool 1 hour longer. Cover and freeze overnight.
4. Remove from the freezer and let stand for 30 minutes. Place cracker crumbs in a shallow bowl. Working quickly, scoop out 1-in. balls of cheesecake; roll each in cracker crumbs and insert a lollipop stick. Place on waxed paper-lined baking sheets. Freeze for 1 hour or until firm.
5. In a microwave, melt white chips and shortening at 70% power; stir until smooth. Place toppings in shallow bowls. Dip cheesecake pops in the white chip mixture; allow excess to drip off. Roll in toppings. Place on waxed paper; let stand until set. Store in the refrigerator.

1 cake pop: 203 cal., 14g fat (8g sat. fat), 37mg chol., 80mg sod., 18g carb. (16g sugars, 0 fiber), 3g pro.

CHEESECAKE POPS

MINI BARBECUED HAM SANDWICHES

These flavorful sandwiches make a perfect mini snack or appetizer. Your guests won't be able to eat just one!
—*Susanne Roupe, East Fairfield, VT*

TAKES: 20 min. • **MAKES:** 2 dozen

- 1 cup chili sauce
- ½ cup water
- 2 Tbsp. sugar
- 2 Tbsp. cider vinegar
- 1 Tbsp. Worcestershire sauce
- 1 tsp. onion powder
- 1 lb. fully cooked ham, very thinly sliced
- 24 dinner rolls, split

In a large saucepan, combine the first 6 ingredients. Bring to a boil. Reduce heat; simmer, uncovered, 6-8 minutes or until slightly thickened. Stir in ham; heat through. Serve on rolls.

1 serving: 143 cal., 3g fat (1g sat. fat), 24mg chol., 513mg sod., 23g carb. (5g sugars, 1g fiber), 7g pro.

SUPER SAUSAGE DIP

SUPER SAUSAGE DIP

I love spicy food, but I married a man who grew up in Tennessee and did not share my love of Mexican-style food. When we moved to the Southwest, he decided to give it a chance. Now he likes foods hotter than I can handle!
—*Kaye Christiansen, Freistatt, MO*

PREP: 15 min. • **COOK:** 35 min.
MAKES: 5 cups

- 1 lb. bulk pork sausage
- 1 small onion, chopped
- ½ cup chopped green pepper
- 3 medium tomatoes, chopped
- 1 can (4 oz.) chopped green chiles
- 1 pkg. (8 oz.) cream cheese, cubed
- 2 cups sour cream
  Green onions, optional
  Tortilla chips

1. In a large skillet, cook sausage, onion and green pepper over medium heat until meat is no longer pink, 5-7 minutes, breaking sausage into crumbles; drain.
2. Stir in tomatoes and chiles. Bring to a boil. Reduce heat; simmer, uncovered, 30 minutes, stirring occasionally.
3. Add cream cheese; stir until melted. Stir in sour cream; heat through. (Do not boil.) Transfer to a fondue pot and keep warm. If desired, garnish with green onions. Serve with chips.
2 Tbsp.: 75 cal., 7g fat (3g sat. fat), 20mg chol., 103mg sod., 2g carb. (1g sugars, 0 fiber), 2g pro.

TEST KITCHEN TIP

If you don't have a fondue pot, keep this sausage dip warm in a slow cooker set to low heat (or on the warm setting) so you don't overcook or dry out the dip too much. Make sure to stir the dip occasionally.

CREAMY BUFFALO CHICKEN DIP

This slightly spicy dip cleverly captures the flavor of Buffalo chicken wings. Using canned chicken eases preparation.
—Allyson DiLascio, Saltsburg, PA

TAKES: 30 min. • **MAKES:** 5 cups

- 1 pkg. (8 oz.) cream cheese, softened
- 1 cup Louisiana-style hot sauce
- 1 cup ranch salad dressing
- 3 cans (4½ oz. each) chunk white chicken, drained and shredded
- 1 cup shredded cheddar cheese
  Thinly sliced green onions, optional
  Corn or tortilla chips
  Celery sticks

1. In a small bowl, combine the cream cheese, hot sauce and salad dressing. Stir in chicken.
2. Spread into an ungreased 11x7-in. baking dish. Sprinkle with cheddar cheese. Bake, uncovered, at 350° for 20-22 minutes or until heated through. If desired, sprinkle with green onions. Serve with chips and celery sticks.

2 Tbsp.: 69 cal., 6g fat (2g sat. fat), 15mg chol., 156mg sod., 1g carb. (0 sugars, 0 fiber), 3g pro.

READER RAVES

"I've been making this recipe for years and it's alway a crowd pleaser. I use pepper jack cheese for a little extra kick."

—ASH CRIMMINS, TASTEOFHOME.COM

CREAMY BUFFALO CHICKEN DIP

 MA
ITALIAN PASTA SAUCE

When my daughter got married, her husband made a batch of this sauce for their wedding. His grandma brought the recipe from Italy nearly 100 years ago.
—*Judy Braun, Juneau, WI*

PREP: 25 min. • **COOK:** 2 hours
MAKES: 20 servings

- 4 lbs. ground beef
- 1 lb. bulk Italian sausage
- 1 large onion, finely chopped
- 3 celery ribs, finely chopped
- 4 garlic cloves, minced
- 2 Tbsp. olive oil
- 3 cans (28 oz. each) crushed tomatoes in puree
- 3 cans (6 oz. each) tomato paste
- 3 cups chicken or beef broth
- 1 lb. fresh mushrooms, sliced
- ¾ cup minced fresh parsley
- 1 Tbsp. sugar
- 2 to 3 tsp. salt
- ½ tsp. pepper
- ½ tsp. ground allspice, optional
  Hot cooked pasta

1. In a Dutch oven or soup kettle, cook and crumble beef in 2 batches over medium heat until no longer pink; drain and set aside. Cook and crumble sausage over medium heat until no longer pink; drain and set aside. In same pan, saute the onion, celery and garlic in oil until the vegetables are tender.
2. Return beef and sausage to the pan. Add next 9 ingredients, including allspice if desired, and bring to a boil. Reduce heat; cover and simmer until the sauce reaches desired thickness, stirring occasionally, 2-3 hours. Serve over pasta.
Freeze option: Freeze cooled sauce in freezer containers. To use, partially thaw in the refrigerator overnight. Heat through in a saucepan, stirring occasionally. Add a little broth or water if necessary.
1 cup: 284 cal., 15g fat (5g sat. fat), 57mg chol., 821mg sod., 16g carb. (9g sugars, 3g fiber), 23g pro.

SMOKED-ALMOND CHEESE TOASTS

I created my recipe for appetizer toasts while planning the menu for a friend's bridal luncheon. Smoked almonds add a special touch to the chunky spread.
—*Laura Stricklin, Jackson, MS*

TAKES: 30 min. • **MAKES:** 3 dozen

- ¾ cup whipped cream cheese, softened
- 2 Tbsp. 2% milk
- 1 cup shredded sharp cheddar cheese
- 1 cup shredded Swiss cheese
- ¾ cup chopped smoked almonds
- ½ cup soft sun-dried tomato halves (not packed in oil), chopped
- ⅛ tsp. pepper
- 1 French bread baguette (10½ oz.), cut into ¼-in. slices
  Chopped fresh chives, optional

1. Preheat oven to 350°. In a large bowl, beat cream cheese and milk until smooth. Stir in the cheeses, almonds, tomato and pepper; spread over bread slices.
2. Place on ungreased baking sheets. Bake until cheese is melted, 10-12 minutes. If desired, top with chopped fresh chives.
1 appetizer: 81 cal., 5g fat (2g sat. fat), 9mg chol., 103mg sod., 6g carb. (1g sugars, 1g fiber), 3g pro.

JOLLY JELLY DOUGHNUTS

with jelly. Fill each doughnut with about 1 tsp. jelly. Carefully roll warm doughnuts in sugar. Serve warm.

1 doughnut: 185 cal., 5g fat (1g sat. fat), 36mg chol., 125mg sod., 31g carb. (9g sugars, 1g fiber), 4g pro.

POLYNESIAN MEATBALLS

With pretty bits of pineapple, these meatballs are sure to attract attention—and the sweet-tart sauce brings people back for seconds.
—*Carol Wakley, North East, PA*

PREP: 30 min. • **COOK:** 15 min.
MAKES: 6 dozen

- 1   can (5 oz.) evaporated milk
- ⅓   cup chopped onion
- ⅔   cup crushed saltines
- 1   tsp. seasoned salt
- 1½   lbs. lean ground beef
SAUCE
- 1   can (20 oz.) pineapple tidbits
- 2   Tbsp. cornstarch
- ½   cup cider vinegar
- 2   Tbsp. soy sauce
- 2   Tbsp. lemon juice
- ½   cup packed brown sugar

1. In a bowl, combine the milk, onion, saltines and seasoned salt. Crumble beef over mixture and mix lightly but thoroughly. With wet hands, shape into 1-in. balls. In a large skillet over medium heat, brown meatballs in small batches, turning often. Remove with a slotted spoon and keep warm. Drain skillet.
2. Drain pineapple, reserving juice; set the pineapple aside. Add enough water to juice to measure 1 cup. In a bowl, combine the cornstarch, pineapple juice mixture, vinegar, soy sauce, lemon juice and brown sugar until smooth. Add to skillet. Bring to a boil; cook and stir until thickened, about 2 minutes. Add meatballs. Reduce heat; cover and simmer for 15 minutes. Add the pineapple; heat through.

1 meatball: 37 cal., 1g fat (1g sat. fat), 9mg chol., 61mg sod., 4g carb. (3g sugars, 0 fiber), 3g pro.

JOLLY JELLY DOUGHNUTS

Plump and filled with jelly, these sugar-coated doughnuts will disappear as fast as you can churn them out.
—*Lee Bremson, Kansas City, MO*

PREP: 25 min. + rising • **COOK:** 30 min.
MAKES: 2½ dozen

- 2   pkg. (¼ oz. each) active dry yeast
- 2   cups warm 2% milk (110° to 115°)
- 7   cups all-purpose flour
- 4   large egg yolks, room temperature
- 1   large egg, room temperature
- ½   cup sugar
- 1   tsp. salt
- 2   tsp. grated lemon zest
- ½   tsp. vanilla extract
- ½   cup butter, melted
      Oil for deep-fat frying
      Red jelly of your choice
      Additional sugar

1. In a large bowl, dissolve yeast in warm milk. Add 2 cups flour; mix well. Let stand in a warm place for 30 minutes. Add the egg yolks, egg, sugar, salt, lemon zest and vanilla; mix well. Beat in the butter and remaining flour. Do not knead. Cover and let rise in a warm place until doubled, about 45 minutes.
2. Punch dough down. On a lightly floured surface, roll out to ½-in. thickness. Cut with a 2½-in. biscuit cutter. Place cutouts on lightly greased baking sheets. Cover and let rise until nearly doubled, about 35 minutes.
3. In a deep-fat fryer or electric skillet, heat oil to 375°. Fry doughnuts, a few at a time, for 1½-2 minutes on each side or until browned. Drain on paper towels.
4. Cool 2-3 minutes; cut a small slit with a sharp knife on 1 side of each doughnut. Cut a small hole in the corner of a pastry bag; insert a very small round tip. Fill bag

POLYNESIAN MEATBALLS

HOVER YOUR CAMERA HERE

4 Secrets to Having the Best Dish at Your Potluck

MINI SWEET POTATO PIES

My son Levi was only 2 years old when he helped me create this delicious recipe, and it was the first time he told me I love you! I'll always remember making these with him.

—*Emily Butler, South Williamsport, PA*

PREP: 45 min.
BAKE: 20 min. + cooling • **MAKES:** 2 dozen

- 2 large sweet potatoes, peeled and cut into ¾-in. cubes
- 2 sheets refrigerated pie crust
- ¼ cup all-purpose flour
- 3 Tbsp. cold unsalted butter, cubed
- 1 cup packed brown sugar, divided

1. Preheat oven to 400°. Place sweet potatoes in a greased 15x10x1-in. baking pan; bake until tender, 35-40 minutes.
2. Meanwhile, on a work surface, unroll 1 crust. Using a 2½-in. round cutter, cut out 12 circles. Press circles onto bottoms and up sides of 12 nonstick mini muffin cups. Repeat with second crust. Chill until filling is ready.
3. In a food processor, pulse flour, butter and ¼ cup brown sugar until crumbly; set aside for topping. Add baked sweet potatoes and remaining ¾ cup brown sugar to food processor; pulse until almost smooth. Fill crust-lined cups three-fourths full. Sprinkle with topping.
4. Decrease the oven setting to 325°. Bake until the crusts are golden brown, 20-24 minutes. Cool 5-10 minutes before removing from pan to a wire rack.
1 mini pie: 156 cal., 6g fat (3g sat. fat), 7mg chol., 67mg sod., 25g carb. (12g sugars, 1g fiber), 1g pro.

MINI SWEET POTATO PIES

SMOKED BRISKET

sheet. Cover and refrigerate overnight or up to 2 days. Meanwhile, in a small saucepan, combine the mop sauce ingredients. Simmer 15 minutes, stirring occasionally. Refrigerate sauce until ready to grill.

2. Soak hickory and mesquite chips or pellets; add to smoker according to the manufacturer's directions. Heat to 225°. Uncover brisket. Place brisket in smoker fat side up; smoke 2 hours. Brush brisket generously with mop sauce; turn meat. Smoke 2 more hours; brush generously with mop sauce again. Wrap brisket securely in heavy-duty aluminum foil; smoke until a thermometer inserted in beef reads 190°, 4-5 more hours.

3. Let beef stand 20-30 minutes before slicing; cut diagonally across the grain into thin slices.

Note: This is a fresh beef brisket, not corned beef.

4 oz. cooked beef: 252 cal., 11g fat (3g sat. fat), 68mg chol., 472mg sod., 2g carb. (0 sugars, 1g fiber), 33g pro.
Diabetic exchanges: 4 lean meat.

TEST KITCHEN TIP

Brisket can become tough and chewy if it's not cooked properly. It is important to cook it low and slow at 225° for the entire process. Trying to speed it up will only cause the meat to seize up and become tough. Finishing it for the last few hours in a covered foil pan with liquid will also help ensure the beef turns out tender.

SMOKED BRISKET

This is always a crowd favorite—it truly melts in your mouth!
—*Jodi Abel, La Jolla, CA*

PREP: 20 min. + marinating
GRILL: 8 hours + standing
MAKES: 20 servings

- 2 Tbsp. olive oil
- 1 fresh beef brisket (7 to 8 lbs.)

RUB
- 2 Tbsp. garlic powder
- 2 Tbsp. onion powder
- 2 Tbsp. chili powder
- 1 Tbsp. ground mustard
- 1 Tbsp. ground cumin
- 1 Tbsp. paprika
- 1 Tbsp. smoked sea salt

MOP SAUCE
- 2 cups beef broth
- ¼ cup olive oil
- 2 Tbsp. Worcestershire sauce
- 2 Tbsp. hickory-flavored liquid smoke

1. Brush olive oil over brisket. Combine rub ingredients; rub over both sides of beef. Place brisket on a rimmed baking

FESTIVE MEAT LOAF PINWHEEL

Dress up basic meat loaf for a special occasion dinner when company is visiting. This crowd-sized pinwheel features deli ham, Swiss cheese and a homemade tomato sauce.
—Vera Sullivan, Amity, OR

PREP: 20 min. • **BAKE:** 1¼ hours
MAKES: 20 servings

- 3 large eggs
- 1 cup dry bread crumbs
- ½ cup finely chopped onion
- ½ cup finely chopped green pepper
- ¼ cup ketchup
- 2 tsp. minced fresh parsley
- 1 tsp. dried basil
- 1 tsp. dried oregano
- 1 garlic clove, minced
- 2 tsp. salt
- ½ tsp. pepper
- 5 lbs. lean ground beef (90% lean)
- ¾ lb. thinly sliced deli ham
- ¾ lb. thinly sliced Swiss cheese

TOMATO PEPPER SAUCE

- ½ cup finely chopped onion
- 2 celery ribs, chopped
- ½ cup chopped green pepper
- 1 garlic clove, minced
- 1 to 2 tsp. olive oil
- 2 cups chopped fresh tomatoes
- 1 cup beef broth
- 1 bay leaf
- 1 tsp. sugar
- ¼ tsp. salt
- ¼ tsp. dried thyme
- 1 Tbsp. cornstarch
- 2 Tbsp. cold water

1. Preheat oven to 350°. In a large bowl, combine the first 11 ingredients. Crumble beef over mixture and mix lightly but thoroughly. On a piece of heavy-duty foil, pat beef mixture into a 17x15-in. rectangle. Cover with ham and cheese slices to within ½ in. of edges.

2. Roll up tightly jelly-roll style, starting with a short side. Place seam side down in a roasting pan. Bake, uncovered, until a thermometer reads 160°, 1¼-1½ hours.

3. In a large saucepan, saute the onion, celery, green pepper and garlic in oil until tender, 3-5 minutes. Add tomatoes, broth, bay leaf, sugar, salt and thyme. Simmer, uncovered, for 30 minutes. Discard the bay leaf.

4. Combine cornstarch and water until smooth; stir into tomato sauce. Bring to a boil; cook and stir until thickened, about 2 minutes. Drain meat loaf. Serve meat loaf with sauce.

1 piece: 319 cal., 17g fat (7g sat. fat), 124mg chol., 732mg sod., 8g carb. (2g sugars, 1g fiber), 32g pro.

SICILIAN
POTATO SALAD

SICILIAN POTATO SALAD

Fresh basil is the star of this mayo-free, Italian-inspired take on potato salad.
—*Susan Falk, Sterling Heights, MI*

PREP: 20 min. • **COOK:** 20 min.
MAKES: 26 servings

- 10 small russet potatoes, unpeeled
- 1½ tsp. salt, divided
- ½ lb. fresh green beans, cut into 1½-in. pieces
- ¼ tsp. pepper
- 2 medium cucumbers, halved lengthwise and cut into ¼-in. slices
- ½ lb. cherry tomatoes, halved
- 1 large red onion, halved and thinly sliced
- 1 cup thinly sliced fresh basil leaves, divided
- ½ cup olive oil
- 4 Tbsp. cider vinegar
- 3 garlic cloves, minced

1. Place the potatoes and ½ tsp. salt in a Dutch oven; add water to cover. Bring to a boil. Reduce heat; cook, uncovered, until tender, 12-15 minutes. Drain; rinse with cold water. Pat dry.
2. Meanwhile, in a small saucepan, bring 1 cup water to a boil. Add beans; cook, uncovered, just until crisp-tender, 3-4 minutes. Drain; immediately drop into ice water. Drain and pat dry.
3. Peel and cube potatoes; sprinkle with remaining salt and the pepper. Transfer to a serving bowl. Add beans, cucumbers, tomatoes, onion and ¾ cup basil leaves. Whisk together the oil, vinegar and garlic. Drizzle over the vegetables; toss to coat. Sprinkle with remaining basil.
¾ cup: 96 cal., 4g fat (1g sat. fat), 0 chol., 143mg sod., 13g carb. (2g sugars, 2g fiber), 2g pro. **Diabetic exchanges:** 1 starch, 1 fat.

CINNAMON-CANDY COOKIES

BACON-COLBY LASAGNA

My grandmother added bacon to her cheesy lasagna. I learned so much cooking by her side.
—*Cathy McCartney, Davenport, IA*

PREP: 30 min. • **BAKE:** 45 min. + standing
MAKES: 2 lasagnas (12 servings each)

- 24 uncooked lasagna noodles
- 2 lbs. lean ground beef (90% lean)
- 2 medium onions, chopped
- 1½ lbs. bacon strips, cooked and crumbled
- 2 cans (15 oz. each) tomato sauce
- 2 cans (14½ oz. each) diced tomatoes, undrained
- 2 Tbsp. sugar
- 1 tsp. salt
- 8 cups shredded Colby-Monterey Jack cheese

1. Preheat oven to 350°. Cook noodles according to package directions for al dente; drain.
2. In a 6-qt. stockpot, cook beef and onions over medium-high heat until beef is no longer pink, 10-12 minutes, breaking beef into crumbles; drain. Stir in the bacon, tomato sauce, tomatoes, sugar and salt; heat through.
3. Spread 1 cup tomato sauce into each of 2 greased 13x9-in. baking dishes. Layer each dish with 4 noodles, overlapping as needed, 1⅔ cups sauce and 1⅓ cups cheese. Repeat layers twice.
4. Bake, covered, 40 minutes. Uncover; bake until bubbly, 5-10 minutes longer. Let stand 15 minutes before serving.

Freeze option: Cool unbaked lasagnas; cover and freeze. To use, partially thaw in refrigerator overnight. Remove from refrigerator 30 minutes before baking. Preheat oven to 350°. Bake the lasagna as directed, increasing time as necessary to heat through and for a thermometer inserted in center to read 165°.

1 piece: 357 cal., 18g fat (11g sat. fat), 67mg chol., 744mg sod., 25g carb. (4g sugars, 2g fiber), 23g pro.

CINNAMON-CANDY COOKIES

These unique Christmas cookies were inspired by my brother's love of Red Hots. Their flavor packs a punch!
—*Wendy Rusch, Cameron, WI*

PREP: 20 min. + chilling
BAKE: 10 min./batch + cooling
MAKES: about 5 dozen

- ⅔ cup Red Hots
- 2⅓ cups all-purpose flour
- 1 cup butter, softened
- 1 cup sugar
- 1 tsp. vanilla extract

FROSTING
- 2 cups confectioners' sugar
- ½ cup butter, softened
- ½ tsp. vanilla or cinnamon extract
- ⅛ tsp. salt
- 4 to 6 Tbsp. 2% milk

1. Place Red Hots in a food processor; process until fine and powdery. Add flour; pulse to combine.
2. In a large bowl, cream butter and sugar until light and fluffy, 5-7 minutes. Beat in vanilla. Gradually beat in the flour mixture. Shape into two 8-in. rolls; wrap each roll in waxed paper. Refrigerate until firm, about 1 hour.
3. Preheat the oven to 350°. Unwrap and cut into ¼-in. slices. Place 2 in. apart on ungreased baking sheets. Bake cookies until edges are just lightly browned, 7-9 minutes. Cool cookies on pans for 2 minutes before removing to wire racks to cool completely.
4. For frosting, in a small bowl, beat confectioners' sugar, butter, extract, salt and enough milk to reach desired consistency. Decorate cookies as desired.

Freeze option: Place wrapped logs in a freezer container; freeze. To use, unwrap frozen dough logs and cut into slices. If necessary, let dough stand a few minutes at room temperature before cutting. Bake and decorate cookies as directed.

1 cookie: 98 cal., 5g fat (3g sat. fat), 12mg chol., 42mg sod., 14g carb. (9g sugars, 0 fiber), 1g pro.

DUO TATER BAKE

Cut down on holiday prep time with this creamy potato dish that combines sweet potatoes with regular spuds. I served this for Thanksgiving, and it was a winner with my family.
—*Joan McCulloch, Abbotsford, BC*

PREP: 40 min. • **BAKE:** 20 min.
MAKES: 2 casseroles (10 servings each)

4 lbs. russet or Yukon Gold potatoes, peeled and cubed
3 lbs. sweet potatoes, peeled and cubed
2 cartons (8 oz. each) spreadable chive and onion cream cheese, divided
1 cup sour cream, divided
¼ cup shredded Colby-Monterey Jack cheese
⅓ cup 2% milk
¼ cup shredded Parmesan cheese
½ tsp. salt
½ tsp. pepper

TOPPING
1 cup shredded Colby-Monterey Jack cheese
½ cup chopped green onions
¼ cup shredded Parmesan cheese

1. Place russet potatoes in a Dutch oven and cover with water. Bring to a boil. Reduce the heat; cover and cook until tender, 10-15 minutes.
2. Meanwhile, place sweet potatoes in a large saucepan; cover with water. Bring to a boil. Reduce heat; cover and cook until tender, 10-15 minutes. Drain; mash with half the cream cheese and sour cream, and the Colby-Monterey Jack cheese.
3. Drain russet potatoes; mash with the remaining cream cheese and sour cream. Stir in the milk, Parmesan cheese, salt and pepper.
4. Spread 1⅓ cups russet potato mixture into each of 2 greased 11x7-in. baking dishes. Layer each with 2 cups sweet potato mixture. Repeat layers. Spread with remaining russet potato mixture.
5. Bake, uncovered, at 350° until heated through, about 15 minutes. Combine the topping ingredients; sprinkle over casseroles. Bake until cheese is melted, 2-3 minutes longer.

¾ cup: 236 cal., 12g fat (8g sat. fat), 38mg chol., 246mg sod., 25g carb. (7g sugars, 2g fiber), 5g pro.

DUO TATER BAKE

EASY MACARONI SALAD

EASY MACARONI SALAD

This hearty pasta salad is sure to please appetites of all ages—and it serves a lot of folks!
—*LaVerna Mjones, Moorhead, MN*

PREP: 15 min. + chilling
MAKES: 34 servings

- 2 lbs. uncooked elbow macaroni
- 12 hard-boiled large eggs, chopped
- 2½ lbs. fully cooked ham, cubed
- 1 pkg. (16 oz.) frozen peas, thawed
- 3 cups sliced celery
- 1 large green pepper, chopped
- ½ cup chopped onion
- 1 jar (4 oz.) diced pimientos, drained
- 4 cups mayonnaise

1. Cook macaroni according to package directions. Rinse in cold water; drain and cool completely.

2. Place in a large bowl; stir in remaining ingredients. Cover and refrigerate for at least 3 hours.

1 cup: 380 cal., 26g fat (4g sat. fat), 102mg chol., 615mg sod., 23g carb. (2g sugars, 2g fiber), 13g pro.

BRING IT

When taking this salad to a picnic or potluck, set the bowl on a bed of ice. Add a couple of ice cubes to a larger bowl and place your smaller serving bowl inside. This will keep the salad cold and won't take up too much additional space on the buffet table at the party.

SOUR CREAM SUGAR COOKIE CAKE

My husband requested a giant sugar cookie for his birthday. I wanted to do something a bit more exciting than birthday cookies, so I came up with this sugar cookie cake. The secret to a dense yet cakelike texture is to make sure you don't overbake the cake.
—Carmell Childs, Orangeville, UT

PREP: 20 min. • **BAKE:** 20 min. + cooling
MAKES: 20 servings

- ½ cup butter, softened
- 1½ cups sugar
- 2 large eggs, room temperature
- 1 tsp. vanilla extract
- 3 cups all-purpose flour
- ¾ tsp. salt
- ½ tsp. baking powder
- ½ tsp. baking soda
- 1 cup sour cream
- 1 can (16 oz.) vanilla frosting
  Optional: Coarse sugar, sprinkles and additional frosting

1. Preheat oven to 350°. In a large bowl, cream butter and sugar until light and fluffy, 5-7 minutes. Beat in eggs and vanilla. In another bowl, whisk flour, salt, baking powder and baking soda; add to creamed mixture alternately with sour cream, beating after each addition just until combined. Spread into a greased 13x9-in. baking pan.

2. Bake until a toothpick inserted in the center comes out clean, 20-25 minutes. Cool completely on a wire rack. Spread frosting over top. Decorate with optional toppings as desired.

1 piece: 295 cal., 11g fat (6g sat. fat), 34mg chol., 228mg sod., 46g carb. (29g sugars, 1g fiber), 3g pro.

SOUR CREAM
SUGAR COOKIE CAKE

BEEF STEW FOR A CROWD

Beef stew always seems to be popular at large gatherings. Everyone likes this hearty combination of beef, potatoes, carrots, celery and onion in a savory tomato-to-beef broth.
—*Jackie Holland, Gillette, WY*

PREP: 30 min. • **COOK:** 2 hours
MAKES: 22 servings (5½ qt.)

2½ lbs. beef stew meat,
    cut into ½-in. cubes
3 Tbsp. canola oil
12 cups water
2 cans (15 oz. each) tomato sauce
¼ cup beef bouillon granules
1 tsp. salt, optional
½ tsp. pepper
3½ lbs. potatoes, peeled and cubed
4 medium carrots, sliced
3 celery ribs, sliced
2 medium onions, coarsely chopped
¾ cup all-purpose flour
1½ cups cold water

1. In a soup kettle, brown the beef in oil; drain. Stir in water, tomato sauce, bouillon, salt if desired and the pepper. Bring to a boil. Reduce the heat; cover and simmer for 1½ hours or until the meat is tender.
2. Add potatoes, carrots, celery and onions. Return to a boil. Reduce heat; cover and simmer for 25-30 minutes or until the vegetables are tender.
3. Combine flour and cold water until smooth; gradually stir into stew. Bring to a boil; cook and stir for 2 minutes or until thickened.
1 cup: 183 cal., 6g fat (2g sat. fat), 32mg chol., 739mg sod., 22g carb. (0 sugars, 3g fiber), 13g pro. **Diabetic exchanges:** 1½ lean meat, 1 starch, 1 vegetable.

BAKLAVA TARTLETS

Want a quick treat that's delicious and easy to make? These tartlets will do the trick. You can serve them right away, but they're even better after chilling for about an hour in the refrigerator.
—*Ashley Eagon, Kettering, OH*

TAKES: 25 min. • **MAKES:** 45 tartlets

¾ cup honey
½ cup butter, melted
1 tsp. ground cinnamon
1 tsp. lemon juice
¼ tsp. ground cloves
2 cups finely chopped walnuts
3 pkg. (1.9 oz. each) frozen miniature
    phyllo tart shells

In a small bowl, mix the first 5 ingredients until blended; stir in walnuts. Spoon 2 tsp. mixture into each tart shell. Refrigerate until serving.
1 tartlet: 76 cal., 5g fat (1g sat. fat), 5mg chol., 24mg sod., 6g carb. (4g sugars, 0 fiber), 2g pro.

CHERRY ICEBOX COOKIES

CREAMY GRAPE SALAD

Folks rave when I bring this refreshing, creamy salad to potlucks. For a special finishing touch, sprinkle it with brown sugar and pecans.
—*Marge Elling, Jenison, MI*

TAKES: 20 min. • **MAKES:** 24 servings

- 1 pkg. (8 oz.) cream cheese, softened
- 1 cup sour cream
- ⅓ cup sugar
- 2 tsp. vanilla extract
- 2 lbs. seedless red grapes
- 2 lbs. seedless green grapes
- 3 Tbsp. brown sugar
- 3 Tbsp. chopped pecans

1. In a large bowl, beat cream cheese, sour cream, sugar and vanilla until blended. Add grapes and toss to coat.
2. Transfer to a serving bowl. Cover and refrigerate until serving. Sprinkle with brown sugar and pecans just before serving.
¾ cup: 131 cal., 6g fat (3g sat. fat), 17mg chol., 35mg sod., 19g carb. (18g sugars, 1g fiber), 2g pro.

TEST KITCHEN TIP

For extra flavor, toast the nuts before sprinkling them on the salad. Or add chopped Snickers or Heath candy bars for a little extra crunch and sweetness to contrast the grapes.

CHERRY ICEBOX COOKIES

Maraschino cherries add colorful flecks to these cookies. As a home economics teacher, I often supplied treats for school functions. These delectable cookies were always popular.
—*Patty Courtney, Jonesboro, TX*

PREP: 20 min. + chilling
BAKE: 10 min./batch • **MAKES:** 16 dozen

- 1 cup butter, softened
- 1 cup sugar
- ¼ cup packed brown sugar
- 1 large egg, room temperature
- ¼ cup maraschino cherry juice
- 4½ tsp. lemon juice
- 1 tsp. vanilla extract
- 3¼ cups all-purpose flour
- ½ tsp. baking soda
- ½ tsp. ground cinnamon
- ¼ tsp. cream of tartar
- ½ cup chopped walnuts
- ½ cup chopped maraschino cherries

1. In a large bowl, cream butter and sugars until light and fluffy, 5-7 minutes. Beat in the egg, cherry and lemon juices, and vanilla. Combine dry ingredients; gradually add to creamed mixture and mix well. Stir in nuts and cherries.
2. Shape into four 12-in. rolls; securely wrap each in waxed paper. Refrigerate for 4 hours or until firm.
3. Unwrap and cut into ¼-in. slices. Place 2 in. apart on ungreased baking sheets. Bake at 375° until the edges begin to brown, 8-10 minutes. Remove to wire racks to cool.
1 cookie: 66 cal., 3g fat (2g sat. fat), 10mg chol., 37mg sod., 9g carb. (4g sugars, 0 fiber), 1g pro.

CREAMY GRAPE SALAD

PEANUT BUTTER GRANOLA MINI BARS

Kids will flip over this deliciously oaty, sweet snack! What's not to love about a batch of peanut butter-honey-oatmeal bars? And at fewer than 100 calories, you can afford to have seconds.
—*Vivian Levine, Summerfield, FL*

PREP: 20 min. • **BAKE:** 15 min. + cooling
MAKES: 3 dozen

- ½   cup reduced-fat creamy peanut butter
- ⅓   cup honey
- 1   large egg
- 2   Tbsp. canola oil
- 1   tsp. vanilla extract
- 3½   cups old-fashioned oats
- ½   cup packed brown sugar
- ¾   tsp. salt
- ⅓   cup peanut butter chips
- ⅓   cup miniature semisweet chocolate chips

1. Preheat oven to 350°. In a large bowl, beat peanut butter, honey, egg, oil and vanilla until blended. Combine the oats, brown sugar and salt; add to the peanut butter mixture and mix well. Stir in chips. (Batter will be sticky.)

2. Press into a greased 13x9-in. baking pan. Bake until mixture is set and edges are lightly browned, 12-15 minutes. Cool on a wire rack. Cut into bars.

1 piece: 96 cal., 4g fat (1g sat. fat), 5mg chol., 78mg sod., 14g carb. (8g sugars, 1g fiber), 3g pro. **Diabetic exchanges:** 1 starch, 1 fat.

PEANUT BUTTER
GRANOLA MINI BARS

CHICKEN CAKES WITH AVOCADO MANGO SAUCE

1. In a large bowl, combine the first 8 ingredients; mix lightly but thoroughly. Shape into forty-eight ½-in.-thick patties. Heat oil in a large cast-iron skillet; fry the patties in batches until a thermometer inserted reads 165°, 3-5 minutes on each side.

2. Meanwhile, place sauce ingredients in a blender; cover and process until smooth. Serve with chicken patties.

1 cake with 2 tsp. sauce: 51 cal., 3g fat (1g sat. fat), 13mg chol., 98mg sod., 3g carb. (1g sugars, 1g fiber), 3g pro.

CONEY DOGS

My mom and I always make these top dogs for get-togethers. Leftovers are no problem—there never are any!
—*Donna Sternthal, Sharpsville, PA*

PREP: 15 min. • **COOK:** 30 min.
MAKES: 24 servings

- 2 lbs. ground beef
- 3 small onions, chopped
- 3 cups water
- 1 can (12 oz.) tomato paste
- 5 tsp. chili powder
- 2 tsp. rubbed sage
- 2 tsp. salt
- 1 tsp. pepper
- ½ tsp. garlic salt
- ½ tsp. dried oregano
- ¼ tsp. cayenne pepper
- 24 hot dogs, cooked
- 24 hot dog buns
  Shredded cheddar cheese, optional

1. In a Dutch oven, cook beef and onions over medium heat until meat is no longer pink, breaking it into crumbles; drain. Stir in water, tomato paste and seasonings.

2. Cover and simmer for 30 minutes, stirring occasionally. Serve over hot dogs on buns; sprinkle with cheese if desired.

1 hot dog: 358 cal., 20g fat (8g sat. fat), 49mg chol., 962mg sod., 27g carb. (6g sugars, 2g fiber), 17g pro.

CHICKEN CAKES WITH AVOCADO MANGO SAUCE

Here's a fabulous appetizer for your next party. Or serve these chicken cakes for dinner with a side of hot rice and your favorite vegetable.
—*Rachael Nodes, La Barge, WY*

PREP: 15 min.
COOK: 10 min./batch
MAKES: 4 dozen (2 cups sauce)

- 2 lbs. ground chicken
- 1 cup dry whole wheat bread crumbs
- ½ cup unsweetened crushed pineapple
- ½ cup finely chopped sweet red pepper
- ½ cup finely chopped red onion
- 1 garlic clove, minced
- 1 tsp. salt
- ½ tsp. pepper
- 3 Tbsp. canola oil

AVOCADO MANGO SAUCE

- 1 medium ripe avocado, peeled and pitted
- ½ cup chopped peeled mango
- 3 Tbsp. unsweetened crushed pineapple
- 2 Tbsp. chopped red onion
- 1 garlic clove, halved
- ½ tsp. salt
- ¼ tsp. ground cumin
- ¼ tsp. pepper

SLOW-COOKED FAVORITES

Looking for a fuss-free dish to pass? These tasty, crowd-pleasing slow-cooker potluck recipes do all the work for you!

P. 239

P. 263

P. 258

MIDNIGHT CARIBBEAN PORK SANDWICHES

1. In a large skillet, heat oil over medium-high heat. Add the onions; cook and stir until tender, 6-8 minutes. Add the beer, brown sugar, 8 garlic cloves, cumin, 5 tsp. chipotle peppers, salt and pepper; cook and stir until combined.
2. Place roast in a 5- or 6-qt. slow cooker. Pour the onion mixture over the meat. Cook, covered, on low 6-8 hours, until pork is tender.
3. Meanwhile, combine mayonnaise, cilantro, and remaining 2 garlic cloves and chipotle peppers. Cover and refrigerate until serving.
4. Remove roast; shred with 2 forks. Strain the cooking juices. Reserve vegetables and 1 cup juices; discard remaining juices. Skim the fat from reserved juices. Return the pork and reserved vegetables and cooking juices to the slow cooker; heat through. Serve on buns with avocado and mayonnaise mixture.

Freeze option: Place the shredded pork and vegetables in freezer containers; top with cooking juices. Cool and freeze. To use, partially thaw in refrigerator overnight. Heat through in a covered saucepan; stir gently. Add broth if necessary.

1 sandwich: 484 cal., 29g fat (7g sat. fat), 71mg chol., 400mg sod., 36g carb. (15g sugars, 3g fiber), 18g pro.

READER RAVES
"This was a very good and flavorful recipe."

—CORWIN44, TASTEOFHOME.COM

MIDNIGHT CARIBBEAN PORK SANDWICHES

These easy sandwiches have nice depth of flavor—savory, sweet, piquant, subtle and sublime. They're worth the wait.
—*Elizabeth Bennett, Mill Creek, WA*

PREP: 25 min. • COOK: 6 hours
MAKES: 12 servings

- 1 Tbsp. canola oil
- 3 medium onions, cut into ½-in. slices
- 1 bottle (12 oz.) amber beer or 1½ cups chicken broth
- ¼ cup packed brown sugar
- 10 garlic cloves, minced and divided
- 2 Tbsp. ground cumin
- 7 tsp. minced chipotle peppers in adobo sauce, divided
- ½ tsp. salt
- ½ tsp. pepper
- 1 boneless pork shoulder butt roast (2 to 3 lbs.)
- 1 cup mayonnaise
- ½ cup minced fresh cilantro
- 12 Hawaiian sweet hamburger buns
- 2 medium ripe avocados, peeled and sliced

GREEN OLIVE DIP

SLOPPY JOE TATER TOT CASSEROLE

This simple casserole is an easy dinner. Serve with carrot and celery sticks for a fuss-free feast. You can also stir in some spicy brown mustard if the adults want more zing.
—*Laura Wilhelm, West Hollywood, CA*

PREP: 20 min. • **COOK:** 4 hours + standing
MAKES: 10 servings

- 1 bag (32 oz.) frozen Tater Tots, divided
- 2 lbs. ground beef or turkey
- 1 can (15 oz.) tomato sauce
- 1 bottle (8 oz.) sweet chili sauce
- 2 Tbsp. packed brown sugar
- 1 Tbsp. Worcestershire sauce
- 1 Tbsp. dried minced garlic
- 1 Tbsp. dried minced onion
- ½ tsp. salt
- ½ tsp. pepper
- 1¼ cups shredded Colby-Monterey Jack cheese
- ¼ tsp. paprika

Place half the Tater Tots in bottom of 5-qt. slow cooker. In a large skillet, cook beef over medium-high heat until no longer pink, 5-6 minutes, breaking into crumbles. Drain. Stir in the next 8 ingredients; reduce the heat and simmer 2-3 minutes. Place the beef mixture in slow cooker; top with remaining Tater Tots. Cook, covered, on low 4 hours. Top with cheese. Sprinkle with paprika. Let stand, uncovered, for 15 minutes before serving.

1 cup: 466 cal., 24g fat (9g sat. fat), 69mg chol., 1332mg sod., 41g carb. (18g sugars, 4g fiber), 22g pro.

GREEN OLIVE DIP

Olive fans will love this dip. It's cheesy and full of beef and beans. It could even be used as a filling for taco shells.
—*Beth Dunahay, Lima, OH*

PREP: 30 min. • **COOK:** 3 hours
MAKES: 8 cups

- 1 lb. ground beef
- 1 medium sweet red pepper, chopped
- 1 small onion, chopped
- 1 can (16 oz.) refried beans
- 1 jar (16 oz.) mild salsa
- 2 cups shredded part-skim mozzarella cheese
- 2 cups shredded cheddar cheese
- 1 jar (5¾ oz.) sliced green olives with pimientos, drained
   Tortilla chips

In a large skillet, cook beef, pepper and onion over medium heat until meat is no longer pink, 5-7 minutes, crumbling meat; drain. Transfer to a greased 3-qt. slow cooker. Add the beans, salsa, cheeses and olives. Cover and cook on low for 3-4 hours or until cheese is melted, stirring occasionally. Serve with chips.

¼ cup: 96 cal., 6g fat (3g sat. fat), 21mg chol., 262mg sod., 4g carb. (1g sugars, 1g fiber), 7g pro.

**SLOPPY JOE
TATER TOT CASSEROLE**

CHICKEN CORDON BLEU SLIDERS

I'm always searching for new ideas for sandwiches because they're my favorite food. I created these sliders with the flavors of a classic dish. This was one taste experiment that met with the family's approval.
—*Carolyn Eskew, Dayton, OH*

PREP: 20 min.
COOK: 2½ hours + standing
MAKES: 2 dozen

- 1½ lbs. boneless skinless chicken breasts
- 1 garlic clove, minced
- ¼ tsp. salt
- ¼ tsp. pepper
- 1 pkg. (8 oz.) cream cheese, cubed
- 2 cups shredded Swiss cheese
- 1¼ cups finely chopped fully cooked ham
- 2 pkg. (12 oz. each) Hawaiian sweet rolls, split
  Chopped green onions

1. Place the chicken in a greased 3-qt. slow cooker; sprinkle with garlic, salt and pepper. Top with cream cheese. Cook, covered, on low 2½-3 hours or until a thermometer inserted in chicken reads 165°. Remove chicken; shred with 2 forks. Return to slow cooker.
2. Stir in Swiss cheese and ham. Cover and let stand for 15 minutes or until the cheese is melted. Stir before serving on rolls. Sprinkle with green onions.
1 slider: 209 cal., 10g fat (5g sat. fat), 53mg chol., 254mg sod., 17g carb. (6g sugars, 1g fiber), 14g pro.

CHICKEN CORDON BLEU SLIDERS

¼ tsp. salt
¼ tsp. pepper
1 small cucumber, peeled, seeded and finely chopped
½ cup fat-free plain Greek yogurt
   Additional snipped fresh dill
   Baked pita chips or assorted fresh vegetables

Process beans and water in a food processor until smooth. Transfer to a greased 1½-qt. slow cooker. Add next 8 ingredients. Cook, covered, on low until heated through, 2-3 hours. Stir in cucumber and yogurt; cool slightly. Sprinkle with additional dill. Serve dip warm or cold with chips or assorted fresh vegetables.

Freeze option: Omitting the cucumber, yogurt and additional dill, freeze cooled dip in freezer containers. To use, thaw in the refrigerator overnight. Stir in the cucumber and yogurt; sprinkle with additional dill.

¼ cup: 86 cal., 3g fat (0 sat. fat), 0 chol., 260mg sod., 11g carb. (1g sugars, 3g fiber), 4g pro. **Diabetic exchanges:** 1 starch, ½ fat.

TEST KITCHEN TIP

To seed a cucumber, cut it in half lengthwise. Gently scoop out the seeds with the tip of a spoon or butter knife. Be careful not to remove too much of the flesh.

HEALTHY GREEK BEAN DIP

HEALTHY GREEK BEAN DIP

Folks will love to eat their veggies when they can dip them in this zesty, fresh alternative to hummus.
—*Kelly Silvers, Edmond, OK*

PREP: 15 min.
COOK: 2 hours
MAKES: 3 cups

2 cans (15 oz. each) cannellini beans, rinsed and drained
¼ cup water
¼ cup finely chopped roasted sweet red peppers
2 Tbsp. finely chopped red onion
2 Tbsp. olive oil
2 Tbsp. lemon juice
1 Tbsp. snipped fresh dill
2 garlic cloves, minced

WARM ROCKY ROAD CAKE

When served warm, this reminds me of super moist lava cake. And until I made this, I didn't think a slow-cooker cake could be so attractive. It's a real winner.
—*Scarlett Elrod, Newnan, GA*

PREP: 20 min. • **COOK:** 3 hours
MAKES: 16 servings

- 1 pkg. German chocolate cake mix (regular size)
- 1 pkg. (3.9 oz.) instant chocolate pudding mix
- 1 cup sour cream
- ⅓ cup butter, melted
- 3 large eggs, room temperature
- 1 tsp. vanilla extract
- 3¼ cups 2% milk, divided
- 1 pkg. (3.4 oz.) cook-and-serve chocolate pudding mix
- 1½ cups miniature marshmallows
- 1 cup semisweet chocolate chips
- ½ cup chopped pecans, toasted
  Vanilla ice cream, optional

1. In a large bowl, combine the first 6 ingredients; add 1¼ cups milk. Beat on low speed 30 seconds. Beat on medium 2 minutes. Transfer to a greased 4- or 5-qt. slow cooker. Sprinkle cook-and-serve pudding mix over batter.
2. In a small saucepan, heat remaining milk until bubbles form around the side of pan; gradually pour over contents of slow cooker.
3. Cook, covered, on high 3-4 hours or until a toothpick inserted in cake portion comes out with moist crumbs.
4. Turn off the slow cooker. Sprinkle marshmallows, chocolate chips and pecans over cake; let stand, covered, until the marshmallows begin to melt, about 5 minutes. Serve warm. If desired, serve with ice cream.
¾ cup: 386 cal., 17g fat (8g sat. fat), 59mg chol., 431mg sod., 55g carb. (34g sugars, 2g fiber), 6g pro.

READER RAVES
"I made this for work, and it was a big hit!"

—JBIESTER, TASTEOFHOME.COM

CHEESEBURGER DIP

CHEESEBURGER DIP

This fun dip recipe uses ingredients I always have in the fridge, so it's easy to throw together on short notice.
—*Cindi DeClue, Anchorage, AK*

PREP: 25 min. • **COOK:** 1¾ hours
MAKES: 16 servings

- 1   lb. lean ground beef (90% lean)
- 1   medium onion, chopped
- 1   pkg. (8 oz.) cream cheese, cubed
- 2   cups shredded cheddar cheese, divided
- 1   Tbsp. Worcestershire sauce
- 2   tsp. prepared mustard
- ¼   tsp. salt
- ⅛   tsp. pepper
- 1   medium tomato, chopped
- ¼   cup chopped dill pickles
-     Tortilla chips

1. In a large skillet, cook beef and onion over medium-high heat until the beef is no longer pink and onion is tender, 6-8 minutes, breaking beef into crumbles; drain. Transfer to a greased 1½- or 3-qt. slow cooker. Stir in the cream cheese, 1½ cups cheddar cheese, Worcestershire sauce, mustard, salt and pepper. Sprinkle with remaining ½ cup cheese.
2. Cook dip, covered, on low until mixture is heated through and cheese is melted, 1¾-2¼ hours. Top with the tomato and pickles. Serve with tortilla chips.
¼ cup: 157 cal., 12g fat (6g sat. fat), 46mg chol., 225mg sod., 2g carb. (1g sugars, 0 fiber), 10g pro.

TEST KITCHEN TIP

Keep an eye on the dip toward the end of cooking. If it goes too long, the edges will get dark.

SLOW-COOKED BEEF BURRITOS WITH GREEN CHILES

SLOW-COOKED BEEF BURRITOS WITH GREEN CHILES

I created this recipe years ago, and it has become a favorite. The wonderful aroma as it cooks makes my family instantly happy. This hearty, flavorful and easy meal uses the long, slow cooking method that truly defines comfort food.
—*Sally J. Pahler, Palisade, CO*

PREP: 20 min. • **COOK:** 7 hours
MAKES: 14 servings

- 2 garlic cloves, minced
- 1 tsp. salt
- 2 tsp. ground cumin
- 1 tsp. cayenne pepper
- 1 boneless beef chuck roast (4 lbs.)
- 1 can (28 oz.) diced tomatoes
- 4 cans (7 oz. each) whole green chiles, drained and coarsely chopped
- 1 large onion, diced
- 14 whole wheat tortillas (8 in.), warmed
  Optional toppings: Shredded cheddar cheese, salsa, sour cream, sliced ripe olives

1. In a small bowl, combine garlic, salt, cumin and cayenne; rub over roast. Place in a 5- or 6-qt. slow cooker. Add tomatoes, chiles and onion. Cook, covered, on low until meat is tender, 7-8 hours.

2. Remove roast from slow cooker; shred with 2 forks. Remove vegetables with a slotted spoon; discard the cooking juices. Return beef and vegetables to slow cooker and heat through. Serve in tortillas, with toppings as desired.

1 burrito: 355 cal., 13g fat (5g sat. fat), 84mg chol., 499mg sod., 28g carb. (4g sugars, 4g fiber), 30g pro. **Diabetic exchanges:** 4 lean meat, 2 starch.

TEST KITCHEN TIP

To save time, use cans of diced green chiles instead of chopping whole chiles.

BACON & SWISS BREAKFAST

BACON & SWISS BREAKFAST

When we have overnight guests, I like to prepare things ahead of time so we can enjoy our company. It often gets crazy when everyone first wakes up, and I like to have food available whenever people are ready to eat. I devised this slow-cooker recipe when I was feeding 22 people breakfast at a destination wedding.
—*Donna Gribbins, Shelbyville, KY*

PREP: 15 min. • **COOK:** 4 hours + standing
MAKES: 12 servings

- 1 pkg. (28 oz.) frozen potatoes O'Brien, thawed
- 1 lb. bacon strips, cooked and crumbled
- 2 cups shredded Swiss cheese
- 12 large eggs
- 2 cups 2% milk
- 1 tsp. seasoned salt
- 1 tsp. pepper
  Minced chives, optional

In a greased 4- or 5-qt. slow cooker, layer potatoes, bacon and cheese. In a large bowl, whisk eggs, milk, seasoned salt and pepper; pour over top. Cook, covered, on low 4-5 hours or until eggs are set. Turn off slow cooker. Remove the crock insert to a wire rack; let stand, uncovered, 30 minutes before serving. Garnish with minced chives if desired.

1 serving: 277 cal., 16g fat (7g sat. fat), 220mg chol., 507mg sod., 13g carb. (3g sugars, 2g fiber), 18g pro.

PINEAPPLE UPSIDE-DOWN DUMP CAKE

No matter the season, this dump cake is wonderful! It works well with gluten-free and sugar-free cake mixes, too.
—*Karin Gatewood, Dallas, TX*

PREP: 10 min.
COOK: 2 hours + standing
MAKES: 10 servings

- ¾ cup butter, divided
- ⅔ cup packed brown sugar
- 1 jar (6 oz.) maraschino cherries, drained
- ½ cup chopped pecans, toasted
- 1 can (20 oz.) unsweetened pineapple tidbits or crushed pineapple, undrained
- 1 pkg. yellow cake mix (regular size) Vanilla ice cream, optional

1. In a microwave, melt ½ cup butter; stir in the brown sugar. Spread evenly onto bottom of a greased 5-qt. slow cooker. Sprinkle with cherries and pecans; top with pineapple. Sprinkle evenly with dry cake mix. Melt remaining butter; drizzle over top.
2. Cook, covered, on high 2 hours or until fruit mixture is bubbly. (To avoid scorching, rotate slow-cooker insert a half turn midway through cooking, lifting carefully with oven mitts.)
3. Turn off the slow cooker; let stand, uncovered, 30 minutes before serving. If desired, serve with ice cream.
½ cup: 455 cal., 22g fat (10g sat. fat), 37mg chol., 418mg sod., 66g carb. (47g sugars, 1g fiber), 3g pro.

PINEAPPLE UPSIDE-DOWN DUMP CAKE

CHOCOLATE LAVA CAKE

Everyone who tries this dessert falls in love with it. Using a slow cooker liner makes cleanup a breeze.
—*Latona Dwyer, Palm Beach Gardens, FL*

PREP: 15 min. • **COOK:** 3 hours
MAKES: 12 servings

- 1 pkg. devil's food cake mix (regular size)
- 1⅔ cups water
- 3 large eggs, room temperature
- ⅓ cup canola oil
- 2 cups cold 2% milk
- 1 pkg. (3.9 oz.) instant chocolate pudding mix
- 2 cups semisweet chocolate chips Whipped cream, optional

1. In a large bowl, combine the cake mix, water, eggs and oil; beat on low speed for 30 seconds. Beat on medium 2 minutes. Transfer to a greased 4-qt. slow cooker.
2. In another bowl, whisk milk and pudding mix for 2 minutes. Let stand until soft-set, about 2 minutes. Spoon over cake batter; sprinkle with chocolate chips. Cover and cook on high for 3-4 hours or until a toothpick inserted in cake portion comes out with moist crumbs. Serve warm.
¾ cup: 215 cal., 10g fat (4g sat. fat), 28mg chol., 254mg sod., 32g carb. (22g sugars, 2g fiber), 3g pro.

CRISPY SNACK MIX

CRISPY SNACK MIX

This recipe proves that you can make just about anything in the slow cooker, even a delightfully crispy snack mix.
—*Jane Pair Sims, De Leon, TX*

PREP: 10 min. • **COOK:** 2½ hours
MAKES: about 13 servings (2½ qt.)

> 4½ cups crispy chow mein noodles
> 4 cups Rice Chex
> 1 can (9¾ oz.) salted cashews
> 1 cup sweetened shredded coconut, toasted
> ½ cup butter, melted
> 2 Tbsp. reduced-sodium soy sauce
> 2¼ tsp. curry powder
> ¾ tsp. ground ginger

1. In a 5-qt. slow cooker, combine noodles, cereal, cashews and coconut. In a small bowl, whisk the butter, soy sauce, curry powder and ginger; drizzle over cereal mixture and mix well.
2. Cover and cook on low for 2½ hours, stirring every 30 minutes. Serve warm or at room temperature.
¾ cup: 298 cal., 22g fat (8g sat. fat), 16mg chol., 420mg sod., 21g carb. (4g sugars, 2g fiber), 5g pro.

READER RAVES
"Great taste. I've already made it twice."

—KGW3, TASTEOFHOME.COM

MA

ASIAN PULLED PORK BUNS

My pulled pork is a happy flavor mash-up of Vietnamese pho noodle soup and a banh mi sandwich. It's one seriously delicious slow-cooker dish.
—*Stacie Anderson, Virginia Beach, VA*

PREP: 15 min. • **COOK:** 7 hours
MAKES: 18 servings

- ½ cup hoisin sauce
- ¼ cup seasoned rice vinegar
- ¼ cup reduced-sodium soy sauce
- ¼ cup honey
- 2 Tbsp. tomato paste
- 1 Tbsp. Worcestershire sauce
- 2 garlic cloves, minced
- 4 lbs. boneless pork shoulder roast
- 18 French dinner rolls (about 1¾ oz. each), split and warmed
  Optional toppings: Shredded cabbage, julienned carrot, sliced jalapeno pepper, fresh cilantro or basil, and Sriracha chili sauce

1. In a bowl, whisk the first 7 ingredients until blended. Place roast in a 4- or 5-qt. slow cooker. Pour sauce mixture over top. Cook, covered, on low until pork is tender, 7-9 hours.

2. Remove roast; cool slightly. Skim fat from cooking juices. Coarsely shred pork with 2 forks. Return pork to slow cooker; heat through. Using tongs, serve pork on rolls, adding toppings as desired.

Freeze option: Freeze the cooled meat mixture in freezer containers. To use, partially thaw in refrigerator overnight. Heat through in a saucepan, stirring occasionally; add broth if necessary. Serve as directed.

1 sandwich: 350 cal., 12g fat (4g sat. fat), 60mg chol., 703mg sod., 35g carb. (8g sugars, 1g fiber), 23g pro.

ASIAN PULLED PORK BUNS

CILANTRO & LIME CHICKEN WITH SCOOPS

I came up with this recipe when I was preparing for a large party, and I wanted a healthy Tex-Mex chicken to serve in tortilla cups. You can make this party dish ahead of time to free yourself for time-sensitive dishes. Serve it in tortilla chip cups or any other savory crispy cup you like. Enjoy leftovers over salad greens or wrapped up in tortillas for burritos.
—Lori Terry, Chicago, IL

PREP: 15 min. • **COOK:** 3½ hours
MAKES: 16 servings (4 cups)

- 1 lb. boneless skinless chicken breasts
- 2 tsp. chili powder
- 2 Tbsp. lime juice
- 1½ cups frozen petite corn (about 5 oz.), thawed
- 1½ cups chunky salsa
- 1½ cups (6 oz.) finely shredded cheddar cheese
- 1 medium sweet red pepper, finely chopped
- 4 green onions, thinly sliced
  Minced fresh cilantro
  Baked tortilla chip scoops

1. Place chicken in a 1½-qt. slow cooker; sprinkle with chili powder and lime juice. Cook, covered, on low for 3-4 hours or until tender.
2. Remove chicken; discard cooking juices. Shred chicken with 2 forks; return to slow cooker. Add corn and salsa; cook, covered, on low 30 minutes or until heated through, stirring occasionally.
3. Stir in the cheese, pepper and green onions. Sprinkle with cilantro; serve with tortilla scoops.
¼ cup chicken mixture: 97 cal., 4g fat (2g sat. fat), 26mg chol., 183mg sod., 5g carb. (2g sugars, 1g fiber), 9g pro. **Diabetic exchanges:** 1 medium-fat meat.

MULLED GRAPE CIDER

I came up with this recipe one year when I attempted to make grape jelly and ended up with 30 jars of delicious grape syrup instead. I simmered the syrup with spices to make this pretty drink.
—Sharon Harmon, Orange, MA

PREP: 20 min. • **COOK:** 3 hours
MAKES: 12 servings (3 qt.)

- 5 lbs. Concord grapes
- 8 cups water, divided
- 1½ cups sugar
- 8 whole cloves
- 4 cinnamon sticks (4 in.)
  Dash ground nutmeg

1. In a large saucepan, combine grapes and 2 cups water; bring to a boil, stirring constantly. Press through a strainer. Reserve juice; discard skins and seeds.
2. Pour juice through a double layer of cheesecloth into a 5-qt. slow cooker. Add the sugar, cloves, cinnamon sticks, nutmeg and remaining water. Cover and cook on low for 3 hours. Discard cloves and cinnamon sticks.
1 cup: 231 cal., 1g fat (0 sat. fat), 0 chol., 4mg sod., 59g carb. (56g sugars, 0 fiber), 1g pro.

**CREAMY CHEESE
POTATOES**

SPICY TOUCHDOWN CHILI

Football, cool weather and chili just
seem to go together. Whether I'm
cheering on the local team on a Friday
night or enjoying a Saturday afternoon
of Oklahoma Sooner football, I enjoy
serving this chili on game day.
—*Chris Neal, Quapaw, OK*

PREP: 30 min. • **COOK:** 4 hours
MAKES: 12 servings (3 qt.)

- 1   lb. ground beef
- 1   lb. bulk pork sausage
- 2   cans (16 oz. each) kidney beans,
      rinsed and drained
- 2   cans (15 oz. each) pinto beans, rinsed
      and drained
- 2   cans (14½ oz. each) diced tomatoes
      with mild green chiles, undrained
- 1   can (14½ oz.) diced tomatoes with
      onions, undrained
- 1   can (12 oz.) beer
- 6   bacon strips, cooked and crumbled
- 1   small onion, chopped
- ¼   cup chili powder
- ¼   cup chopped pickled jalapeno slices
- 2   tsp. ground cumin
- 2   garlic cloves, minced
- 1   tsp. dried basil
- ¾   tsp. cayenne pepper
      Optional: Shredded cheddar cheese,
      sour cream and chopped green
      onions

1. In a large skillet, cook beef over medium
heat until no longer pink, 6-8 minutes,
crumbling beef; drain. Transfer to a 6-qt.
slow cooker. Repeat with sausage.
2. Stir in the next 13 ingredients. Cook,
covered, on low until heated through,
4-5 hours. If desired, top individual
servings with cheese, sour cream
and green onions.
1 cup: 365 cal., 15g fat (5g sat. fat), 48mg
chol., 901mg sod., 34g carb. (7g sugars,
9g fiber), 22g pro.

CREAMY CHEESE POTATOES

This easy potato dish is a comfort-food
classic. It's popular at gatherings.
—*Greg Christiansen, Parker, KS*

PREP: 10 min. • **COOK:** 3¼ hours
MAKES: 10 servings

- 1   can (10¾ oz.) condensed cream
      of chicken soup, undiluted
- 1   can (10¾ oz.) condensed cream
      of mushroom soup, undiluted
- 3   Tbsp. butter, melted
- 1   pkg. (30 oz.) frozen shredded hash
      brown potatoes, thawed
- 2   cups shredded cheddar cheese
- 1   cup sour cream
      Minced fresh parsley, optional

1. In a 3-qt. slow cooker coated with
cooking spray, combine the soups and
butter. Stir in potatoes.
2. Cover and cook on low for 3-4 hours
or until the potatoes are tender. Stir in
cheese and sour cream. Cover and cook
15-30 minutes longer or until heated
through. If desired, top with additional
shredded cheddar cheese and minced
fresh parsley.
¾ cup: 278 cal., 17g fat (10g sat. fat), 52mg
chol., 614mg sod., 21g carb. (2g sugars,
2g fiber), 9g pro.

SPICY TOUCHDOWN CHILI

HOVER YOUR CAMERA HERE
How to Host a
Chili Cook-Off

ITALIAN SAUSAGES WITH PROVOLONE

Here's an easy recipe everyone will rave about. These tangy sausages with their pepper and onion topping will go quickly. Better make a double batch!
—*Shelly Bevington, Hermiston, OR*

PREP: 15 min. • **COOK:** 4 hours
MAKES: 10 servings

- 10 Italian sausage links (4 oz. each)
- 1 Tbsp. canola oil
- 1 each small sweet red, yellow and orange peppers, cut into strips
- 2 medium onions, halved and sliced
- 2 cups Italian salad dressing
- 10 slices provolone cheese
- 10 brat buns, split

1. In a large skillet, brown sausages, in batches, in the oil. Drain. Transfer to a 5-qt. slow cooker. Add the peppers, onions and salad dressing. Cover and cook on low for 4-5 hours or until a thermometer reads 160° and vegetables are tender.
2. Place the sausages and cheese in buns; using a slotted spoon, top with pepper mixture.
1 serving: 543 cal., 31g fat (10g sat. fat), 60mg chol., 1267mg sod., 41g carb. (9g sugars, 2g fiber), 25g pro.

ITALIAN
SAUSAGES WITH
PROVOLONE

**SLOW-COOKER
ARTICHOKE-SPINACH DIP**

HAWAIIAN KIELBASA

Savory sausage teams up with juicy, tangy pineapple for a winning combination that you can prep in a flash. The sweet barbecue-style sauce ties them together.
—*Louise Kline, Fort Myers, FL*

PREP: 15 min. • **COOK:** 2½ hours
MAKES: 12 servings

- 2 lbs. smoked kielbasa or Polish sausage, cut into 1-in. pieces
- 1 can (20 oz.) unsweetened pineapple chunks, undrained
- ½ cup ketchup
- 2 Tbsp. brown sugar
- 2 Tbsp. yellow mustard
- 1 Tbsp. cider vinegar
- ¾ cup lemon-lime soda
- 2 Tbsp. cornstarch
- 2 Tbsp. cold water

1. Place the sausage in a 3- or 4-qt. slow cooker. Drain pineapple, reserving ¾ cup juice; set pineapple aside. In a small bowl, whisk the ketchup, brown sugar, mustard and vinegar. Stir in soda and reserved pineapple juice. Pour the mixture over the sausage; stir to coat. Cover and cook on low until heated through, 2-3 hours.
2. Stir in the pineapple. In a small bowl, combine the cornstarch and water until smooth. Stir into slow cooker. Cover and cook until the sauce is thickened, about 30 minutes longer. Serve with toothpicks if desired.
½ cup: 289 cal., 21g fat (7g sat. fat), 51mg chol., 975mg sod., 15g carb. (12g sugars, 0 fiber), 10g pro.

SLOW-COOKER
ARTICHOKE-SPINACH DIP

Little extras like crumbled feta and red wine vinegar take this creamy dip of artichoke hearts, spinach and Parmesan to the next level. Just throw the whole nine yards into a slow cooker, and it's good to go on game day.
—*Alyssa Janis, Green Bay, WI*

PREP: 20 min. • **COOK:** 2 hours
MAKES: 24 servings

- 2 cans (14 oz. each) water-packed artichoke hearts, drained and chopped
- 1 pkg. (10 oz.) frozen chopped spinach, thawed and squeezed dry
- 1 cup sour cream
- 1 small onion, chopped
- 2 garlic cloves, minced
- ¾ cup grated Parmesan cheese
- ¾ cup 2% milk
- ½ cup crumbled feta cheese
- ⅓ cup mayonnaise
- 1 Tbsp. red wine vinegar
- ¼ tsp. coarsely ground pepper
- 1 pkg. (8 oz.) cream cheese, cubed
  Sweet red pepper slices and
  tortilla chip scoops

1. Combine first 11 ingredients until well blended. Add cream cheese.
2. Place artichoke mixture in a greased 3- or 4-qt. slow cooker; cook, covered, on low for 2 hours. Stir; cover and keep warm. Serve with red pepper slices and tortilla chip scoops.
¼ cup: 112 cal., 9g fat (4g sat. fat), 22mg chol., 217mg sod., 4g carb. (1g sugars, 0 fiber), 4g pro.

SPICY SAUSAGE HASH BROWNS

I love to develop my own recipes and have people calling for them often. My family members and friends from our church tend to be my favorite and most honest critics, and they love this dish!
—Angela Sheridan, Opdyke, IL

PREP: 15 min. • COOK: 5 hours
MAKES: 9 servings

- 1   lb. bulk spicy pork sausage
- 1   pkg. (30 oz.) frozen shredded hash brown potatoes, thawed
- 2   cups sour cream
- 1   jar (16 oz.) double-cheddar cheese sauce
- 2   cans (4 oz. each) chopped green chiles
- ½   tsp. crushed red pepper flakes

In a large skillet, cook the sausage over medium heat until no longer pink; drain. Transfer to a 4-qt. slow cooker. Stir in the remaining ingredients. Cover and cook on low for 5-6 hours or until heated through.
1 cup: 368 cal., 25g fat (12g sat. fat), 73mg chol., 723mg sod., 22g carb. (4g sugars, 2g fiber), 10g pro.

APPLE CIDER PULLED PORK

For potlucks and tailgates, we slow-cook pork with cider, onions and spices. These tangy sliders make a winning meal with sweet potato fries.
—Rachel Lewis, Danville, VA

PREP: 15 min. • COOK: about 6¼ hours
MAKES: 12 servings

- 2   tsp. seasoned salt
- ½   tsp. ground mustard
- ½   tsp. paprika
- ¼   tsp. ground coriander
- ¼   tsp. pepper
- 2   medium Granny Smith apples, peeled and coarsely chopped
- 1   medium onion, chopped
- 1   celery rib, chopped
- 1½ cups apple cider or juice
- 1   boneless pork shoulder butt roast (3 lbs.)
- 2   Tbsp. cornstarch
- 2   Tbsp. water
- 24 mini buns, warmed
     Additional apple slices, optional

1. In a small bowl, mix first 5 ingredients. Place apples, onion, celery and cider in a 5-qt. slow cooker; top with roast. Sprinkle roast with the seasoning mixture. Cook, covered, on low until tender, 6-8 hours.
2. Remove roast; shred with 2 forks. Skim fat from cooking juices. Mix cornstarch and water; stir into the cooking juices. Cook, covered, on high until thickened, 10-15 minutes; stir in pork. Serve on buns. If desired, top with apple slices.
Freeze option: Freeze cooled meat mixture in freezer containers. To use, partially thaw in refrigerator overnight. Heat through in a saucepan, stirring occasionally; add broth or water if necessary.
2 sliders: 375 cal., 15g fat (5g sat. fat), 69mg chol., 563mg sod., 35g carb. (9g sugars, 2g fiber), 25g pro.

STEAK STROGANOFF

STEAK STROGANOFF

This slow-cooker recipe makes a traditional dinner so easy. Serve tender sirloin steak with a flavorful gravy over noodles for a home-style meal that your whole family will request time and again.
—*Lisa VanEgmond, Annapolis, IL*

PREP: 25 min. • **COOK:** 7 hours
MAKES: 12 servings

- 3 to 4 lbs. beef top sirloin steak, cubed
- 2 cans (14½ oz. each) chicken broth
- 1 lb. sliced fresh mushrooms
- 1 can (12 oz.) regular cola
- ½ cup chopped onion
- 1 envelope onion soup mix
- 1 to 2 tsp. garlic powder
- 2 tsp. dried parsley flakes
- ½ tsp. pepper
- 2 envelopes country gravy mix
- 2 cups sour cream
  Hot cooked noodles
  Minced fresh parsley, optional

1. In a 5-qt. slow cooker, combine the first 9 ingredients. Cover and cook on low for 7-8 hours or until beef is tender.
2. With a slotted spoon, remove beef and mushrooms. Place gravy mix in a large saucepan; gradually whisk in cooking liquid. Bring to a boil; cook and stir until thickened, about 2 minutes. Remove from the heat; stir in sour cream. Add the beef and mushrooms to the gravy. Serve with noodles. If desired, sprinkle with parsley.
1 cup: 345 cal., 20g fat (11g sat. fat), 65mg chol., 840mg sod., 11g carb. (7g sugars, 1g fiber), 29g pro.

CRANBERRY CHILI
MEATBALLS

CRANBERRY CHILI MEATBALLS

Using packaged meatballs helps save time in the kitchen, and they are just as tasty as homemade. My friends look forward to enjoying these meatballs at our holiday gatherings, and there are never any leftovers! The sauce is tangy yet sweet, and the festive color is perfect for any holiday party.
—Amy Scamerhorn, Indianapolis, IN

PREP: 10 min. • **COOK:** 2 hours
MAKES: about 5 dozen

- 1 can (14 oz.) jellied cranberry sauce
- 1 bottle (12 oz.) chili sauce
- ¾ cup packed brown sugar
- ½ tsp. chili powder
- ½ tsp. ground cumin
- ¼ tsp. cayenne pepper
- 1 pkg. (32 oz.) frozen fully cooked homestyle meatballs, thawed

In a saucepan over medium heat, combine the first 6 ingredients; stir until sugar is dissolved. Place the meatballs in a 4-qt. slow cooker. Add the sauce and gently stir to coat. Cook, covered, on low until heated through, 2-3 hours.

Freeze option: Freeze the cooled meatball mixture in freezer containers. To use, partially thaw in refrigerator overnight. Microwave mixture, covered, on high in a microwave-safe dish until heated through, stirring occasionally; add water or broth if necessary.

1 meatball: 74 cal., 4g fat (2g sat. fat), 6mg chol., 191mg sod., 8g carb. (5g sugars, 0 fiber), 2g pro.

SLOW-COOKED PORK ROAST

SLOW-COOKED PORK ROAST

Here's a tasty meal that's wonderful for summer because the oven never needs to heat up. It is so flavorful and is sure to become a favorite.
—Marion Lowery, Medford, OR

PREP: 20 min. • **COOK:** 6 hours + standing
MAKES: 12 servings

- 2 cans (8 oz. each) unsweetened crushed pineapple, undrained
- 1 cup barbecue sauce
- 2 Tbsp. unsweetened apple juice
- 1 Tbsp. minced fresh rosemary or 1 tsp. dried rosemary, crushed
- 1 tsp. minced garlic
- 2 tsp. grated lemon zest
- 1 tsp. liquid smoke, optional
- ½ tsp. salt
- ¼ tsp. pepper
- 2 Tbsp. olive oil
- 1 boneless pork loin roast (3 to 4 lbs.)

1. In a large saucepan, combine the first 9 ingredients. Bring to a boil. Reduce the heat; simmer, uncovered, for 3 minutes.
2. Meanwhile, cut the roast in half. In a nonstick skillet, heat the oil over medium heat; add pork and brown on all sides.
3. Place pork in a 5-qt. slow cooker; pour sauce over pork and turn to coat. Cover and cook on low for 6-7 hours or until meat is tender. Let stand for 10 minutes before slicing.

3 oz. cooked pork: 205 cal., 5g fat (2g sat. fat), 57mg chol., 364mg sod., 16g carb. (13g sugars, 1g fiber), 22g pro.

COUNTRY-STYLE BARBECUE RIBS

These ribs get a good sear under the broiler, then go into the slow cooker to become fall-apart tender. Enjoy them with great sides, or shredded on a bun. Either way, they're the most amazing ribs you'll ever have.

—Shannon Copley, Upper Arlington, OH

PREP: 15 min. • **COOK:** 3 hours
MAKES: 10 servings

- 2 Tbsp. paprika
- 2 Tbsp. brown sugar
- 2 tsp. salt
- 2 tsp. garlic powder
- 2 tsp. chili powder
- 1 tsp. onion powder
- 1 tsp. ground chipotle pepper
- 1 tsp. pepper
- ¾ tsp. dried thyme
- 4 lbs. boneless country-style pork ribs
- 1 bottle (18 oz.) barbecue sauce
- ¾ cup amber beer or reduced-sodium chicken broth

1. Preheat broiler. Mix first 9 ingredients. Place pork in a foil-lined 15x10x1-in. pan; rub generously with seasoning mixture. Broil 4-5 in. from the heat until browned, 2-3 minutes per side.

2. Transfer to a 5-qt. slow cooker. Whisk together barbecue sauce and beer; pour over ribs. Cook, covered, on low until tender, 3-4 hours.

3. Remove ribs. Reserve 2 cups cooking juices; discard remaining juices. Skim fat from reserved juices. Serve with ribs.

1 serving: 393 cal., 17g fat (6g sat. fat), 105mg chol., 1098mg sod., 26g carb. (20g sugars, 1g fiber), 33g pro.

TEST KITCHEN TIP
Country-style are the meatiest of all pork ribs. Look for highly marbled ribs; they might be labeled pork shoulder country-style ribs.

COUNTRY-STYLE BARBECUE RIBS

SLOW-COOKER BACON MAC & CHEESE

I'm all about easy slow-cooker meals. Using lots of cheese, I developed an addictive spin on a casserole favorite.
—*Kristen Heigl, Staten Island, NY*

PREP: 20 min. • **COOK:** 3 hours + standing
MAKES: 18 servings

- 2 large eggs, lightly beaten
- 4 cups whole milk
- 1 can (12 oz.) evaporated milk
- ¼ cup butter, melted
- 1 Tbsp. all-purpose flour
- 1 tsp. salt
- 1 pkg. (16 oz.) small pasta shells
- 1 cup shredded provolone cheese
- 1 cup shredded Manchego or Monterey Jack cheese
- 1 cup shredded white cheddar cheese
- 8 bacon strips, cooked and crumbled

1. In a large bowl, whisk first 6 ingredients until blended. Stir in pasta and cheeses; transfer to a 4- or 5-qt. slow cooker.
2. Cook, covered, on low until the pasta is tender, 3-3½ hours. Turn off slow cooker; remove the insert. Let stand, uncovered, 15 minutes before serving. Top with bacon.

½ cup: 272 cal., 14g fat (8g sat. fat), 59mg chol., 400mg sod., 24g carb. (5g sugars, 1g fiber), 13g pro.

SLOW-COOKER BACON MAC & CHEESE

BBQ BRATS

In Wisconsin, brats are a food group! We are always looking for new ways to cook them. This recipe is easy and a hit at tailgate parties or cookouts no matter the time of year.
—*Jessica Abnet, DePere, WI*

PREP: 20 min. • **COOK:** 3 hours
MAKES: 10 servings

- 10 uncooked bratwurst links
- 1 bottle (12 oz.) **beer** or 1½ cups chicken broth
- 1 cup ketchup
- 1 cup honey barbecue sauce
- 10 hot dog buns, split
     Spicy brown mustard

1. Grill bratwursts, covered, on a greased rack over medium heat or broil 4 in. from the heat 10 minutes, turning frequently. Transfer to a 5-qt. slow cooker.
2. In a large bowl, mix the beer, ketchup and barbecue sauce; pour over the bratwursts. Cook, covered, on low until cooked through, 3-4 hours. Place the bratwursts in buns. Serve with mustard and, if desired, cooking liquid.
1 serving: 480 cal., 27g fat (9g sat. fat), 64mg chol., 1659mg sod., 41g carb. (20g sugars, 1g fiber), 16g pro.

BBQ BRATS

VEGETARIAN BUFFALO DIP

A friend made Buffalo chicken dip and that got me thinking about creating a vegetarian dip with the same flavors. This addictive dip is so amazing, no one will miss the meat.
—Amanda Silvers, Oldfort, TN

PREP: 10 min. • **COOK:** 1½ hours
MAKES: 6 cups

- 1 cup sour cream
- 8 oz. cream cheese, softened
- 1 envelope ranch salad dressing mix
- 2 cups shredded sharp cheddar cheese
- 1 can (15 oz.) black beans, rinsed and drained
- 8 oz. fresh mushrooms, chopped
- 1 cup Buffalo wing sauce
  Optional: Sliced green onions and tortilla chips

Combine sour cream, cream cheese and ranch dressing mix in a bowl until smooth. Stir in the next 4 ingredients. Transfer to a 3- or 4-qt. slow cooker. Cook, covered, on high for 1½ hours. If desired, sprinkle with green onions and serve with tortilla chips.
¼ cup: 113 cal., 8g fat (5g sat. fat), 21mg chol., 526mg sod., 5g carb. (1g sugars, 1g fiber), 4g pro.

BRING IT
Make this dip a few hours before you leave for the party, then keep the slow cooker on the warm setting at the event.

GARDEN GREEN BEANS & POTATOES

Fresh green beans paired with red potatoes make for an easy and filling side dish. To make it even better, add crumbled bacon!
—Kelly Zinn, Cicero, IN

PREP: 10 min. • **COOK:** 6 hours
MAKES: 16 servings

- 2 lbs. fresh green beans, trimmed
- 1½ lbs. red potatoes, quartered
- 1 medium onion, chopped
- ½ cup beef broth
- 1½ tsp. salt
- 1 tsp. dried thyme
- ½ tsp. pepper
- ¼ cup butter, softened
- 1 Tbsp. lemon juice

In a 6-qt. slow cooker, combine the first 7 ingredients. Cook, covered, on low for 6-8 hours or until beans are tender. Stir in butter and lemon juice. Remove with a slotted spoon.
¾ cup: 77 cal., 3g fat (2g sat. fat), 8mg chol., 278mg sod., 12g carb. (2g sugars, 3g fiber), 2g pro. **Diabetic exchanges:** 1 vegetable, ½ starch, ½ fat.

**LOADED
BROCCOLI-CHEESE
POTATO CHOWDER**

SLOW-COOKER TURKEY BREAST WITH GRAVY

This quick-prep recipe lets you feast on turkey at any time of year. We save the rich broth for gravy, noodles and soup making.
—*Joyce Hough, Annapolis, MD*

PREP: 25 min. • **COOK:** 5 hours + standing
MAKES: 12 servings

- 2 tsp. dried parsley flakes
- 1 tsp. salt
- 1 tsp. poultry seasoning
- ½ tsp. paprika
- ½ tsp. pepper
- 2 medium onions, chopped
- 3 medium carrots, cut into ½-in. slices
- 3 celery ribs, coarsely chopped
- 1 bone-in turkey breast (6 to 7 lbs.), skin removed
- ¼ cup all-purpose flour
- ½ cup water

1. Mix the first 5 ingredients in a small bowl. Place vegetables in a 6- or 7-qt. slow cooker; top with turkey. Rub turkey with seasoning mixture.
2. Cook, covered, on low 5-6 hours or until a thermometer inserted in turkey reads at least 170°. Remove from slow cooker; let stand, covered, 15 minutes before slicing.
3. Meanwhile, strain cooking juices into a small saucepan. Mix flour and water until smooth; stir into cooking juices. Bring to a boil; cook and stir until thickened, 1-2 minutes. Serve with turkey.

6 oz. cooked turkey with 3 Tbsp. gravy: 200 cal., 1g fat (0 sat. fat), 117mg chol., 270mg sod., 2g carb. (0 sugars, 0 fiber), 43g pro. **Diabetic exchanges:** 6 lean meat.

LOADED BROCCOLI-CHEESE POTATO CHOWDER

For anyone who loves baked potatoes or broccoli cheese soup, this is the best of both worlds. If you have bacon lovers, offer crumbled cooked bacon as a topping. Then everyone is happy, carnivore or not!
—*Vivi Taylor, Middleburg, FL*

PREP: 15 min. • **COOK:** 6 hours 10 min.
MAKES: 8 servings (2 qt.)

- 1 pkg. (20 oz.) refrigerated hash brown potatoes O'Brien
- 1 garlic clove, minced
- 2 cups reduced-fat sour cream
- ¼ cup all-purpose flour
- ½ tsp. pepper
- ⅛ tsp. ground nutmeg
- 3 cups vegetable stock
- 1 pkg. (12 oz.) frozen broccoli florets, thawed
- 4 cups shredded cheddar cheese
- ½ cup finely chopped green onions

1. Combine the hash browns and garlic in a 5- or 6-qt. slow cooker. In a large bowl, whisk the sour cream, flour, pepper and nutmeg until smooth; stir in stock. Pour into slow cooker; stir to combine. Cook, covered, on low until hash browns are tender, 6-8 hours.
2. Add the broccoli and 3 cups cheese; cover and cook until cheese is melted, about 10 minutes longer. Serve with green onions and remaining cheese.
1 cup: 386 cal., 23g fat (13g sat. fat), 62mg chol., 921mg sod., 26g carb. (6g sugars, 2g fiber), 20g pro.

TEST KITCHEN TIP

If your slow cooker lid is a bit loose, cover the cooker with a piece of parchment before adding the lid. Doing so will keep the lid more firmly in place.

SLOW-COOKER
TURKEY BREAST
WITH GRAVY

HOVER YOUR
CAMERA HERE
Simple & Fun
Friendsgiving
Ideas

SLOW-COOKED REUBEN SPREAD

I'm a big fan of Reuben sandwiches and anything with that flavor combination. For an appetizer, I blend corned beef with Swiss to make a spread for rye bread or crackers.
—*June Herke, Watertown, SD*

PREP: 10 min. • **COOK:** 4 hours
MAKES: 3¾ cups

- 2 pkg. (8 oz. each) cream cheese, cubed
- 4 cups shredded Swiss cheese
- 1 can (14 oz.) sauerkraut, rinsed and well drained
- 4 pkg. (2 oz. each) thinly sliced deli corned beef, chopped
- ½ cup Thousand Island salad dressing
  Snack rye bread or rye crackers

1. Place first 5 ingredients in a 3-qt. slow cooker; stir to combine. Cook, covered, on low 4-4½ hours or until heated through.
2. Stir to blend. Serve spread with bread or crackers.

2 Tbsp.: 137 cal., 12g fat (6g sat. fat), 33mg chol., 285mg sod., 2g carb. (1g sugars, 0 fiber), 6g pro.

SLOW-COOKED REUBEN SPREAD

CHRISTMAS PUNCH

SLOW-COOKER CHORIZO BREAKFAST CASSEROLE
My children ask for this slow-cooked casserole for breakfast and dinner. I've served it with white country gravy or salsa— it's delightful either way.
—*Cindy Pruitt, Grove, OK*

PREP: 25 min. • **COOK:** 4 hours + standing
MAKES: 8 servings

- 1 lb. fresh chorizo or bulk spicy pork sausage
- 1 medium onion, chopped
- 1 medium sweet red pepper, chopped
- 2 jalapeno peppers, seeded and chopped
- 1 pkg. (30 oz.) frozen shredded hash brown potatoes, thawed
- 1½ cups shredded Mexican cheese blend
- 12 large eggs
- 1 cup 2% milk
- ½ tsp. pepper
  Optional: Chopped avocado and tomato

1. In a large skillet, cook chorizo, onion, red pepper and jalapenos over medium heat until cooked through and vegetables are tender, 7-8 minutes, breaking chorizo into crumbles; drain. Cool slightly.
2. In a greased 5-qt. slow cooker, layer a third of the potatoes, chorizo mixture and cheese. Repeat layers twice. In a large bowl, whisk eggs, milk and pepper until blended; pour over top.
3. Cook, covered, on low until eggs are set and a thermometer reads 160°, 4-4½ hours. Uncover and let stand 10 minutes before serving. If desired, top with chopped avocado and tomato.
Note: Wear disposable gloves when cutting hot peppers; the oils can burn skin. Avoid touching your face.
1½ cups: 512 cal., 32g fat (12g sat. fat), 350mg chol., 964mg sod., 25g carb. (4g sugars, 2g fiber), 30g pro.

CHRISTMAS PUNCH
This holiday, why not indulge in a warm ruby red punch made in the slow cooker? We use cinnamon sticks and Red Hots candies to give it that cozy spiced flavor and welcome-home aroma.
—*Angie Goins, Tazewell, TN*

PREP: 5 min. • **COOK:** 3 hours
MAKES: 10 servings

- 4 cups unsweetened pineapple juice
- 4 cups cranberry juice
- ⅓ cup Red Hots
- 2 cinnamon sticks (3 in.)
  Fresh cranberries and additional cinnamon sticks

In a 3- or 4-qt. slow cooker, combine the first 4 ingredients. Cook, covered, on low until heated through and candies are melted, 3-4 hours. Garnish the punch with the cranberries and additional cinnamon sticks.
¾ cup: 129 cal., 0 fat (0 sat. fat), 0 chol., 4mg sod., 33g carb. (28g sugars, 0 fiber), 1g pro.

EASY & ELEGANT HAM

I love to serve my large family this moist, tender ham. It can be readied quickly in the morning, frees up my oven, tastes outstanding and feeds a crowd. Pineapple, cherries and an orange glaze make it a showstopper.
—*Denise DiPace, Medford, NJ*

PREP: 5 min. • COOK: 6 hours
MAKES: 20 servings

- 2 cans (20 oz. each) sliced pineapple
- 1 fully cooked boneless ham (about 6 lbs.), cut in half
- 1 jar (6 oz.) maraschino cherries, well drained
- 1 jar (12 oz.) orange marmalade

1. Drain pineapple, reserving juice; set juice aside. Place half of the pineapple in an ungreased 6-qt. slow cooker. Top with ham. Add cherries, remaining pineapple and reserved pineapple juice. Spoon the marmalade over ham. Cover and cook on low until heated through, 6-7 hours.
2. Remove the ham to a warm serving platter. Serve with pineapple and cherries.
5 oz.: 212 cal., 5g fat (2g sat. fat), 69mg chol., 1424mg sod., 18g carb. (18g sugars, 0 fiber), 25g pro.

SEAFOOD CHEESE DIP

This cheesy recipe has a nice combination of seafood flavors and clings beautifully to slices of bread.
—*Michelle Domm, Atlanta, NY*

PREP: 15 min. • COOK: 1½ hours
MAKES: 5 cups

- 1 pkg. (32 oz.) Velveeta, cubed
- 2 cans (6 oz. each) lump crabmeat, drained
- 1 can (10 oz.) diced tomatoes and green chiles, undrained
- 1 cup frozen cooked salad shrimp, thawed
  French bread baguette, sliced and toasted, and assorted fresh vegetables

In a greased 3-qt. slow cooker, combine the Velveeta, crab, tomatoes and shrimp. Cover and cook on low for 1½-2 hours or until the cheese is melted, stirring occasionally. Serve with baguette slices and vegetables.
¼ cup: 172 cal., 12g fat (7g sat. fat), 77mg chol., 791mg sod., 4g carb. (3g sugars, 0 fiber), 12g pro.

SWEET & SPICY MEATBALLS

SWEET & SPICY MEATBALLS

You'll usually find a batch of these meatballs in my freezer. The slightly sweet sauce nicely complements the spicy pork sausage.
—*Genie Brown, Roanoke, VA*

PREP: 25 min. • **BAKE:** 15 min.
MAKES: about 4 dozen

- 2 lbs. bulk spicy pork sausage
- 1 large egg, lightly beaten
- 1 cup packed brown sugar
- 1 cup red wine vinegar
- 1 cup ketchup
- 1 Tbsp. soy sauce
- 1 tsp. ground ginger

1. In a large bowl, combine sausage and egg. Shape into 1-in. balls. Place on a greased rack in a shallow baking pan. Bake at 400° for 15-20 minutes or until a thermometer reads 160°; drain.
2. Meanwhile, in a saucepan, combine the remaining ingredients. Bring to a boil. Reduce heat; simmer, uncovered, until sugar is dissolved.
3. Transfer meatballs to a 3-qt. slow cooker. Add sauce and stir gently to coat. Cover and keep warm on low until serving.
1 meatball: 70 cal., 4g fat (1g sat. fat), 14mg chol., 200mg sod., 6g carb. (6g sugars, 0 fiber), 2g pro.

PHILLY CHEESE
SANDWICHES

PHILLY CHEESE SANDWICHES

I'm a big fan of Philly sandwiches, so this throw-together recipe is right up my alley. And my slow cooker does all the work. Win-win!
—*Christina Addison, Blanchester, OH*

PREP: 20 min. • **COOK:** 8 hours
MAKES: 8 servings

- 1 boneless beef chuck roast (2½ to 3 lbs.), trimmed and cut into 1-in. cubes
- 2 medium onions, halved and sliced
- ¼ cup Worcestershire sauce
- 2 garlic cloves, minced
- 1 tsp. dried oregano
- ½ tsp. dried basil
- 1 medium sweet red pepper, sliced
- 1 medium green pepper, sliced
- 8 slices American cheese or pepper jack cheese
- 8 hoagie buns, split and toasted

1. In a 3- or 4-qt. slow cooker, combine first 6 ingredients. Cook, covered, on low 7 hours. Stir in peppers; cook, covered, until the meat and peppers are tender, 1-3 hours.
2. Stir to break up the meat. Serve beef mixture and cheese on buns.
1 sandwich: 546 cal., 23g fat (9g sat. fat), 97mg chol., 754mg sod., 42g carb. (9g sugars, 2g fiber), 40g pro.

TEST KITCHEN TIP

For a bit of crunchiness, you can toast the split hoagie buns under the broiler for 2-3 minutes. But watch carefully—they go from perfect to burnt in a hurry!

SAUSAGE JALAPENO DIP

SAUSAGE JALAPENO DIP

This creamy dip cooks up like a dream in the slow cooker. Scoop it up with crunchy tortilla chips or raw veggies.
—*Gina Fensler, Cincinnati, OH*

PREP: 15 min. • **COOK:** 5½ hours
MAKES: 6 cups

- 1 lb. bulk Italian sausage
- 2 large sweet red peppers, finely chopped
- 3 jalapeno peppers, finely chopped
- 1 cup whole milk
- 2 pkg. (8 oz. each) cream cheese, softened
- 1 cup shredded part-skim mozzarella cheese
  Tortilla chips

1. In a skillet, cook sausage over medium heat until no longer pink, 6-8 minutes, breaking it into crumbles; drain.
2. Place the red peppers, jalapenos and sausage in a 3-qt. slow cooker; add milk. Cook, covered, on low until peppers are tender, 5-6 hours.
3. Stir in cheeses. Cook, covered, on low until cheese is melted, about 30 minutes longer. Serve with tortilla chips.
Note: Wear disposable gloves when cutting hot peppers; the oils can burn skin. Avoid touching your face.
¼ cup: 137 cal., 12g fat (6g sat. fat), 33mg chol., 211mg sod., 3g carb. (2g sugars, 0 fiber), 5g pro.

BOEUF BOURGUIGNON FROM THE SLOW COOKER

I'd wanted to make boeuf bourguignon (beef Burgundy) ever since I got one of Julia Child's cookbooks, but I wanted to find a way to fix it in a slow cooker. My version of is still rich, hearty and delicious, but without the need to watch it on the stovetop or in the oven.
—*Crystal Jo Bruns, Iliff, CO*

PREP: 30 min. + marinating
COOK: 8 hours
MAKES: 12 servings

- 3 lbs. beef stew meat
- 1¾ cups dry red wine
- 3 Tbsp. olive oil
- 3 Tbsp. dried minced onion
- 2 Tbsp. dried parsley flakes
- 1 bay leaf
- 1 tsp. dried thyme
- ¼ tsp. pepper
- 8 bacon strips, chopped
- 1 lb. whole fresh mushrooms, quartered
- 24 pearl onions, peeled (about 2 cups)
- 2 garlic cloves, minced
- ⅓ cup all-purpose flour
- 1 tsp. salt
  Hot cooked whole wheat egg noodles, optional

1. Place beef in a large resealable bowl; add wine, oil and seasonings. Turn to coat. Cover; refrigerate overnight.
2. In a skillet, cook bacon over medium heat until crisp, stirring occasionally. Remove with a slotted spoon; drain on paper towels. Discard drippings, reserving 1 Tbsp. in pan.
3. Add the mushrooms and onions to the drippings; cook and stir over medium-high heat until tender. Add garlic; cook 1 minute longer.
4. Drain the beef, reserving marinade; transfer beef to a 4- or 5-qt. slow cooker. Sprinkle beef with flour and salt; toss to coat. Top with the bacon and mushroom mixture. Add reserved marinade.
5. Cook, covered, on low until the beef is tender, 8-10 hours. Remove bay leaf. If desired, serve stew with noodles.

⅔ cup beef mixture: 289 cal., 15g fat (5g sat. fat), 77mg chol., 350mg sod., 8g carb. (2g sugars, 1g fiber), 25g pro. **Diabetic exchanges:** 3 lean meat, 1½ fat, 1 vegetable.

TEST KITCHEN TIP

To peel pearl onions, place in boiling water; boil 2 minutes. Drain and submerge in an ice water bath, When cool, pinch the stem end to remove the peel.

BOEUF BOURGUIGNON FROM THE SLOW COOKER

SLOW-COOKED
CARNITAS

SLOW-COOKED CARNITAS

Simmer succulent pork the slow-cooker way. Sometimes, instead of using tortillas, I put the meat on top of shredded lettuce for a tasty salad.
—*Lisa Glogow, Aliso Viejo, CA*

PREP: 20 min. • **COOK:** 6 hours
MAKES: 12 servings

- 1 boneless pork shoulder butt roast (3 to 4 lbs.)
- 3 garlic cloves, thinly sliced
- 2 tsp. olive oil
- ½ tsp. salt
- ½ tsp. pepper
- 1 bunch green onions, chopped
- 1½ cups minced fresh cilantro
- 1 cup salsa
- ½ cup chicken broth
- ½ cup tequila or additional chicken broth
- 2 cans (4 oz. each) chopped green chiles
- 12 flour tortillas (8 in.) or corn tortillas (6 in.), warmed
  Optional: Fresh cilantro leaves, sliced red onion and chopped tomatoes

1. Cut roast in half; place in a 5-qt. slow cooker. Sprinkle with the garlic, oil, salt and pepper. Add onions, cilantro, salsa, broth, tequila and chiles. Cover, cook on low until meat is tender, 6-8 hours.
2. Remove meat; cool slightly. Shred with 2 forks and return to the slow cooker; heat through. Spoon about ⅔ cup meat mixture onto each tortilla; serve with toppings of your choice.
1 carnita: 363 cal., 15g fat (5g sat. fat), 67mg chol., 615mg sod., 28g carb. (1g sugars, 1g fiber), 24g pro.

MA

BUTTERNUT SQUASH & BARLEY SOUP

I love to use my garden produce in this veggie-packed soup. Serve it with bread or oatmeal dinner rolls, and you've got a delicious, healthy dinner.
—*Julie Sloan, Osceola, IN*

PREP: 25 min. • **COOK:** 5¼ hours
MAKES: 12 servings (3 qt.)

- 1 small butternut squash (2½ to 3 lbs.), peeled and cut into 1-in. cubes (about 6 cups)
- 4 cups water
- 1 carton (32 oz.) reduced-sodium chicken broth
- ¾ cup medium pearl barley
- 2 medium carrots, chopped
- 2 celery ribs, chopped
- 1 small onion, chopped
- 2 Tbsp. minced fresh parsley or 2 tsp. dried parsley flakes
- 2 garlic cloves, minced
- 1 tsp. rubbed sage
- 1¼ tsp. salt
- ½ tsp. curry powder
- ¼ tsp. pepper
- 1 cup cubed cooked turkey

1. Place all ingredients except turkey in a 5- or 6-qt. slow cooker. Cook, covered, on low 5-7 hours or until squash and barley are tender.

2. Stir in turkey; cook, covered, 15 minutes or until heated through.

Freeze option: Transfer soup to three 1-qt. freezer containers; cool. Cover and freeze for up to 3 months. To use frozen soup, thaw in refrigerator. Place in a saucepan and heat through.

1 cup: 120 cal., 1g fat (0 sat. fat), 12mg chol., 493mg sod., 23g carb. (4g sugars, 6g fiber), 7g pro. **Diabetic exchanges:** 1½ starch.

TEST KITCHEN TIP
Adjust the amount of curry powder to suit your taste.

BUTTERNUT SQUASH & BARLEY SOUP

MA
POTLUCK BEANS

It was the morning of our family potluck and I still needed something to take for the buffet. I threw together this recipe while drinking my morning coffee. By the end of the gathering, the beans were all gone and someone had even washed the slow cooker for me!
—*Mary Anne Thygesen, Portland, OR*

PREP: 10 min. • **COOK:** 4 hours
MAKES: 12 servings

- 1 cup brewed coffee
- ½ cup packed brown sugar
- ¼ cup spicy brown mustard
- 2 Tbsp. molasses
- 2 cans (16 oz. each) butter beans
- 2 cans (16 oz. each) kidney beans
- 2 cans (16 oz. each) navy beans

In a greased 3- or 4-qt. slow cooker, mix first 4 ingredients. Rinse and drain beans; stir into coffee mixture. Cook, covered, on low until flavors are blended, 4-5 hours.
Freeze option: Freeze cooled beans in freezer containers. To use, partially thaw in refrigerator overnight. Heat through in a covered saucepan, stirring occasionally; add water if necessary.
½ cup: 243 cal., 0 fat (0 sat. fat), 0 chol., 538mg sod., 50g carb. (13g sugars, 10g fiber), 14g pro.

SLOW-COOKER SAUSAGE & APPLES

This recipe belongs to my friend Patty, who made me a wonderful cookbook of her dishes. This is one of her most popular recipes. I often double it for parties.
—*Tammy Zywicki, Elmira, NY*

PREP: 10 min. • **COOK:** 3 hours
MAKES: 24 servings

- 2 lbs. smoked kielbasa or Polish sausage, sliced
- 1 jar (24 oz.) chunky applesauce
- ½ cup packed brown sugar
- ½ cup chopped onion

Combine all ingredients in a 4- or 5-qt. slow cooker. Cook, covered on low, until heated through, 3-4 hours.
¼ cup: 155 cal., 10g fat (4g sat. fat), 25mg chol., 254mg sod., 11g carb. (9g sugars, 0 fiber), 5g pro.

JALAPENO MAC & CHEESE

BLACK-EYED PEAS & HAM

Every New Year's Day, we have these slow-cooked black-eyed peas to bring good luck for the coming year.
—*Dawn Legler, Fort Morgan, CO*

PREP: 20 min. + soaking • **COOK:** 5 hours
MAKES: 12 servings

- 1 pkg. (16 oz.) dried black-eyed peas, rinsed and sorted
- ½ lb. fully cooked boneless ham, finely chopped
- 1 medium onion, finely chopped
- 1 medium sweet red pepper, finely chopped
- 5 bacon strips, cooked and crumbled
- 1 large jalapeno pepper, seeded and finely chopped
- 2 garlic cloves, minced
- 1½ tsp. ground cumin
- 1 tsp. reduced-sodium chicken bouillon granules
- ½ tsp. salt
- ½ tsp. cayenne pepper
- ¼ tsp. pepper
- 6 cups water
  Minced fresh cilantro, optional
  Hot cooked rice

1. Soak the black-eyed peas according to package directions.
2. Transfer peas to a 6-qt. slow cooker; add the next 12 ingredients. Cover and cook on low 5-7 hours, until peas are tender. Sprinkle with cilantro if desired. Serve with rice.
Note: Wear disposable gloves when cutting hot peppers; the oils can burn skin. Avoid touching your face.
¾ cup: 170 cal., 3g fat (1g sat. fat), 13mg chol., 386mg sod., 24g carb. (5g sugars, 7g fiber), 13g pro. **Diabetic exchanges:** 1½ starch, 1 lean meat.

JALAPENO MAC & CHEESE

After I had surgery, a friend brought me a big pan of mac and cheese. I've tweaked the recipe over the years, most recently adding jalapenos at the request of my son.
—*Teresa Gustafson, Elkton, MD*

PREP: 25 min. • **COOK:** 3 hours
MAKES: 15 servings

- 1 pkg. (16 oz.) uncooked elbow macaroni
- 6 Tbsp. butter, divided
- 4 jalapeno peppers, seeded and finely chopped
- 3 cups shredded cheddar cheese
- 2 cups shredded Colby-Monterey Jack cheese
- 2 cups whole milk
- 1 can (10¾ oz.) condensed cream of onion soup, undiluted
- 1 can (10¾ oz.) condensed cheddar cheese soup, undiluted
- ½ cup mayonnaise
- ¼ tsp. pepper
- 1 cup crushed Ritz crackers (about 25 crackers)

1. Cook macaroni according to package directions for al dente; drain. Transfer to a greased 5-qt. slow cooker.
2. Melt 2 Tbsp. butter in a large skillet over medium-high heat. Add jalapenos; cook and stir until crisp-tender, about 5 minutes. Add to the slow cooker. Stir in the cheeses, milk, soups, mayonnaise and pepper.
3. Cook, covered, on low until cheese is melted and mixture is heated through, about 3 hours. Melt remaining 4 Tbsp. butter; stir in crackers. Sprinkle over macaroni mixture.
Note: Wear disposable gloves when cutting hot peppers; the oils can burn skin. Avoid touching your face.
¾ cup: 428 cal., 27g fat (13g sat. fat), 53mg chol., 654mg sod., 33g carb. (5g sugars, 2g fiber), 14g pro.

BLACK-EYED PEAS & HAM

HOVER YOUR CAMERA HERE

12 Essential Tips that Make Traveling with Food So Much Easier

SO-EASY STICKY CHICKEN WINGS

My neighbor once shared these tangy wings with me at a potluck, and they have been a family favorite ever since.
—*Jo Vanderwolf, Lillooet, BC*

PREP: 20 min. • **COOK:** 3 hours
MAKES: 40 pieces

- 4 lbs. chicken wings
- 1 cup barbecue sauce
- 1 cup soy sauce
- 6 green onions, chopped, divided
- 1 Tbsp. sesame seeds

Using a sharp knife, cut through the 2 joints on each wing ; discard the wing tips. Place the remaining wing pieces in a 4- or 5-qt. slow cooker. Stir in barbecue sauce, soy sauce and ¼ cup chopped green onions. Cook, covered, on high 3-4 hours or until tender. Sprinkle with sesame seeds and the remaining green onions.

1 piece: 68 cal., 4g fat (1g sat. fat), 14mg chol., 452mg sod., 3g carb. (2g sugars, 0 fiber), 6g pro.

SO-EASY STICKY
CHICKEN WINGS

1. In a large skillet, brown each roast in oil on all sides. Drain. Transfer meat to a 7-qt. slow cooker. Combine the water, onion, garlic, salad dressing and gravy mixes, pepper flakes, Italian seasoning and Worcestershire sauce; pour over beef. Cover and cook on low for 8-10 hours or until meat is tender.

2. Remove beef; cool slightly. Skim fat from cooking juices. Pour juices into a large bowl. Shred the beef with 2 forks; add to bowl. Using a slotted spoon, place ½ cup on each bun. Top with cheese and giardiniera if desired.

Freeze option: Cool the meat and juices; transfer to freezer containers. Freeze for up to 3 months. To use, thaw in refrigerator overnight. Place in a Dutch oven; heat through. Using a slotted spoon, place ½ cup on each bun. Top with cheese and giardiniera if desired.

1 sandwich: 450 cal., 16g fat (5g sat. fat), 89mg chol., 969mg sod., 39g carb. (8g sugars, 1g fiber), 37g pro.

READER RAVES

"I made it for a dinner party, and there literally was nothing left."

—JENNIFER, TASTEOFHOME.COM

MOM'S ITALIAN BEEF SANDWICHES

MOM'S ITALIAN BEEF SANDWICHES

My mom made the best Italian beef. There were never any leftovers when she made these sandwiches for family reunions.
—*Mary McVey, Colfax, NC*

PREP: 20 min. • **COOK:** 8 hours
MAKES: 16 servings

- 1 boneless beef rump roast or bottom round roast (2 lbs.), halved
- 1 boneless beef chuck roast (2 lbs.), halved
- 1 beef sirloin tip roast (1 lb.)
- 2 Tbsp. canola oil
- 2 cups water
- 1 medium onion, chopped
- 4 garlic cloves, minced
- 2 envelopes Italian salad dressing mix
- 1 envelope zesty Italian salad dressing mix
- 1 envelope (0.87 oz.) brown gravy mix
- 1 to 2 Tbsp. crushed red pepper flakes
- 1 Tbsp. Italian seasoning
- 2 tsp. Worcestershire sauce
- 16 hoagie buns, split
  Optional: Sliced provolone cheese and giardiniera

CINCINNATI-STYLE CHILI

My husband had this type of chili when visiting a friend in Ohio and was super thrilled when I made it at home. You can have it two-way, with just chili and spaghetti, but our favorite is five-way, when you add all three toppings: beans, cheese and onion.

—*Tari Ambler, Shorewood, IL*

PREP: 35 min. • **COOK:** 6 hours
MAKES: 10 servings

- 2 lbs. extra-lean ground turkey
- 2 medium onions, finely chopped
- 4 garlic cloves, minced
- 2 cans (8 oz. each) no-salt-added tomato sauce
- 1 can (14½ oz.) reduced-sodium beef broth
- 2 Tbsp. cider vinegar
- ½ oz. unsweetened chocolate, chopped
- 3 Tbsp. chili powder
- 1 bay leaf
- 2 tsp. Worcestershire sauce
- 1 tsp. ground cumin
- ¾ tsp. salt
- ¾ tsp. ground cinnamon
- ¼ tsp. ground allspice
- ⅛ tsp. ground cloves
- ⅛ tsp. cayenne pepper
- 1 pkg. (16 oz.) whole wheat spaghetti

TOPPINGS

- 1 can (16 oz.) kidney beans, rinsed and drained
- 1¼ cups shredded reduced-fat cheddar cheese
- 1 medium onion, chopped

1. In a Dutch oven coated with cooking spray, cook turkey, onions and garlic until turkey is no longer pink. Transfer to a 3-qt. slow cooker.

2. In a large bowl, combine tomato sauce, broth, vinegar, chocolate and seasonings; pour over turkey mixture. Cook, covered, on low 6-8 hours.

3. Cook spaghetti according to package directions; drain. Remove bay leaf from the chili. For each serving, place ¾ cup spaghetti in a bowl. Top with about ⅔ cup chili, 3 Tbsp. kidney beans, 2 Tbsp. cheese and 1 Tbsp. chopped onion.

1 serving: 388 cal., 6g fat (3g sat. fat), 47mg chol., 523mg sod., 52g carb. (9g sugars, 10g fiber), 37g pro.

BRING IT

Make this chili a day ahead and reheat in the microwave before you head out. Cook the spaghetti just before leaving, tossing it lightly with a little oil while warm to prevent sticking.

MIXED VEGGIES & RICE

MIXED VEGGIES & RICE

To add variety to sides for those who don't care for potatoes, I came up with this colorful dish. It's an easy slow-cooker recipe that you can put right onto the buffet table.
—*Judy Batson, Tampa, FL*

PREP: 5 min. • **COOK:** 3 hours
MAKES: 8 servings

- 4 pkg. (10 oz. each) frozen long grain white rice with mixed vegetables
- 12 oz. frozen mixed vegetables
- ½ cup vegetable broth or light beer
- 1 tsp. onion powder
- 1 tsp. garlic powder
- 1 tsp. seasoned salt
  Butter, optional

In a 5-qt. slow cooker, combine the first 6 ingredients. Cook, covered, on low for 3-4 hours or until heated through. If desired, serve with butter.
¾ cup: 120 cal., 0 fat (0 sat. fat), 0 chol., 254mg sod., 26g carb. (3g sugars, 3g fiber), 3g pro. **Diabetic exchanges:** 1½ starch.

THE SWEETEST TREATS

Bring sweetness to the party with these crowd-pleasing goodies.
It's easy to step up your dessert game with any of these showstoppers!

P. 292

P. 305

P. 280

BANANA CRUMB PUDDING

1. In a large heavy saucepan, mix sugar and cornstarch. Whisk in milk. Cook and stir over medium heat until thickened and bubbly. Reduce heat to low; cook and stir 2 minutes longer. Remove from heat.
2. In a bowl, whisk a small amount of the hot mixture into egg yolks; return all to pan, whisking constantly. Bring to a gentle boil; cook and stir for 2 minutes. Remove from heat. Stir in butter, vanilla and salt. Cool 15 minutes, stirring occasionally.
3. Reserve 1 cup of whole wafers and 1 banana for topping. Crush 2 cups wafers and set aside. In a 13x9-in. baking dish, arrange a single layer of whole wafers, filling the gaps with crushed wafers. Layer with a third of the bananas and pudding. Repeat layers twice. Press waxed paper onto the surface of pudding. Refrigerate, covered, overnight.
4. For topping, beat heavy cream until it begins to thicken. Add sugar; beat until soft peaks form (do not overmix). Just before serving, remove waxed paper and spread whipped cream over pudding; top with reserved banana and wafers.

¾ cup: 535 cal., 27g fat (13g sat. fat), 121mg chol., 370mg sod., 70g carb. (46g sugars, 1g fiber), 7g pro.

TEST KITCHEN TIP
Want to change things up? Add 2 Tbsp. spiced rum along with the vanilla extract for an unexpected flavor.

(MA)

BANANA CRUMB PUDDING
Friends and family ask me to make my thick and creamy banana pudding for all occasions. They can't get enough of the wonderful flavor of the fruit and the vanilla wafer crumbs. You can also top the classic southern treat with meringue instead of whipped cream.
—*Yvonnia Butner, Pinnacle, NC*

PREP: 15 min. • **COOK:** 20 min. + chilling
MAKES: 15 servings

- 1 cup sugar
- ½ cup cornstarch
- 6 cups 2% milk
- 5 large egg yolks
- ¼ cup butter, cubed
- 2 tsp. vanilla extract
- 1 tsp. kosher salt
- 2 pkg. (11 oz. each) vanilla wafers
- 7 medium bananas, sliced

TOPPING
- 2 cups heavy whipping cream
- 6 Tbsp. sugar

CHOCOLATE HAZELNUT PUDDING TORTE

TART CRANBERRY CAKE

You can't beat this recipe to showcase true fall flavor. The ruby cranberries stay bright and beautiful, and their tartness is irresistible. I've made this cake many times to share.
—*Marilyn Paradis, Woodburn, OR*

PREP: 15 min. • **BAKE:** 45 min.
MAKES: 20 servings

- 3 large eggs, room temperature
- 2 cups sugar
- ¾ cup butter, softened
- 1 tsp. almond extract
- 2 cups all-purpose flour
- 2½ cups fresh or frozen cranberries, thawed
- ⅔ cup chopped pecans
  Optional: Whipped cream and cranberries

1. Preheat oven to 350°. In a large bowl, beat eggs and sugar until slightly thickened and lemon-colored, about 5 minutes. Add butter and extract; beat 2 minutes. Gradually stir in flour just until combined. Stir in cranberries and pecans. Spread in a greased 13x9-in. baking dish.
2. Bake until a toothpick inserted in the center comes out clean, 45-50 minutes. If desired, serve each piece with whipped cream and a cranberry.
1 piece: 227 cal., 10g fat (5g sat. fat), 46mg chol., 66mg sod., 32g carb. (21g sugars, 1g fiber), 3g pro.

TEST KITCHEN TIP

If you use frozen cranberries for this recipe, measure them while they're frozen. Frozen cranberries are the same shape and size as fresh, but once they're thawed they'll shrink and take up less space—so you'll risk adding too many cranberries if you thaw them before measuring.

MA

CHOCOLATE HAZELNUT PUDDING TORTE

This recipe is a busy mom's twist on a favorite dessert—tiramisu. The dish is simple to assemble and perfect to make the day before you want to serve it. The hardest thing about this recipe is waiting for it to chill so you can eat it!
—*Cheryl Snavely, Hagerstown, MD*

PREP: 15 min. + chilling
MAKES: 8 servings

- 24 soft ladyfingers, divided
- ½ cup Nutella, divided
- 1½ cups half-and-half cream
- 1 pkg. (3.4 oz.) instant French vanilla pudding mix
- 1 carton (12 oz.) frozen whipped topping, thawed
  Grated or shaved chocolate

1. Arrange 12 ladyfingers in an 11x7-in. dish. Spread with half the Nutella.
2. In a large bowl, whisk the cream and pudding mix for 2 minutes. Stir in whipped topping. Spread half the mixture over the Nutella. Top with remaining ladyfingers; spread with remaining Nutella and then remaining pudding mixture. Sprinkle with grated or shaved chocolate. Refrigerate, covered, for 8 hours or overnight. Refrigerate any leftovers.
1 piece: 390 cal., 18g fat (11g sat. fat), 67mg chol., 347mg sod., 46g carb. (37g sugars, 1g fiber), 5g pro.

TART CRANBERRY CAKE

TRADITIONAL CHEESECAKE

Here's a basic cheesecake that tastes great alone or with garnishes and sauces.
—Taste of Home *Test Kitchen*

PREP: 20 min. • **BAKE:** 55 min. + chilling
MAKES: 12 servings

- 1 cup graham cracker crumbs
- 1 Tbsp. sugar
- 3 Tbsp. cold butter

FILLING

- 4 pkg. (8 oz. each) cream cheese, softened
- 1¼ cups sugar
- 1 Tbsp. lemon juice
- 2 tsp. vanilla extract
- 3 large eggs, room temperature, lightly beaten
  Raspberry sauce, optional

1. Preheat oven to 350°. In a small bowl, combine cracker crumbs and sugar; cut in butter until crumbly. Grease the side only of a 9-in. springform pan; press crumb mixture onto the bottom of pan. Place on a baking sheet. Bake for 10 minutes. Cool on a wire rack.
2. In a large bowl, beat cream cheese and sugar until smooth. Beat in lemon juice and vanilla. Add eggs; beat on low speed just until combined. Pour filling onto crust. Return pan to baking sheet.
3. Bake 45-55 minutes or until center is almost set. Cool on wire rack 10 minutes. Carefully run a knife around the inside edge of pan to loosen; cool 1 hour longer.
4. Refrigerate overnight. Serve with Raspberry sauce if desired. Refrigerate any leftovers.
1 piece: 424 cal., 31g fat (19g sat. fat), 144mg chol., 311mg sod., 30g carb. (24g sugars, 0 fiber), 8g pro.
Raspberry Sauce: In a small saucepan, combine ⅔ cup sugar and 4 tsp. cornstarch; stir in ¼ cup water until smooth. Add 2½ cups fresh or frozen raspberries. Bring to a boil; cook and until thickened, about 2 minutes. Remove from heat; strain, then stir in 2 tsp. lemon juice.

TRADITIONAL CHEESECAKE

ZUCCHINI WALNUT CAKE

1 tsp. vanilla extract
2 cups confectioners' sugar
   Chopped toasted walnuts, optional

1. Preheat oven to 350°. Grease a 13x9-in. baking pan; set aside.
2. In a large bowl, beat the zucchini, sugar, oil and eggs until well blended. Combine the flour, cinnamon, salt, baking powder and baking soda; gradually beat into the zucchini mixture until blended. Fold in walnuts if desired.
3. Pour batter into prepared pan. Bake until a toothpick inserted in the center comes out clean, 35-40 minutes. Cool completely on a wire rack.
4. For frosting, in a small bowl, beat the cream cheese, butter, milk and vanilla until smooth. Add confectioners' sugar and mix well. Frost cake. Sprinkle with nuts if desired. Store in the refrigerator.

1 piece: 275 cal., 13g fat (3g sat. fat), 45mg chol., 174mg sod., 37g carb. (26g sugars, 1g fiber), 3g pro.

TEST KITCHEN TIP

To make a chocolate version of this cake, add ½ cup of cocoa powder to the dry flour mixture, then follow the recipe as published. For other variations, try using toasted pecans instead of walnuts or adding 1 cup of chocolate chips to the top of the cake before baking. You could also try adding 1 can (20 oz.) of crushed pineapple, drained, to the wet zucchini mixture.

ZUCCHINI WALNUT CAKE

What gardener doesn't have extra zucchini? When it's abundant, I shred and freeze plenty so I have it on hand to bake this moist sheet cake all year long. I've made this cake for the last 13 years, and it's a winner! The cream cheese frosting is yummy, and the big panful always goes fast at picnic or potluck. I have a friend who started growing zucchini just to make this cake!
—*Marie Hoyer, Hodgenville, KY*

PREP: 20 min. • **BAKE:** 35 min. + cooling
MAKES: 24 servings

2   cups shredded zucchini
2   cups sugar
1   cup canola oil
4   large eggs, room temperature
2½ cups all-purpose flour
1½ tsp. ground cinnamon
1   tsp. salt
½   tsp. baking powder
½   tsp. baking soda
½   cup chopped toasted walnuts, optional
FROSTING
3   oz. cream cheese, softened
¼   cup butter, softened
1   Tbsp. 2% milk

CHOCOLATE-COVERED STRAWBERRY COBBLER

This cobbler came about because I love chocolate-covered strawberries. Top it with whipped cream, either plain or with a little chocolate syrup stirred in.
—*Andrea Bolden, Unionville, TN*

PREP: 15 min. • **BAKE:** 35 min. + standing
MAKES: 12 servings

1	cup butter, cubed
1½	cups self-rising flour
2¼	cups sugar, divided
¾	cup 2% milk
1	tsp. vanilla extract
⅓	cup baking cocoa
4	cups fresh strawberries, quartered
2	cups boiling water
	Whipped cream and additional strawberries

1. Preheat oven to 350°. Place butter in a 13x9-in. baking pan; heat pan in oven for 3-5 minutes or until butter is melted. Meanwhile, in a large bowl, combine flour, 1¼ cups sugar, milk and vanilla until well blended. In a small bowl, mix cocoa and remaining 1 cup sugar.
2. Remove baking pan from oven; add batter. Sprinkle with strawberries and cocoa mixture; pour boiling water evenly over top (do not stir). Bake 35-40 minutes or until a toothpick inserted into cake portion comes out clean.
3. Let stand 10 minutes. Serve warm, with whipped cream and additional strawberries.
1 serving: 368 cal., 16g fat (10g sat. fat), 42mg chol., 316mg sod., 55g carb. (41g sugars, 2g fiber), 3g pro.

CHOCOLATE-COVERED STRAWBERRY COBBLER

CLASSIC CHOCOLATE CAKE

This recipe appeared on a can of Hershey's Cocoa way back in 1943. I tried it, my boys liked it and I've been making it ever since. I make all my cakes from scratch, and this is one of the best!
—*Betty Follas, Morgan Hill, CA*

PREP: 15 min. • **BAKE:** 35 min. + cooling
MAKES: 15 servings

- ⅔ cup butter, softened
- 1⅔ cups sugar
- 3 large eggs, room temperature
- 2 cups all-purpose flour
- ⅔ cup baking cocoa
- 1¼ tsp. baking soda
- 1 tsp. salt
- 1⅓ cups 2% milk
  Confectioners' sugar or favorite frosting

1. Preheat oven to 350°. Cream butter and sugar until light and fluffy, 5-7 minutes. Add eggs, 1 at a time, beating well after each addition. Combine flour, cocoa, baking soda and salt; add to creamed mixture alternately with milk, beating until smooth after each addition. Pour batter into a greased and floured 13x9-in. baking pan.
2. Bake until a toothpick inserted in center comes out clean, 35-40 minutes. Cool completely on a wire rack. When cake is cool, dust with confectioners' sugar or top with your favorite frosting.
1 piece: 257 cal., 10g fat (6g sat. fat), 67mg chol., 368mg sod., 38g carb. (23g sugars, 1g fiber), 4g pro.

TEST KITCHEN TIP

Unsweetened cocoa powder is recommended for this cake. It is rich in cocoa butter and dissolves into the batter to create a nice, smooth texture and strong chocolate flavor.

CHOCOLATE MARSHMALLOW PEANUT BUTTER SQUARES

I combined a couple of recipes to create these crunchy, chocolaty bars that burst with peanut butter flavor, marshmallows and pretzel pieces. The bars could also pass for fudge!
—*Dawn Lowenstein, Huntingdon Valley, PA*

PREP: 15 min. • **COOK:** 5 min. + chilling
MAKES: 5 dozen

- 1 can (14 oz.) sweetened condensed milk
- 1 pkg. (11 oz.) peanut butter and milk chocolate chips
- ½ cup milk chocolate chips
- ½ cup creamy peanut butter
- 1 tsp. vanilla extract
- 1½ cups miniature marshmallows
- 1 cup broken miniature pretzels
- 1 cup Rice Krispies

1. Place first 5 ingredients in a large heavy saucepan; cook and stir over low heat until smooth and blended, about 5 minutes (mixture will be very thick). Remove from heat; stir in the remaining ingredients. Spread into a greased 13x9-in. pan.
2. Refrigerate, covered, until firm, about 4 hours. Cut into squares. Store in an airtight container in the refrigerator.
1 square: 85 cal., 4g fat (2g sat. fat), 3mg chol., 50mg sod., 12g carb. (8g sugars, 0 fiber), 1g pro.

NUTTY PIE-CRUST COOKIES

NUTTY PIE-CRUST COOKIES

I like Italian cream cake, so I used it as inspiration for this cookie recipe. The splash of orange liqueur in the filling makes it special.
—Sonji McCarty-Onezine, Beaumont, TX

PREP: 15 min. + chilling
BAKE: 10 min./batch + cooling
MAKES: about 3 dozen

- 1 cup butter, softened
- 1¾ cups all-purpose flour
- ¼ cup confectioners' sugar
- ⅛ tsp. salt
- ⅓ cup heavy whipping cream
FILLING
- ½ cup finely chopped pecans, toasted
- ½ cup sweetened shredded coconut, toasted
- ½ cup butter, softened
- ½ cup cream cheese, softened
- ⅛ tsp. salt
- 2 tsp. orange liqueur, optional
- ¾ cup confectioners' sugar

1. In a large bowl, beat butter, flour, confectioners' sugar and salt until crumbly. Beat in cream. Divide dough in half. Shape each into a disk; wrap and refrigerate for 30 minutes or until firm enough to roll.
2. Preheat oven to 350°. On a lightly floured surface, roll each portion of dough to ¼-in. thickness. Cut with a floured 1½-in. round cookie cutter. Place circles 1 in. apart on ungreased baking sheets.
3. Bake 10-12 minutes or until edges begin to brown. Cool on pans 2 minutes. Remove to wire racks to cool completely.
4. For filling, place pecans and coconut in a small bowl; toss to combine. Reserve ½ cup coconut mixture. In another bowl,

beat butter, cream cheese, salt and, if desired, liqueur until creamy. Gradually beat in confectioners' sugar until smooth. Fold in remaining coconut mixture.
5. Spread filling over bottoms of half of the cookies; cover with remaining cookies. Place reserved the coconut mixture in a shallow bowl. Roll sides of the cookies in the mixture.
Freeze option: Transfer wrapped disks to a resealable container; freeze. To use, thaw dough in refrigerator until soft enough to roll. Prepare, bake and fill cookies as directed.
1 sandwich cookie: 120 cal., 10g fat (6g sat. fat), 24mg chol., 79mg sod., 8g carb. (3g sugars, 0 fiber), 1g pro.

BANANA FUDGE PIE

This dessert, which is like a banana sundae, is both light and good. I make it often.
—Myra Innes, Auburn, KS

PREP: 20 min. • **BAKE:** 30 min. + chilling
MAKES: 8 servings

- 1 sheet refrigerated pie crust
- ½ cup miniature semisweet chocolate chips, melted
- 3 cups whipped topping, divided
- 2 large eggs
- ¼ cup sugar
- 2 to 3 bananas, sliced
  Additional miniature chocolate chips, optional

1. Preheat oven to 350°. Unroll crust into a 9-in. pie plate; flute edge. In a large bowl, combine melted chocolate, 1 cup whipped topping, eggs and sugar. Mix well. Pour into crust. Bake until center is set, about 30 minutes. Cool for 10 minutes, then refrigerate for 1 hour.
2. Layer sliced bananas over pie and top with remaining 2 cups whipped topping. Sprinkle miniature chocolate chips on top if desired. Chill until serving.
1 piece: 317 cal., 16g fat (10g sat. fat), 58mg chol., 117mg sod., 39g carb. (22g sugars, 1g fiber), 3g pro.

BANANA FUDGE PIE

DUTCH APPLE CAKE

My husband and I came to Canada from Holland more than 40 years ago. This traditional Dutch recipe is a family favorite and has frequently gone along with me to potluck suppers and other get-togethers.
—*Elizabeth Peters, Martintown, ON*

PREP: 15 min. + standing
BAKE: 1½ hours + cooling
MAKES: 12 servings

- 3 medium tart apples, peeled and cut into ¼-in. slices (3 cups)
- 3 Tbsp. plus 1 cup sugar, divided
- 1 tsp. ground cinnamon
- ⅔ cup butter, softened
- 4 large eggs, room temperature
- 1 tsp. vanilla extract
- 2 cups all-purpose flour
- ⅛ tsp. salt

1. In a large bowl, combine the apples, 3 Tbsp. sugar and cinnamon; let stand for 1 hour.

2. Preheat oven to 300°. In a second bowl, cream butter and the remaining 1 cup sugar until light and fluffy, 5-7 minutes. Add eggs, 1 at a time, beating well after each addition. Add vanilla. Combine flour and salt; gradually add to creamed mixture and beat until smooth.

3. Transfer to a greased 9x5-in. loaf pan. Push apple slices vertically into batter, placing them close together.

4. Bake until a toothpick inserted in the center comes out clean, 1½-1¾ hours. Cool for 10 minutes before removing from pan to a wire rack. Serve warm.

1 piece: 282 cal., 12g fat (7g sat. fat), 97mg chol., 120mg sod., 40g carb. (24g sugars, 1g fiber), 4g pro.

DUTCH APPLE CAKE

PINK LEMONADE STAND CAKE

PINK LEMONADE STAND CAKE

If you love a moist and creamy cake, this is it! Lemon juice and lemonade give the layers a tangy, citrusy touch, and the cream cheese frosting with sprinkles makes it extra pretty.
—*Lauren McAnelly, Des Moines, IA*

PREP: 50 min. • **BAKE:** 20 min. + cooling
MAKES: 12 servings

- 1 cup buttermilk
- 2 Tbsp. lemon juice
- 2 Tbsp. seedless strawberry jam, warmed
- 2 Tbsp. thawed pink lemonade concentrate
- 2 Tbsp. grenadine syrup
- 1 cup unsalted butter, softened
- 1¼ cups sugar
- 3 Tbsp. grated lemon zest
- 4 large eggs, room temperature
- ½ tsp. vanilla extract
- 2½ cups all-purpose flour
- 1 tsp. baking powder
- ½ tsp. baking soda
- ½ tsp. salt

FROSTING
- 1 cup unsalted butter, softened
- 1 pkg. (8 oz.) cream cheese, softened
- 1 Tbsp. grated lemon zest
- 4 cups confectioners' sugar
- ⅓ cup thawed pink lemonade concentrate

ASSEMBLY
- 3 Tbsp. thawed pink lemonade concentrate
  Pink sprinkles

1. Preheat oven to 350°. Line 3 greased 8-in. round baking pans with parchment; grease parchment.
2. Whisk first 5 ingredients until blended. In a large bowl, cream butter, sugar and lemon zest for 5-7 minutes or until light and fluffy. Add eggs, 1 at a time, beating well after each addition. Beat in vanilla. In another bowl, whisk flour, baking powder, baking soda and salt; add to creamed mixture alternately with buttermilk mixture, beating well after each addition.
3. Transfer batter to prepared pans. Bake until a toothpick inserted in center comes out clean, 20-24 minutes. Cool in pans for 10 minutes before removing to wire racks; remove parchment. Cool completely.
4. For frosting, in a large bowl, beat the butter, cream cheese and lemon zest until smooth. Gradually beat in confectioners' sugar and ⅓ cup lemonade concentrate. If necessary, refrigerate until spreadable, up to 1 hour.
5. Place 1 layer on a serving plate. Brush 1 Tbsp. lemonade concentrate over cake; spread with ½ cup frosting. Repeat layers. Top with remaining cake layer; brush remaining lemonade concentrate over top. Spread remaining frosting over top and side of cake. Decorate with sprinkles. Refrigerate until serving.
1 piece: 732 cal., 39g fat (24g sat. fat), 172mg chol., 291mg sod., 91g carb. (68g sugars, 1g fiber), 7g pro.
For cupcakes: Make batter as directed; fill 24 paper-lined muffin cups three-fourths full. Bake at 350° until a toothpick comes out clean, 16-19 minutes. Cool in pans 10 minutes; remove to wire racks to cool completely. Prepare frosting as directed, omitting 3 Tbsp. lemonade concentrate for brushing layers; pipe or spread frosting over tops. Yield: 2 dozen cupcakes.

**CHOCOLATE
PEANUT TREATS**

CHOCOLATE PEANUT TREATS
(PICTURED ON COVER)
When I was in high school, I took these squares to bake sales—and they were always the first to sell out. I still make them for loved ones who love the classic combo of chocolate and peanut butter.
—*Christy Asher, Colorado Springs, CO*

PREP: 20 min. + chilling
MAKES: about 2 dozen

- ¾   cup graham cracker crumbs
- ½   cup butter, melted
- 2   cups confectioners' sugar
- ½   cup chunky peanut butter
- 1   cup semisweet chocolate chips

1. In a bowl, combine cracker crumbs and butter. Stir in the sugar and peanut butter. Press mixture into a greased 8-in. square pan.

2. In a microwave or double boiler, melt the chocolate chips and stir until smooth. Spread over peanut butter layer. Chill for 30 minutes; cut into squares. Chill until firm, about 30 minutes longer. Store in the refrigerator.
1 serving: 148 cal., 9g fat (4g sat. fat), 10mg chol., 81mg sod., 18g carb. (14g sugars, 1g fiber), 2g pro.

MA
DIRTY BANANA TRIFLE
What could be better than bananas, cookies and Kahlua? You can adjust this to suit your taste, depending on how strong you like your Kahlua flavor.
—*Laurie Handlin, Ocean View, DE*

PREP: 40 min. + chilling
MAKES: 24 servings

- 2   pkg. (8 oz. each) cream cheese, softened, divided
- 2   cans (14 oz. each) sweetened condensed milk, divided
- 1½   cups Kahlua (coffee liqueur), chilled
- 2½   cups cold 2% milk, divided
- 2   pkg. (3.9 oz. each) instant chocolate pudding mix
- 3   cartons (8 oz. each) frozen whipped topping, thawed, divided
- 9   whole chocolate graham crackers, coarsely crushed
- 2   pkg. (3.4 oz. each) instant banana cream pudding mix
- 1½   cups coarsely crushed vanilla wafers (about 45 wafers)
- 5   medium bananas, sliced
   Additional wafers, crushed chocolate graham crackers and sliced bananas

1. In a large bowl, beat 1 package cream cheese and 1 can condensed milk until blended. Beat in Kahlua, ½ cup milk and chocolate pudding mixes until thickened, about 2 minutes. Fold in 1 carton whipped topping, then chocolate graham crackers.
2. In another large bowl, beat remaining package of cream cheese and can of condensed milk until blended. Beat in the remaining 2 cups milk and banana pudding mixes until thickened, about 2 minutes. Fold in 1 carton whipped topping, vanilla wafers and bananas.
3. Spread chocolate pudding mixture in the bottom of a 6- or 7-qt. trifle bowl or glass bowl. Layer with 1½ cups whipped topping and banana pudding mixture; top with remaining 1½ cups whipped topping. Cover and refrigerate overnight.
4. Garnish with additional wafers, crushed chocolate graham crackers and sliced bananas before serving.
1 cup: 381 cal., 16g fat (11g sat. fat), 33mg chol., 326mg sod., 46g carb. (33g sugars, 1g fiber), 5g pro.

DIRTY BANANA TRIFLE

OLD-FASHIONED WHOOPIE PIES

Who can resist soft chocolate sandwich cookies filled with a layer of fluffy white frosting? Mom has made these for years. They're a treat that never lasted very long with me and my two brothers around.
—*Maria Costello, Monroe, NC*

PREP: 35 min. + chilling
BAKE: 10 min./batch + cooling
MAKES: 2 dozen

- ½ cup baking cocoa
- ½ cup hot water
- ½ cup shortening
- 1½ cups sugar
- 2 large eggs, room temperature
- 1 tsp. vanilla extract
- 2⅔ cups all-purpose flour
- 1 tsp. baking powder
- 1 tsp. baking soda
- ¼ tsp. salt
- ½ cup buttermilk

FILLING
- 3 Tbsp. all-purpose flour
  Dash salt
- 1 cup 2% milk
- ¾ cup shortening
- 1½ cups confectioners' sugar
- 2 tsp. vanilla extract

1. Preheat oven to 350°. In a small bowl, combine cocoa and water. Let cool for 5 minutes.
2. In a large bowl, cream shortening and sugar until light and fluffy, 5-7 minutes. Beat in the eggs, vanilla and cocoa mixture. Combine the dry ingredients; gradually add to the creamed mixture alternately with buttermilk, beating well after each addition.
3. To form cookies, drop 2 Tbsp. of batter 2 in. apart onto greased baking sheets. Bake until firm to the touch, 10-12 minutes. Remove to wire racks to cool.
4. For filling, in a small saucepan, combine flour and salt. Gradually whisk in milk until smooth; cook and stir over medium-high heat until thickened, 5-7 minutes. Remove from heat. Cover and refrigerate until completely cool.
5. In a small bowl, cream the shortening, confectioners' sugar and vanilla until light and fluffy, 5-7 minutes. Add milk mixture; beat until fluffy, about 7 minutes. Spread the filling on half the cookies; top with remaining cookies. Store in refrigerator.
1 whoopie pie: 244 cal., 11g fat (3g sat. fat), 19mg chol., 116mg sod., 33g carb. (20g sugars, 1g fiber), 3g pro.

TEST KITCHEN TIP

There are plenty of different fillings you could try with this whoopie pie recipe. We recommend substituting a raspberry, maple or cream cheese filling for the classic frosting. You can also try mixing in chocolate chips or crushed peppermint (perfect for the holidays!) to add a bit of bite.

OLD-FASHIONED WHOOPIE PIES

HEALTHY BLACKBERRY COBBLER

HEALTHY BLACKBERRY COBBLER

This tasty treat has helped my family stay healthy, lose weight and still be able to enjoy dessert! Other kinds of berries or even fresh peaches are just as delicious in this cobbler.
—Leslie Browning, Lebanon, KY

PREP: 15 min. + standing • **BAKE:** 45 min.
MAKES: 10 servings

- ½ cup sugar
- 4½ tsp. quick-cooking tapioca
- ¼ tsp. ground allspice
- 5 cups fresh or frozen blackberries, thawed
- 2 Tbsp. orange juice

DOUGH

- 1 cup all-purpose flour
- ⅓ cup plus 1 Tbsp. sugar, divided
- ¼ tsp. baking soda
- ¼ tsp. salt
- ⅓ cup vanilla yogurt
- ⅓ cup fat-free milk
- 3 Tbsp. butter, melted

1. Preheat oven to 350°. In a large bowl, combine sugar, tapioca and allspice. Add blackberries and orange juice; toss to coat. Let stand for 15 minutes. Spoon into a greased 2-qt. baking dish.

2. In a large bowl, combine flour, ⅓ cup sugar, the baking soda and salt. Combine yogurt, milk and butter; stir into the dry ingredients until smooth. Spread over the berry mixture.

3. Bake for 20 minutes; sprinkle with remaining 1 Tbsp. sugar. Bake until golden brown, 25-30 minutes. Serve warm.

1 serving: 194 cal., 4g fat (2g sat. fat), 10mg chol., 128mg sod., 38g carb. (23g sugars, 4g fiber), 3g pro.

HOLIDAY PRETZEL SALAD

I gave a classic summer salad a holiday twist by making green, white and red layers. The combination of salty, sweet, creamy and fruity is always a hit!
—Renee Conneally, Northville, MI

PREP: 35 min. + chilling • **BAKE:** 10 min.
MAKES: 15 servings

- ¾ cup butter, melted
- 3 Tbsp. sugar
- 2 cups crushed pretzels

LIME LAYER
- 1 cup boiling water
- 1 pkg. (3 oz.) lime gelatin
- 1 pkg. (8 oz.) cream cheese, softened
- 1 carton (8 oz.) frozen whipped topping, thawed
- 14 drops green food coloring, optional

CREAM CHEESE LAYER
- 1 pkg. (8 oz.) cream cheese, softened
- ½ cup sugar
- 1 carton (8 oz.) frozen whipped topping, thawed

STRAWBERRY LAYER
- 2 cups boiling water
- 2 pkg. (3 oz. each) strawberry gelatin
- 4 cups sliced fresh strawberries
  Optional: Additional whipped topping, strawberries and miniature pretzels

1. Preheat oven to 350°. Mix melted butter and sugar; stir in pretzels. Press onto bottom of an ungreased 13x9-in. baking dish. Bake 10 minutes. Cool completely on a wire rack.

2. Meanwhile, for lime layer, in a large bowl, add boiling water to lime gelatin; stir 2 minutes to completely dissolve. Refrigerate until partially set, about 1 hour. In a bowl, beat cream cheese until smooth. Add cooled lime gelatin mixture; beat until smooth. Fold in the whipped topping; if desired, add green food coloring. Spread over crust. Refrigerate until set but not firm, 25-30 minutes.

3. For cream cheese layer, in a bowl, beat cream cheese and sugar until smooth. Fold in whipped topping. Spread over the lime layer. Refrigerate until set.

4. For strawberry layer, in a large bowl, add boiling water to strawberry gelatin; stir 2 minutes to completely dissolve. Refrigerate until partially set, about 1 hour. Stir in strawberries. Gently spoon over cream cheese layer. Refrigerate, covered, until firm, 2-4 hours. To serve, cut into squares. If desired, top with additional whipped topping, strawberries and miniature pretzels.

1 serving: 407 cal., 25g fat (17g sat. fat), 55mg chol., 368mg sod., 40g carb. (29g sugars, 1g fiber), 5g pro.

READER RAVES

"What a colorful and tasty twist on an old standby! I'm envisioning a blue version for the patriotic holidays!"

—SHAWNBA, TASTEOFHOME.COM

STRAWBERRY LADYFINGER ICEBOX CAKE

MA

STRAWBERRY LADYFINGER ICEBOX CAKE

This cake is inventive and yet familiar. Be sure to use a springform pan so you can easily remove it. If the cake breaks while you're transferring it to the serving plate, just push it back together, pressing gently.
—*Stella Ohanian, Porter Ranch, CA*

PREP: 35 min. + chilling
MAKES: 12 servings

- 6   cups fresh strawberries, sliced
- 4   tsp. balsamic vinegar
- 38 crisp ladyfinger cookies (about 23 oz.)
- 2   cartons (8 oz. each) mascarpone cheese, softened
- 2   cups heavy whipping cream
- ½   cup sugar
- 2   tsp. vanilla extract
- 12 fresh strawberries

1. In a large bowl, mix strawberries and vinegar. Let stand 30 minutes.
2. Meanwhile, line the bottom of a 9-in. ungreased springform pan with parchment. Trim ½ in. off 1 end of each of 22 ladyfingers. Arrange ladyfingers, rounded sides up, along sides of prepared pan. Line bottom of pan with 8 ladyfingers, trimming to fit if necessary.
3. In a large bowl, beat mascarpone cheese on low speed until fluffy. Add cream, sugar and vanilla; beat on medium until stiff peaks form. Spread 1½ cups of the cheese mixture evenly over cookies. With a slotted spoon, spread half the strawberry mixture over top. Repeat layers. Layer with remaining ladyfingers, trimming to fit if necessary. Spread remaining cheese mixture over top.
4. Carefully cover and refrigerate at least 8 hours or overnight. Remove rim from pan; arrange fresh strawberries over top.
1 piece: 456 cal., 33g fat (19g sat. fat), 120mg chol., 72mg sod., 36g carb. (25g sugars, 2g fiber), 7g pro.

MINI S'MORES

DOUBLE BUTTERSCOTCH COCONUT CAKE

I got this recipe from a co-worker years ago, and then I changed it a bit by adding a family favorite: butterscotch. It is super easy to throw together and is a perfect accompaniment to coffee or tea.
—*Marina Castle-Kelley, Canyon Country, CA*

PREP: 20 min. • **BAKE:** 40 min. + cooling
MAKES: 16 servings

- 1   pkg. yellow cake mix (regular size)
- 1   pkg. (3.4 oz.) instant butterscotch pudding mix
- 4   large eggs
- 1   cup canned coconut milk
- ¼   cup canola oil
- 1   cup sweetened shredded coconut
- ½   cup butterscotch chips

GLAZE

- ½   cup butterscotch chips
- 2   Tbsp. heavy whipping cream
- ⅓   cup sweetened shredded coconut, toasted

1. Preheat oven to 350°. Grease and flour a 10-in. fluted tube pan; set aside.
2. In a large bowl, combine cake mix, pudding mix, eggs, coconut milk and oil; beat on low speed for 30 seconds. Beat on medium speed 2 minutes. Stir in the coconut and butterscotch chips. Transfer batter to prepared pan.
3. Bake until a toothpick inserted in the center comes out clean, 40-45 minutes. Cool in pan 10 minutes before removing to a wire rack to cool completely.
4. For glaze, in a microwave, melt the butterscotch chips and cream; stir until smooth. Drizzle over cake; sprinkle with toasted coconut.
1 piece: 327 cal., 15g fat (10g sat. fat), 49mg chol., 359mg sod., 42g carb. (30g sugars, 1g fiber), 4g pro.

MINI S'MORES

Want to sink your teeth into s'mores all year long? Here's the answer! Just combine marshmallow creme, chocolate and graham crackers for an awesome bite any time.
—*Stephanie Tewell, Elizabeth, IL*

PREP: 50 min. + standing • **COOK:** 5 min.
MAKES: about 4 dozen

- 2   cups milk chocolate chips
- ½   cup heavy whipping cream
- 1   pkg. (14.4 oz.) graham crackers, quartered
- 1   cup marshmallow creme
- 2   cartons (7 oz. each) milk chocolate for dipping

1. Place chocolate chips in a small bowl. In a small saucepan, bring cream just to a boil. Pour over chocolate; stir with a whisk until smooth. Cool to room temperature or until mixture reaches a spreading consistency, about 10 minutes.

2. Spread chocolate mixture over half of the graham crackers. Spread the marshmallow creme over the remaining graham crackers; place over chocolate-covered crackers, pressing to adhere.
3. Melt dipping chocolate according to package directions. Dip each s'more halfway into dipping chocolate; allow excess to drip off. Place on waxed paper-lined baking sheets; let stand until dipping chocolate is set. Store in an airtight container in the refrigerator.
1 piece: 145 cal., 7g fat (4g sat. fat), 5mg chol., 66mg sod., 19g carb. (13g sugars, 1g fiber), 2g pro.

TEST KITCHEN TIP

Keep on whisking! At first, the chocolate and cream mixture may look separated. But don't panic—it will smooth out with plenty of whisking. For a hint of richer flavor, mix peanut butter into the marshmallow creme.

DOUBLE
BUTTERSCOTCH
COCONUT CAKE

SOUTHERN PEACH UPSIDE-DOWN CAKE

A dear friend from the South gave me the idea for this peachy cake. I add bourbon to the peaches and top each slice with vanilla or cinnamon ice cream.
—*Trista Jefferson, Batavia, OH*

PREP: 25 min. • **BAKE:** 40 min.
MAKES: 10 servings

- 2 cups sliced peeled fresh or frozen peaches, thawed
- 2 Tbsp. bourbon, optional
- ¼ cup butter
- ½ cup packed brown sugar

BATTER

- ½ cup butter, softened
- ¾ cup sugar
- 1 large egg, room temperature
- 1 tsp. vanilla extract
- 1¼ cups all-purpose flour
- 1¼ tsp. baking powder
- ¼ tsp. salt
- ½ cup 2% milk

1. Preheat oven to 350°. If desired, combine peaches and bourbon; let stand 10 minutes.

2. Place ¼ cup butter in a 10-in. cast-iron or other ovenproof skillet; heat in oven until the butter is melted, 5-7 minutes. Sprinkle brown sugar evenly over butter. Arrange peach slices over brown sugar.

3. For batter, in a large bowl, cream the butter and sugar until light and fluffy, 5-7 minutes. Beat in egg and vanilla. In another bowl, whisk flour, baking powder and salt; add to the creamed mixture alternately with milk, beating after each addition just until combined. Spread batter evenly over peaches.

4. Bake until a toothpick inserted in the center comes out clean, 40-45 minutes. Cool for 5 minutes before inverting onto a serving plate. Serve warm.

1 piece: 306 cal., 15g fat (9g sat. fat), 56mg chol., 235mg sod., 41g carb. (29g sugars, 1g fiber), 3g pro.

SOUTHERN PEACH
UPSIDE-DOWN CAKE

RHUBARB UPSIDE-DOWN CAKE

I've baked this cake every spring for many years, and my family loves it! At potlucks it gets eaten up quickly, even by folks who don't normally go for rhubarb. Use your own fresh rhubarb, hit up a farmers market or find a neighbor who will trade stalks for the recipe!
—*Helen Breman, Mattydale, NY*

PREP: 20 min. • **BAKE:** 35 min.
MAKES: 10 servings

- 3 cups sliced fresh or frozen rhubarb
- 1 cup sugar
- 2 Tbsp. all-purpose flour
- ¼ tsp. ground nutmeg
- ¼ cup butter, melted

BATTER
- ¼ cup butter, melted
- ¾ cup sugar
- 1 large egg, room temperature
- 1½ cups all-purpose flour
- 2 tsp. baking powder
- ½ tsp. ground nutmeg
- ¼ tsp. salt
- ⅔ cup 2% milk
   Sweetened whipped cream, optional

1. Preheat oven to 350°. Place rhubarb in a greased 10-in. cast-iron or other heavy ovenproof skillet. Combine sugar, flour and nutmeg; sprinkle over rhubarb. Drizzle with melted butter.
2. For batter, in a large bowl, beat the butter and sugar until blended. Beat in the egg. Combine the flour, baking powder, nutmeg and salt. Gradually add to egg mixture alternately with milk, beating well after each addition.
3. Spread batter over rhubarb mixture. Bake until a toothpick inserted in the center comes out clean, about 35 minutes. Loosen edge immediately and invert onto a serving dish. Serve warm. If desired, serve with whipped cream.
1 piece: 316 cal., 10g fat (6g sat. fat), 48mg chol., 248mg sod., 53g carb. (36g sugars, 1g fiber), 4g pro.

PINEAPPLE PRETZEL FLUFF

I often bring this special salad to potlucks, and everyone goes crazy for the sweet and crunchy combination. Be sure to add the pretzel mixture right before serving to keep it crispy.
—*Beth Olby, Ashland, WI*

PREP: 15 min. + chilling
BAKE: 10 min. + cooling
MAKES: 12 servings

- 1 cup coarsely crushed pretzels
- ½ cup butter, melted
- 1 cup sugar, divided
- 1 pkg. (8 oz.) cream cheese, softened
- 1 can (20 oz.) unsweetened crushed pineapple, drained
- 1 carton (12 oz.) frozen whipped topping, thawed

1. Preheat oven to 400°. Mix pretzels, melted butter and ½ cup sugar. Press into a 13x9-in. pan. Bake for 7 minutes. Cool completely on a wire rack.
2. Meanwhile, in a large bowl, beat cream cheese and remaining ½ cup sugar until creamy. Fold in pineapple and whipped topping; refrigerate, covered, until serving.
3. To serve, break pretzel mixture into small pieces. Stir into pineapple mixture.
½ cup: 334 cal., 19g fat (13g sat. fat), 39mg chol., 230mg sod., 37g carb. (31g sugars, 1g fiber), 2g pro.

MINT CHOCOLATE CHEESECAKE

I created this mint chocolate cheesecake for our high school's annual fundraiser. We were told that it brought a hefty price and was one of the first desserts to go! If desired, the cookie pieces may be stirred into the batter instead of being added in a layer. Keep the pieces fairly small; if they're too large, they have a tendency to rise to the top.

—Sue Gronholz, Beaver Dam, WI

PREP: 20 min. • **BAKE:** 1¼ hours + chilling
MAKES: 16 servings

- 10 Oreo cookies, finely crushed (about 1 cup)
- 3 Tbsp. sugar
- 2 Tbsp. butter, melted

FILLING

- 4 pkg. (8 oz. each) cream cheese, softened
- 1 cup sugar
- 1 cup white baking chips, melted and cooled
- 6 Tbsp. creme de menthe
- ¼ cup all-purpose flour
- 2 Tbsp. creme de cacao
- ½ tsp. peppermint extract
- 4 large eggs, room temperature, lightly beaten
- 10 Oreo cookies, coarsely crushed (about 1 cup)

GANACHE

- ¾ cup semisweet chocolate chips
- 6 Tbsp. heavy whipping cream

1. Preheat the oven to 325°. Place a greased 9-in. springform pan on a double thickness of heavy-duty foil (about 18 in. square). Wrap foil securely around pan. In a small bowl, mix cookie crumbs and sugar; stir in melted butter. Press onto bottom of prepared pan.

2. For filling, in a large bowl, beat cream cheese and sugar until smooth. Beat in the melted and cooled chips, creme de menthe, flour, creme de cacao and extract. Add eggs; beat on low speed just until blended. Pour half the batter over crust; sprinkle with crushed Oreos. Carefully spoon remaining batter over top. Place springform pan in a larger baking pan; add 1 in. hot water to the larger pan.

3. Bake until the center is just set and the top appears dull, 75-80 minutes. Remove springform pan from water bath. Cool on a wire rack 10 minutes. Loosen rim of pan with a knife; remove foil. Cool 1 hour longer. Refrigerate overnight, covering when completely cooled.

4. Remove rim from pan. For ganache, place chocolate chips in a small bowl. In a small saucepan, bring cream just to a boil. Pour over chocolate; stir with a whisk until smooth. Spread over cheesecake.

1 piece: 518 cal., 33g fat (18g sat. fat), 116mg chol., 296mg sod., 46g carb. (38g sugars, 1g fiber), 7g pro.

MINT CHOCOLATE CHEESECAKE

POTLUCK PUMPKIN TORTE

A local newspaper featured this recipe. A creamy alternative to pumpkin pie, it quickly became one of my favorites.
—*Peggy Shea, Lowell, IN*

PREP: 30 min. • **BAKE:** 25 min. + chilling
MAKES: 15 servings

  1⅔ cups graham cracker crumbs
  ⅓ cup sugar
  ½ cup butter, melted
  CREAM CHEESE FILLING
  2 pkg. (8 oz. each) cream cheese, softened
  ¾ cup sugar
  2 large eggs
  PUMPKIN FILLING
  2 envelopes unflavored gelatin
  ½ cup cold water
  1 can (30 oz.) pumpkin pie filling
  1 can (5½ oz.) evaporated milk
  2 large eggs, lightly beaten
  TOPPING
  1 carton (12 oz.) frozen whipped topping, thawed

1. Preheat oven to 350°. In a small bowl, combine the crumbs, sugar and butter. Press onto the bottom of an ungreased 13x9-in. baking dish; set aside.
2. Beat cream cheese and sugar until smooth. Add eggs; beat on low speed just until combined. Pour over crust. Bake until center is almost set, 25-30 minutes.
3. In a small bowl, sprinkle gelatin over cold water; let stand 1 minute. In a large saucepan, combine the pie filling and evaporated milk. Bring to a boil. Add the gelatin; stir until dissolved. Whisk a small amount of hot mixture into the eggs. Return all to the pan, whisking constantly.
4. Cook, stirring, over low until mixture is thickened and coats the back of a spoon. Cool 10 minutes. Spread over cream cheese layer. Spread whipped topping over top. Refrigerate, covered, overnight.
1 piece: 413 cal., 24g fat (15g sat. fat), 109mg chol., 296mg sod., 42g carb. (32g sugars, 2g fiber), 7g pro.

POTLUCK
PUMPKIN TORTE

EASY FRESH STRAWBERRY PIE

EASY FRESH STRAWBERRY PIE

Often when I make this pie, I'll use whole strawberries and arrange them pointed side up in the pastry shell for a different presentation. It's also is a timesaver because I don't have to slice the berries.
—*Josh Carter, Birmingham, AL*

PREP: 20 min. + cooling
BAKE: 15 min. + chilling
MAKES: 8 servings

- 1 sheet refrigerated pie crust
- ¾ cup sugar
- 2 Tbsp. cornstarch
- 1 cup water
- 1 pkg. (3 oz.) strawberry gelatin
- 4 cups sliced fresh strawberries
  Whipped cream, optional

1. Preheat oven to 450°. Unroll crust into a 9-in. pie plate. Trim edge. Line unpricked crust with a double thickness of heavy-duty foil or parchment. Bake 8 minutes. Remove foil; bake 5 minutes longer. Cool on a wire rack.
2. In a small saucepan, combine sugar, cornstarch and water until smooth. Bring to a boil; cook and stir until thickened, about 2 minutes. Remove from the heat; stir in gelatin until dissolved. Refrigerate until slightly cooled, 15-20 minutes.
3. Meanwhile, arrange strawberries in the crust. Pour gelatin mixture over berries. Refrigerate until set. If desired, serve with whipped cream.

1 piece: 264 cal., 7g fat (3g sat. fat), 5mg chol., 125mg sod., 49g carb. (32g sugars, 2g fiber), 2g pro.

TEST KITCHEN TIP

Using extra refrigerated pie crust to create a decorative braided edge is a beautiful way to enhance this pie!

FRUIT & ALMOND BITES

FRUIT & ALMOND BITES

With big handfuls of dried apricots, cherries, almonds and pistachios, these are seriously tasty and satisfying no-bake treats. You can take them anywhere.
—*Donna Pochoday-Stelmach, Morristown, NJ*

PREP: 40 min. + chilling
MAKES: about 4 dozen

- 3¾ cups sliced almonds, divided
- ¼ tsp. almond extract
- ¼ cup honey
- 2 cups finely chopped dried apricots
- 1 cup finely chopped dried cherries or cranberries
- 1 cup finely chopped pistachios, toasted

1. Place 1¼ cups almonds in a food processor; pulse until finely chopped. Remove almonds to a shallow bowl; reserve for coating.
2. Add the remaining 2½ cups almonds to the food processor; pulse until finely chopped. Add extract. While processing, gradually add honey. Remove to a large bowl; stir in apricots and cherries. Divide mixture into 6 portions; shape each into a ½-in.-thick roll. Wrap and refrigerate until firm, about 1 hour .
3. Unwrap rolls and cut into 1½-in. pieces. Roll half the pieces in reserved almonds, pressing gently to adhere. Roll the other half in pistachios. If desired, wrap each piece individually in waxed paper, twisting ends to close. Store in airtight containers, layered between waxed paper if pieces are unwrapped.

1 piece: 86 cal., 5g fat (0 sat. fat), 0 chol., 15mg sod., 10g carb. (7g sugars, 2g fiber), 2g pro. **Diabetic exchanges:** 1 fat, ½ starch.

PEANUT BUTTER CAKE BARS

Packed with peanut butter and chocolate chips, these cakelike bars are perfect for any occasion. Kids and adults alike are in for a treat with these gems.
—*Charlotte Ennis, Lake Arthur, NM*

PREP: 15 min. • **BAKE:** 45 min. + cooling
MAKES: 2 dozen

- ⅔ **cup butter, softened**
- ⅔ **cup peanut butter**
- 1 **cup sugar**
- 1 **cup packed brown sugar**
- 4 **large eggs, room temperature**
- 2 **tsp. vanilla extract**
- 2 **cups all-purpose flour**
- 2 **tsp. baking powder**
- ½ **tsp. salt**
- 1 **pkg. (11½ oz.) milk chocolate chips**

1. Preheat oven to 350°. In a large bowl, cream butter, peanut butter, sugar and brown sugar. Add eggs, 1 at a time, beating well after each addition. Beat in vanilla. Combine flour, baking powder and salt; gradually add to the creamed mixture. Stir in chocolate chips.

2. Spread into a greased 13x9-in. baking pan. Bake until a toothpick inserted in the center comes out clean, 45-50 minutes. Cool on a wire rack. Cut into bars.

1 bar: 277 cal., 14g fat (6g sat. fat), 52mg chol., 178mg sod., 35g carb. (25g sugars, 1g fiber), 5g pro.

PEANUT BUTTER CAKE BARS

STRAWBERRY
JAM CAKE

addition. Beat in the strawberries, sour cream and, if desired, extract. Combine the flour, baking powder, baking soda and salt; add to the creamed mixture. Transfer batter to prepared pans.

3. Bake until a toothpick inserted in the center comes out clean, 22-26 minutes. Cool for 10 minutes before removing from pans to wire racks to cool completely.

4. For frosting, in a large bowl, beat cream cheese and butter until fluffy. Add the confectioners' sugar, strawberries and, if desired, the extract and red food coloring; beat until smooth.

5. Place bottom cake layer on a serving plate; top with ¼ cup jam and ½ cup frosting. Repeat layers. Top with the remaining cake layer. Spread remaining frosting over top and side of cake. Garnish with strawberries if desired.

1 piece: 783 cal., 28g fat (17g sat. fat), 72mg chol., 416mg sod., 130g carb. (99g sugars, 1g fiber), 6g pro.

TEST KITCHEN TIP

If you have homemade jam or preserves in your cupboard, you can substitute it for the jam in this cake to give it an extra-personal touch. Use just enough to coat the cake layer; too much and your next layer may go sliding.

STRAWBERRY JAM CAKE

When I need a cake for a special occasion, this is my go-to recipe because everyone is crazy about it. Every year I make it for the Relay for Life cake raffle we have at work. It has raised a lot of money for a good cause.
—*Tammy Urbina, Warner Robins, GA*

PREP: 35 min. • **BAKE:** 25 min. + cooling
MAKES: 12 servings

- 1 cup butter, softened
- 1¾ cups sugar
- 5 large egg whites, room temperature
- 2 cups pureed strawberries
- ½ cup sour cream
- 1 tsp. strawberry extract, optional
- 3 cups cake flour
- 2½ tsp. baking powder
- ¼ tsp. baking soda
- ¼ tsp. salt

FROSTING
- 1 pkg. (8 oz.) cream cheese, softened
- ¼ cup butter, softened
- 6 cups confectioners' sugar
- ¼ cup pureed strawberries
- ½ tsp. strawberry extract, optional
- 1 to 3 drops red food coloring, optional

ASSEMBLY
- ½ cup seedless strawberry jam, divided
  Halved or sliced fresh strawberries, optional

1. Preheat oven to 350°. Grease and flour three 9-in. round baking pans; set aside.
2. In a large bowl, cream butter and sugar until light and fluffy, 5-7 minutes. Add egg whites, 1 at a time, beating well after each

FUDGY BROWNIES WITH PEANUT BUTTER PUDDING FROSTING

Rich brownies are topped with a peanut butter frosting to make this recipe that the whole family will love. These are just perfect for a potluck or bake sale, or as a yummy after-dinner treat.
—*Amy Crook, Syracuse, UT*

PREP: 20 min. • **BAKE:** 25 min. + chilling
MAKES: 2½ dozen

- 1 pkg. fudge brownie mix (13x9-in. pan size)
- 1½ cups confectioners' sugar
- ½ cup butter, softened
- 2 to 3 Tbsp. peanut butter
- 2 Tbsp. cold 2% milk
- 4½ tsp. instant vanilla pudding mix
- 1 can (16 oz.) chocolate fudge frosting

1. Prepare and bake brownies according to package directions. Cool on a wire rack.
2. Meanwhile, in a small bowl, beat the confectioners' sugar, butter, peanut butter, milk and pudding mix until smooth. Spread over brownies. Refrigerate for 30 minutes or until firm. Frost with chocolate frosting just before cutting.

1 brownie: 236 cal., 12g fat (4g sat. fat), 23mg chol., 145mg sod., 31g carb. (23g sugars, 1g fiber), 2g pro.

TEST KITCHEN TIP

Need to cut some sugar? Substitute all-natural peanut butter for the standard version.

FUDGY BROWNIES WITH PEANUT BUTTER PUDDING FROSTING

NECTARINE PLUM COBBLER

I live in northern Manitoba, where fresh nectarines and plums are usually available only at summer's end. I make the fruit filling and freeze it for use all winter. My family really enjoys this recipe, and it's wonderful topped with vanilla ice cream.
—*Darlene Jackson, The Pas, MB*

PREP: 30 min. + cooling • **BAKE:** 30 min.
MAKES: 12 servings

- 1¼ cups sugar, divided
- 2 Tbsp. cornstarch
- ¾ cup unsweetened apple juice
- 5 cups sliced peeled fresh plums
- 5 cups sliced peeled nectarines or peaches
- 2½ cups all-purpose flour
- 3 tsp. baking powder
- ½ tsp. baking soda
- ½ tsp. salt
- ½ cup cold butter
- 1½ cups buttermilk
  Vanilla ice cream, optional

1. Preheat the oven to 375°. In a large saucepan, combine ¾ cup sugar and the cornstarch. Gradually stir in apple juice until smooth. Stir in plums and nectarines. Cook and stir until mixture comes to a boil; cook 1-2 minutes longer or until thickened and bubbly. Reduce the heat; simmer, uncovered, for 5 minutes.
2. Remove from heat; cool for 10 minutes. Pour into a greased 13x9-in. baking dish.
3. In a large bowl, whisk flour, baking powder, baking soda, salt and remaining ½ cup sugar. Cut in butter until crumbly. Make a well in the center; stir in buttermilk just until a soft dough forms. Drop by tablespoonfuls over fruit mixture. Bake until golden brown, 30-35 minutes. Serve warm, with ice cream if desired.
1 serving: 333 cal., 9g fat (5g sat. fat), 22mg chol., 361mg sod., 61g carb. (36g sugars, 3g fiber), 5g pro.

HONEY-PEANUT BUTTER COOKIES

It's not unusual for my husband to request these cookies by name. You'll love 'em.
—*Lucile Proctor, Panguitch, UT*

PREP: 15 min. • **BAKE:** 10 min./batch
MAKES: 5 dozen

- ½ cup shortening
- 1 cup creamy peanut butter
- 1 cup honey
- 2 large eggs, room temperature, lightly beaten
- 3 cups all-purpose flour
- 1 cup sugar
- 1½ tsp. baking soda
- 1 tsp. baking powder
- ½ tsp. salt

1. Preheat oven to 350°. In a bowl, mix shortening, peanut butter and honey. Add eggs; mix well. Combine flour, sugar, baking soda, baking powder and salt; add to peanut butter mixture and mix well.
2. Roll into 1½-in. balls and place on ungreased baking sheets. Flatten with a fork dipped in flour. Bake until set, 8-10 minutes. Remove to racks to cool.
1 cookie: 95 cal., 4g fat (1g sat. fat), 6mg chol., 80mg sod., 14g carb. (8g sugars, 0 fiber), 2g pro.

CHOCOLATE ECLAIRS

CHOCOLATE ECLAIRS

With creamy filling and thick, decadent frosting, these eclairs are extra special. Now you can make these classic bakery treats at home!
—*Jessica Campbell, Viola, WI*

PREP: 45 min. • **BAKE:** 35 min. + cooling
MAKES: 9 servings

- 1 **cup water**
- ½ **cup butter, cubed**
- ¼ **tsp. salt**
- 1 **cup all-purpose flour**
- 4 **large eggs**
FILLING
- 2½ **cups cold 2% milk**
- 1 **pkg. (5.1 oz.) instant vanilla pudding mix**
- 1 **cup heavy whipping cream**
- ¼ **cup confectioners' sugar**
- 1 **tsp. vanilla extract**
FROSTING
- 2 **oz. semisweet chocolate**
- 2 **Tbsp. butter**
- 1¼ **cups confectioners' sugar**
- 2 **to 3 Tbsp. hot water**

1. Preheat the oven to 400°. In a large saucepan, bring water, butter and salt to a boil. Add flour all at once and stir until a smooth ball forms. Remove from heat; let stand 5 minutes. Add eggs, 1 at a time, beating well after each addition. Continue beating until mixture is smooth and shiny.
2. Using a tablespoon or a pastry tube with a #10 or large round tip, form dough into nine 4x1½-in. strips on a greased baking sheet. Bake until puffed and golden, 35-40 minutes. Remove to a wire rack. Immediately split eclairs open; remove tops and set aside. Discard soft dough from inside. Cool eclairs.
3. In a large bowl, beat milk and pudding mix according to package directions. In another bowl, whip cream until soft peaks form. Beat in sugar and vanilla; fold into pudding. Fill eclairs (chill any remaining filling for another use). Replace tops.
4. For frosting, in a microwave, melt chocolate and butter; stir until smooth. Stir in sugar and enough hot water to achieve a smooth consistency. Cool slightly. Frost eclairs. Store in refrigerator.
1 eclair: 483 cal., 28g fat (17g sat. fat), 174mg chol., 492mg sod., 52g carb. (37g sugars, 1g fiber), 7g pro.

BERRY-PATCH BROWNIE PIZZA

I just love the combination of fruit, almonds and chocolate that makes this brownie so distinctive. The fruit lightens the chocolate a bit and makes it feel as though you're eating something both decadent and healthy.
—*Sue Kauffman, Columbia City, IN*

PREP: 20 min. + chilling
BAKE: 15 min. + cooling
MAKES: 12 servings

- 1 **pkg. fudge brownie mix (13x9-in. pan size)**
- ⅓ **cup chopped unblanched almonds**
- 1 **tsp. almond extract**
TOPPING
- 1 **pkg. (8 oz.) cream cheese, softened**
- 1 **Tbsp. sugar**
- 1 **tsp. vanilla extract**
- ½ **tsp. grated lemon zest**
- 2 **cups whipped topping**
  Assorted fresh berries
  Optional: Fresh mint leaves and coarse sugar

1. Preheat oven to 375°. Prepare brownie batter according to package directions for fudgelike brownies, adding almonds and almond extract. Spread into a greased 14-in. pizza pan.
2. Bake until a toothpick inserted in center comes out clean, 15-18 minutes. Cool completely on a wire rack.
3. Beat the first 4 topping ingredients until smooth; fold in whipped topping. Spread over crust to within ½ in. of edge; refrigerate, loosely covered, 2 hours.
4. To serve, cut into 12 pieces; top with berries of choice. If desired, top with mint and sprinkle with coarse sugar.
1 piece: 404 cal., 26g fat (8g sat. fat), 51mg chol., 240mg sod., 39g carb. (26g sugars, 2g fiber), 5g pro.

BERRY-PATCH
BROWNIE PIZZA

PEANUT BUTTER PRETZEL BARS

My secret to these rich no-bake bites? Pretzels in the crust. They add a salty crunch to the classic peanut butter and chocolate pairing.
—*Jennifer Beckman, Falls Church, VA*

PREP: 15 min. + chilling • **MAKES:** 4 dozen

- 1 pkg. (16 oz.) miniature pretzels, divided
- 1½ cups butter, melted
- 1½ cups peanut butter
- 3 cups confectioners' sugar
- 2 cups semisweet chocolate chips
- 1 Tbsp. shortening

1. Line a 13x9-in. baking pan with foil, letting ends extend up sides. Set aside 1½ cups pretzels for topping. In a food processor, pulse remaining pretzels until fine crumbs form. In a large bowl, mix butter, peanut butter, confectioners' sugar and pretzel crumbs.

2. Press into the prepared pan. In a microwave, melt chocolate chips and shortening; stir until smooth. Spread over peanut butter layer. Break the reserved pretzels and sprinkle over top; press down gently. Refrigerate, covered, until set, about 1 hour. Lifting with foil, remove from pan. Cut into bars.

1 bar: 201 cal., 13g fat (6g sat. fat), 15mg chol., 233mg sod., 22g carb. (12g sugars, 1g fiber), 3g pro.

TEST KITCHEN TIP

Unless otherwise specified, Taste of Home recipes are tested with lightly salted butter. Unsalted, or sweet, butter is sometimes used to achieve a buttery flavor, such as in shortbread cookies or buttercream frosting. In this recipe, you may prefer to use sweet butter, due to the saltiness of the pretzels.

PEANUT BUTTER PRETZEL BARS

MACAROON CHERRY PIE

MACAROON CHERRY PIE

In summer, I use homegrown cherries in this amazing pie with a crunchy coconut topping. But canned tart cherries yield a dessert that's almost as delicious. I always bake this pie around Presidents Day or Valentine's Day, but it's popular the whole year through.
—Lori Daniels, Beverly, WV

PREP: 25 min. • **BAKE:** 35 min. + chilling
MAKES: 8 servings

    Dough for single-crust pie
3   **cans (14½ oz. each) pitted tart cherries**
1   **cup sugar**
⅓   **cup cornstarch**
½   **tsp. ground cinnamon**
¼   **tsp. red food coloring, optional**

TOPPING
1   **large egg, room temperature, lightly beaten**
2   **Tbsp. 2% milk**
1   **Tbsp. butter, melted**
¼   **tsp. almond extract**
¼   **cup sugar**
⅛   **tsp. salt**
1   **cup sweetened shredded coconut**
½   **cup sliced almonds**

1. Preheat the oven to 400°. On a lightly floured surface, roll dough to a ⅛-in.-thick circle; transfer to a 9-in. cast-iron skillet or deep-dish pie plate. Trim to ½ in. beyond edge of plate; flute edge. Bake 6 minutes; set aside.

2. Drain cherries, reserving 1 cup juice. Set cherries aside. In a large saucepan, combine sugar and cornstarch; gradually stir in cherry juice until blended. Bring to a boil over medium heat; cook and stir until thickened, 2 minutes.

3. Remove from heat; stir in cinnamon and, if desired, food coloring. Gently fold in cherries. Pour into crust. Cover the edge loosely with foil. Bake at 400° 20 minutes.

4. Meanwhile, in a large bowl, combine first 6 topping ingredients. Stir in coconut and almonds.

5. Remove foil from pie; spoon topping over pie. Reduce oven to 350°; bake until topping is lightly browned, 15-20 minutes. Cool on a wire rack 1 hour. Chill 4 hours or overnight before cutting.

Dough for single-crust pie (9 in.): Combine 1¼ cups all-purpose flour and ¼ tsp. salt; cut in ½ cup cold butter until crumbly. Gradually add 3-5 Tbsp. ice water, tossing with a fork until the dough holds together when pressed. Shape into a disk; wrap and refrigerate 1 hour.

1 piece: 434 cal., 16g fat (8g sat. fat), 36mg chol., 199mg sod., 70g carb. (48g sugars, 3g fiber), 5g pro.

Classic Crumb-Topped Cherry Pie: Preheat oven to 425°. Omit the topping ingredients. Mix ½ cup all-purpose flour and ½ cup sugar; cut in ¼ cup cold butter until crumbly. Sprinkle over filling. Bake 35-45 minutes or until crust is golden brown and filling is bubbly. Cover the edge loosely with foil if pie is browning too quickly.

READER RAVES

"A huge hit! I used fresh sour cherries and then added 1 cup of 100% organic tart cherry juice for the juice required. Skipped the food coloring. Easy to make and delicious!"

—GUEST5547, TASTEOFHOME.COM

WATERMELON CUPCAKES

WATERMELON CUPCAKES

My granddaughter and I bake together each week. She was inspired by all of her mommy's flavored syrups, so we came up with this watermelon cupcake. If you have watermelon syrup, it can replace some of the lemon-lime soda in the cake batter and frosting, but the gelatin adds a lot of watermelon flavor on its own. If you are not going to pipe the frosting, you can reduce the amount of frosting by half.
—*Elizabeth Bramkamp, Gig Harbor, WA*

PREP: 30 min. • **BAKE:** 20 min. + cooling
MAKES: 2 dozen

- 1 pkg. white cake mix (regular size)
- 1 cup lemon-lime soda
- 3 large egg whites, room temperature
- ¼ cup canola oil
- 1 pkg. (3 oz.) watermelon gelatin
- 2 drops watermelon oil, optional

FROSTING

- 2 cups butter, softened
- 6 cups confectioners' sugar
- 1 pkg. (3 oz.) watermelon gelatin
- 5 to 6 Tbsp. lemon-lime soda
- 15 drops red food coloring
- 3 Tbsp. miniature semisweet chocolate chips

1. Preheat oven to 350°. Line 24 muffin cups with paper liners. In a large bowl, combine cake mix, soda, egg whites, canola oil, watermelon gelatin and, if desired, watermelon oil; beat on low speed 30 seconds. Beat on medium speed 2 minutes. Transfer to prepared pans. Bake until a toothpick inserted in center comes out clean, 18-21 minutes. Cool in pans 10 minutes before removing to wire racks to cool completely.
2. For frosting, in a large bowl, combine butter, confectioners' sugar, gelatin, soda and food coloring; beat until smooth. Frost cupcakes. Sprinkle with chocolate chips. Store in the refrigerator.
1 cupcake: 385 cal., 19g fat (11g sat. fat), 41mg chol., 282mg sod., 54g carb. (46g sugars, 1g fiber), 2g pro.

BLUEBERRY LEMON TRIFLE

BLUEBERRY LEMON TRIFLE

A refreshing lemon filling and fresh blueberries give this sunny dessert sensation plenty of color.
—*Ellen Peden, Houston, TX*

PREP: 15 min. + chilling
MAKES: 14 servings

- 3 cups fresh blueberries, divided
- 2 cans (15¾ oz. each) lemon pie filling
- 2 cups lemon yogurt
- 1 prepared angel food cake (8 to 10 oz.), cut into 1-in. cubes
- 1 carton (8 oz.) frozen whipped topping, thawed
   Optional: Lemon slices and fresh mint

1. Set aside ¼ cup blueberries for garnish. In a large bowl, combine the lemon pie filling and yogurt.
2. In a 3½-qt. serving or trifle bowl, layer a third each of the cake cubes, lemon mixture and blueberries. Repeat layers twice. Top with whipped topping. Cover and refrigerate for at least 2 hours. Garnish with reserved blueberries and, if desired, lemon and mint.
1 serving: 230 cal., 4g fat (3g sat. fat), 2mg chol., 235mg sod., 44g carb. (27g sugars, 1g fiber), 3g pro.

CRANBERRY NUT COOKIES

In fall, I stock up on fresh cranberries and freeze them so I can make these cookies throughout the year. Tangy cranberries are a nice addition to a buttery cookie.
—Machelle Wall, Rosamond, CA

PREP: 15 min. • **BAKE:** 20 min./batch
MAKES: 5 dozen

- ⅔ cup butter, softened
- 1 cup sugar
- 1 cup packed brown sugar
- 1 large egg, room temperature
- ¼ cup 2% milk
- 2 Tbsp. lemon juice
- 3 cups all-purpose flour
- ¼ cup ground walnuts
- 1 tsp. baking powder
- ½ tsp. salt
- ¼ tsp. baking soda
- 2½ cups halved fresh or frozen cranberries
- 1 cup chopped walnuts

1. Preheat oven to 350°. In a large bowl, cream butter and sugars until light and fluffy, 5-7 minutes. Beat in the egg, milk and lemon juice. Combine flour, ground walnuts, baking powder, salt and baking soda; gradually add to the creamed mixture and mix well. Stir in the cranberries and chopped walnuts.

2. Drop by heaping tablespoonfuls 2 in. apart onto lightly greased baking sheets. Bake until golden brown, 16-18 minutes. Remove to wire racks to cool.

1 cookie: 87 cal., 4g fat (1g sat. fat), 9mg chol., 52mg sod., 13g carb. (7g sugars, 0 fiber), 1g pro.

CRANBERRY NUT COOKIES

CARROT CAKE

CREAM CHEESE FROSTING
- 6 oz. cream cheese, softened
- 6 Tbsp. butter, softened
- 3 cups confectioners' sugar
- 1 tsp. vanilla extract
  Additional chopped nuts

1. Preheat oven to 350°. In a large bowl, combine the flour, sugar, cinnamon, baking soda and salt. Add the eggs, oil, carrots and vanilla; beat until combined. Stir in the pineapple, coconut and nuts.
2. Pour into a greased 13x9-in. baking pan. Bake until a toothpick inserted in the center comes out clean, 50-60 minutes. Cool on a wire rack.
3. For frosting, beat cream cheese and butter in a small bowl until fluffy. Add the confectioners' sugar and vanilla; beat until smooth. Frost cake. Sprinkle with additional nuts. Store in the refrigerator.
1 piece: 819 cal., 49g fat (12g sat. fat), 76mg chol., 346mg sod., 91g carb. (72g sugars, 3g fiber), 8g pro.

TEST KITCHEN TIP
Using room-temperature eggs helps the cake mix more evenly and achieve a higher volume.

CARROT CAKE

This wonderful recipe dates back to my great-grandmother. You will love the texture the cake gets from pineapple, coconut and, of course, carrots! For lighter appetites or to serve more people, cut it into smaller pieces and place the slices in pretty cupcake liners.
—*Debbie Terenzini-Wilkerson, Lusby, MD*

PREP: 20 min. • **BAKE:** 50 min.
MAKES: 12 servings

- 2 cups all-purpose flour
- 2 cups sugar
- 2 tsp. ground cinnamon
- 1 tsp. baking soda
- ½ tsp. salt
- 3 large eggs, room temperature
- 1½ cups canola oil
- 2 cups finely grated carrots
- 1 tsp. vanilla extract
- 1 cup well-drained crushed pineapple
- 1 cup sweetened shredded coconut
- 1 cup chopped nuts

BLUEBERRY ZUCCHINI SQUARES

I saw a bar recipe using apple and lemon zest on a muffin mix box. I tried it from scratch with shredded zucchini and fresh blueberries instead. It's a nifty combo.
—*Shelly Bevington, Hermiston, OR*

PREP: 30 min. • **BAKE:** 30 min. + cooling
MAKES: 2 dozen

- 2 cups shredded zucchini (do not pack)
- ½ cup buttermilk
- 1 Tbsp. grated lemon zest
- 3 Tbsp. lemon juice
- 1 cup butter, softened
- 2½ cups sugar
- 2 large eggs, room temperature
- 3¼ cups plus 2 Tbsp. all-purpose flour, divided
- 1 tsp. baking soda
- ½ tsp. salt
- 2 cups fresh or frozen blueberries

GLAZE
- 2 cups confectioners' sugar
- ¼ cup buttermilk
- 1 Tbsp. grated lemon zest
- 2 tsp. lemon juice
- ⅛ tsp. salt

1. Preheat oven to 350°. Grease a 15x10x1-in. baking pan; set aside.

2. In a small bowl, combine zucchini, buttermilk, lemon zest and lemon juice; toss to combine. In a large bowl, cream butter and sugar until light and fluffy, 5-7 minutes. Beat in eggs, 1 at a time. In another bowl, whisk 3¼ cups flour, baking soda and salt; gradually add to the creamed mixture alternately with zucchini mixture, mixing well after each addition. Toss blueberries with remaining 2 Tbsp. flour; fold into batter.

3. Transfer the batter to prepared pan, spreading evenly (pan will be full). Bake until light golden brown and a toothpick inserted in the center comes out clean, 30-35 minutes. Cool completely in pan on a wire rack.

4. In a small bowl, mix glaze ingredients until smooth; spread over top. Let stand until glaze is set.

1 piece: 270 cal., 8g fat (5g sat. fat), 36mg chol., 197mg sod., 47g carb. (33g sugars, 1g fiber), 3g pro.

TEST KITCHEN TIP

If you don't have buttermilk on hand, make your own by mixing 1 to 2 Tbsp. of lemon juice or white vinegar and enough milk to measure 1 cup. Allow it to sit for 5-10 minutes before using.

CHOCOLATE AMARETTI

CHOCOLATE AMARETTI

These classic almond paste cookies are like ones you'd find in an Italian bakery. My husband and children are always excited when I include these goodies in my holiday baking lineup.
—*Kathy Long, Whitefish Bay, WI*

PREP: 15 min. • **BAKE:** 20 min./batch
MAKES: 2 dozen

- 1¼ **cups almond paste**
- ¾ **cup sugar**
- 2 **large egg whites**
- ½ **cup confectioners' sugar**
- ¼ **cup baking cocoa**

1. Preheat oven to 350°. In the bowl of a stand mixer, crumble the almond paste into small pieces. Add the remaining ingredients; mix on low until combined. Beat on medium until well combined and mixture is smooth, 2-3 minutes.
2. Drop by tablespoonfuls 2 in. apart onto parchment-lined baking sheets. Bake until tops are cracked, 17-20 minutes. Cool for 1 minute before removing from pans to wire racks. Store in an airtight container.
1 cookie: 92 cal., 3g fat (0 sat. fat), 0 chol., 6mg sod., 15g carb. (13g sugars, 1g fiber), 2g pro.

CHOCOLATE-STRAWBERRY CELEBRATION CAKE

CHOCOLATE-STRAWBERRY CELEBRATION CAKE

Although I have some wonderful from-scratch recipes, this one uses a boxed mix with plenty of doctoring. It has become a popular groom's cake that gets more attention than the wedding cake.
—*Nora Fitzgerald, Sevierville, TN*

PREP: 30 min. • **BAKE:** 30 min. + cooling
MAKES: 16 servings

- 1 pkg. chocolate cake mix (regular size)
- 1 pkg. (3.9 oz.) instant chocolate pudding mix
- 4 large eggs, room temperature
- 1 cup sour cream
- ¾ cup water
- ¼ cup canola oil
- 4 oz. semisweet chocolate, melted

FROSTING
- 2 cups butter, softened
- 4 cups confectioners' sugar
- ¾ cup baking cocoa
- ½ cup 2% milk

ASSEMBLY
- 4 oz. semisweet chocolate, chopped
- ½ cup heavy whipping cream
- 1 lb. fresh strawberries, hulled
Seedless strawberry jam, warmed, optional

1. Preheat oven to 350°. Combine the first 7 ingredients; beat on low speed for 30 seconds. Beat on medium for 2 minutes. Transfer to 2 greased and floured 9-in. round baking pans.
2. Bake until a toothpick inserted in the center comes out clean, 28-32 minutes. Cool for 10 minutes before removing from pans to wire racks to cool completely.
3. For frosting, in a large bowl, cream the butter, confectioners' sugar and cocoa until light and fluffy. Beat in milk until smooth. Spread frosting between layers and over top and side of cake.
4. For ganache, place chocolate in a small bowl. Heat cream just to a boil; pour over chocolate and whisk until smooth. Drizzle over top of cake, allowing the ganache to drape down the side. Arrange the strawberries on top of cake. If desired, brush jam onto strawberries.
1 piece: 666 cal., 40g fat (23g sat. fat), 120mg chol., 485mg sod., 69g carb. (50g sugars, 2g fiber), 6g pro.

BUTTERSCOTCH PECAN DESSERT

Light and creamy, this terrific treat never lasts long when I serve it. The fluffy cream cheese layer topped with cool butterscotch pudding makes a lip-smacking combination.
—*Becky Harrison, Albion, IL*

PREP: 15 min. + chilling
BAKE: 20 min. + cooling
MAKES: 20 servings

- ½ cup cold butter, cubed
- 1 cup all-purpose flour
- ¾ cup chopped pecans, divided
- 1 pkg. (8 oz.) cream cheese, softened
- 1 cup confectioners' sugar
- 1 carton (8 oz.) frozen whipped topping, thawed, divided
- 3½ cups cold 2% milk
- 2 pkg. (3.4 or 3.5 oz. each) instant butterscotch or vanilla pudding mix

1. Preheat oven to 350°. In a small bowl, cut the butter into the flour until crumbly; stir in ½ cup pecans. Press crust into an ungreased 13x9-in. baking dish. Bake until lightly browned, about 20 minutes. Cool.
2. In a small bowl, beat cream cheese and confectioners' sugar until fluffy. Fold in 1 cup whipped topping; spread over crust.
3. In a large bowl, whisk milk and pudding mix for 2 minutes. Let stand for 2 minutes or until soft-set; pour over cream cheese layer. Refrigerate until set, 15-20 minutes. Top with remaining whipped topping and pecans. Refrigerate for 1-2 hours.
1 piece: 242 cal., 14g fat (8g sat. fat), 27mg chol., 247mg sod., 23g carb. (18g sugars, 1g fiber), 3g pro.

BUTTERSCOTCH PECAN
DESSERT

INDEX